# LUCIFER 2.0,

## When algorithms unleash the Web demons

BOUSSAD ADDAD

*Boussad Addad*

## *Dedication*

It is the morning of January 1, 2021. I haven't had time to make new resolutions and I'm already caught up in a promise. The day after a lively New Year's Eve spent with my family, far from the rules of a world that is not mine, my 5-year-old son runs to me and wakes me up: "Daddy, Daddy, will you write the poem you promised us?" Knowing his power of insistence, I get up straight away: "My darling, you could have waited a little, we are tired now! But, of course, I'm going to write it to you. And I do it:

** Freedom **

*On my school notebooks*

*On my desk and the trees*

*…*

*Bloodstone paper or ash*

*I write your name*

Two days later, he and his twin brother recited to me by heart those parts of the poem by Paul Eluard, an early actor in the French Resistance during the German occupation of France[1], a text which marked my childhood. It is a poem that I learned when I was twice their age, at the age of 11, that is to say after two years of learning the French language that I discovered in my elementary school perched on the mountains of Kabylia [Algeria].

The poem being learned by my little ones, I tell myself that the year 2021 starts well. I can now sleep with peace of mind and for a long time…

I dedicate this book to them, to my treasures Rayane and Rémy. So that they grow up as free men.

---

[1] During the period of the German occupation of France during World War II, Paul Eluard was part of the resistance. He participated in clandestine literature within the National Committee of Writers. His poem *Liberté (Freedom)* written in 1942 was parachuted in thousands of copies as leaflets by British planes over France occupied territory.

*Boussad Addad*

# INTRODUCTION

*"Your behaviors, you don't realize it but you are programmed. It was unintentional, but now you have to decide how much you are willing to give up your intellectual independence,"*

—Chamath Palihapitiya

I devoted the first volume[2] of this book to the capture of attention by the screens. It is a conditioning process leading to compulsive behaviors, symptoms of the users' addiction to the Web. And unfortunately, nobody is safe, as I have shown. It all started with a questioning of my own behavior that I found abnormal. So, I told my personal experience and detailed a method that I developed and followed to get out of it. It is the fruit of a long work of research and reflection. It has profoundly changed my life, well beyond the use of the Internet. I strongly invite you to read it if you have not already done so.

The harm is actually greater than that of addiction alone. The propaganda that reigns on the Web, and it is the object of this volume 2, is just as devastating. The opaque algorithms that are deployed en masse to sell us *Coca-Cola* are just as formidable and effective in influencing our opinions and even emotions. This is all the more true in times of crisis such as the coronavirus, which will be discussed at length in the last chapter of this book. This opacity acts like fear, paralyzes the rational part of our brain and awakens in us only the primary instincts. Logic and all reflection are reduced to nothing. The Web is like a spiral galaxy, dominated by dark matter, from which it is difficult to escape if one is caught in its gravitational field. Dear reader, dear Internet user, I

---

[2] Boussad Addad, "Digital heroin, the magic secrets behind screen addiction", Independently published, 2023.

welcome you on board for another breathtaking galactic tour! We will probably pass through regions that are already familiar to you and undoubtedly others, full of discoveries. Fasten your seatbelts, immediate takeoff…

*My dive into the chaos…*

Once, while watching a video on YouTube, the author referred to Twitter as "a network of a certain level, elitist, not like Facebook." I heard more or less the same thing from a journalist who said that "Facebook is for old people and less educated people" and Twitter is "the favorite place of a certain influential elite," especially in big cities Paris. And that's why, according to him, journalists and politicians didn't see the French Yellow Vests movement coming, because it was born on Facebook and not on Twitter. "Really?", I wondered. Indeed, I have often heard polemics following publications made on the network of the blue bird by the great of this world, "the elite." "It must be true then," I thought. Donald Trump, the most powerful man in the world, had made it his favorite medium of communication. But given the amount of time he spent on it, I sometimes wondered if the blue bird was not stronger than he was!

In my quest for answers to my questions, I subscribed to Twitter to see what was going on. And there, I get a big slap, much more violent than I imagined.

I want to make it clear that I don't want to teach anyone a lesson. Who am I to allow myself to do so? I just ask myself questions and try to answer them. I am critical, it is true, but, first of all, towards myself as I said at the beginning of the previous volume of the book. Everything started from there. I felt less free than I should in my life and I wanted to understand why. The first door that I had to push on the way to freedom was the one of awareness and that went through the understanding of the ins and outs of the complex mechanisms of the Web. The quest was for me long, as for all the freedoms, but it was well worth the cost. Especially if it allows many readers of this book to reach the same goals, and faster. That is the point here.

Let's go back to Twitter, the network of the "elite" that I scrutinized for a few weeks, without intervening in any way. This is a precaution on my part to avoid any interference that would influence my story. Once a day, in the evening, I observe, read, and analyze the actions and reactions of each and every one. The first observation is alarming. It seems that some people literally live there, so many are their tweets, retweets and comments. And to my sad surprise, there were indeed many doctors among them. After invading TV shows, as they are often reproached for, they are also very active on Twitter. To my astonishment, the urologist Laurent Alexandre, who considers himself a futurologist, convinced and repeating for years the imminence of "the death of death," is among them. Seeing his intense activity on Twitter, I could not help but think of this great lesson of transhumanism—lack of humanism I would say—that he gave during a conference before students of the three famous academic institutions: École Polytechnique, Centrale-Supelec, and Normal Sup. This is how he addressed the silent crowd: "The complex world of tomorrow can only be managed by intellectuals. You in this room will live in a golden age [...] What Harari in *Homo Deus* calls gods and useless. The gods are you, you who master, control, and manage [...] The Yellow Vests are the first manifestation of this unbearable intellectual gap that we are creating between the winners, Harari's gods, and the losers, the useless [...]" And to reduce the gap between "the gods, those who will have the sacred fire of the digital," and "the useless, those subscribers to the universal income who will live locked in their virtual reality helmets," the urologist argues in another forum that the oocytes of "intelligent women" should be frozen to allow them to have more children. "It is urgent to promote babies among intellectual women, engineers and researchers [...] Social Security should reimburse 100% of egg freezing for women scientists to allow them to have late babies after their PhD," he writes[3]. Dear reader, no, you are not dreaming, you are having a nightmare…

---

[3] Laurent Alexandre, "Let's Encourage Gifted Women to Have More Children," www.lexpress.fr, 03/02/2018.

Let's take a look at what's happening in Silicon Valley, the cradle of the digital world, often cited as a reference by the urologist. Speaking to students at the prestigious Stanford University, Chamath Palihapitiya, former vice president (2005–2011) of growth at Facebook, warns about the dangers of social networks and digital platforms[4]: "Your behaviors, you don't realize it, but you are programmed. It was unintentional, but now you have to decide how much intellectual independence you are willing to give up. And don't think,—oh yeah, not me, I'm a fucking genius, I'm at Stanford—you're probably the most likely to fall into the trap. Because you spend your whole damn life checking off boxes." We're a long way from transhumanist hubris and Polytechnic gods here!

To be honest, the deafening silence of the students present and the applause at the end of the lecture bothered me more than the urologist's speech. I probably would have left the lecture hall without looking back if I were there. I successively went through the École Polytechnique and the École Normale Supérieure, and I was ranked first in my class each time, but my god, I don't see myself in this speech at all. And I would like to salute those little hands that work hard, day and night, Yellow Vests or not, without whom we would all have died of hunger during the coronavirus crisis.

Laurent Alexandre is indeed very active on Twitter: "Social networks are simple. You post two or three controversial things a day and after two years, you have at least 30,000 followers," he explains one day to a friend[5]. This is his magic recipe!

It is 2020 and to tell the truth, nothing surprises me anymore. I myself witnessed on the Web, on the professional network LinkedIn, a psychoanalyst who shamelessly mocked a visibly fragile person. Yes, I am talking about the professional who is supposed to help people in difficulty. I couldn't help but call her out, without insulting her, of course, even though there was no lack of desire. But what was she

---

[4] Jennings Brown, "Former Facebook Exec: 'You Don't Realize It But You Are Being Programmed,'" https://gizmodo.com, 12/11/2017.
[5] Jean-Francois Robert, "How the Founder of Doctissimo Became a Futurist," www.vanityfair.fr, MAY 24, 2018.

looking for with her mockery? She is probably a goddess who wants to fight!

There is another one who does not go unnoticed, Gilbert Deray, a nephrologist (kidney specialist) who has literally squatted on TV sets and who distinguishes himself on the Web. He floods Twitter daily with anxiety-provoking posts. Every day of the period I have analyzed contains its share of terror from him: "no treatment," "long COVID in children," "Africa affected more than the official figures," "Africa in danger," "considerable damage in India," "the delta variant is progressing in Europe," etc. Internet users, who are obviously used to this daily dose of anxiety from this doctor, answer him "well, another depressive tweet in 15 seconds," "It was the doom and gloom minute," "What worries me is the anxiety-provoking discourse and the hazardous predictions of everyone for almost a year," "It must be paying well to do so much," etc. And how can we not be offended by such behavior? Isn't reassurance the first thing any doctor should do? Yet it is common knowledge that stress is harmful to the immune system, which is so important in this pandemic period. I don't understand...

It's 2020 and men, just like some gods among them, are chasing subscribers, likes, comments ..., even if it means sowing chaos. If we can't wait to live it in hell, we provoke it on Earth. The Pharaohs thought of Paradise and left pyramids, a wonder of the world, the current generation thinks of hell and will leave ruins. I do not understand...

I don't think that intelligence has evolved in the right direction since antiquity. There is obviously a bug in Darwin's software. I find the definition of the elite and of intelligence drastically misplaced now. Plato said in his time that intelligence was the process that allowed the acquisition of science. And not of Twitter followers indeed! Can we legitimately consider ourselves intellectual when we spend hours on social networks insulting, harassing, mocking, or just wasting our time, without questioning ourselves? We should not be surprised in this case, especially when we promote artificial intelligence -Like the previous God lecturer—without really understanding its mechanisms like most of the speakers on TV shows, to see ourselves one day replaced by robots, especially in tasks that require a minimum of thinking...

But my quest is just beginning. I start by following, becoming a *follower* as they say, of some people. Twitter makes suggestions. I gladly accept them to see where they take me. First observation, all these people seem to have the same opinions on almost everything. They support each other (with *likes*), praise each other, and comment on each other's posts. They even defend themselves when they feel attacked. We are in front of an informational and social bubble. Curious to know a little about the other side, I become a follower of some of its members. From close to close, I become the follower of many people who are, at first sight, quite distant from each other. But a rather clear pattern emerges quite quickly: the network is organized in a tribal pattern, each tribe being an almost hermetic bubble. The only exchanges between them are usually in the form of darts when there is a battle. I use warlike terms on purpose, because this is really more than just a confrontation of ideas or opinions as we will see later. The first bubble I have identified is political, let's call it the "G bubble," which is the one that defends the governmental measures taken during the COVID crisis19. Some people, no doubt out of self-interest, others out of naivety, and others out of simple followership, stubbornly defend even the indefensible. It is astonishing when you see the COVID fiasco and the management of tests, masks, then vaccines. The second bubble I noted, the R (Rebel), is the one that rejects everything the government does, out of mistrust and loss of confidence, which we can legitimately understand. Rejecting everything at once is not serious either. The third bubble, the S, is what I call the sect. It is against the deployment of "5G that would allow tracking us with chips under our skin." It is also relentlessly active in supporting Donald Trump. The fourth bubble, the Z (zeteticians), is the one that doesn't doubt anything while its members should by definition master the art of doubting. I have the impression that for these people [Z], science has stopped and everything is now known. Any new hypothesis is to be discarded for them. Among them there is everything, bloggers without a clear profession, biologists, doctors, computer scientists, etc. The Zs, for example, have staunchly supported the fraud study published in *The Lancet*, without having obviously read it or just misunderstood it. They did the same by showing blind confidence in a treatment [Remdesivir] presented as effective against Covid-19, based on another more than dubious study as I expressed it at the time on LinkedIn. The criteria of the current clinical trial have been changed (mortality is no longer mentioned) without this bothering anyone! A researcher took the liberty of insulting me for having expressed my opinion on this useless drug sold for 3,000 dollars per treatment! The urologist Laurent Alexandre, who does not doubt anything, supported this drug before recognizing his mistake … very late. Time has proven me right and the WHO has even advised against Remdesivir because it is so dangerous for the kidneys and the heart. Some Parisian patients ended up in dialysis after taking this drug! And Europe ordered 1.2 billion worth of it. Thanks to the taxpayer.

We probably reached the height of mediocrity when a member of the Zs, a student who has not even defended his doctoral thesis yet (whose subject is apparently on pollutants in food[6]), posted on Twitter on January 16, 2021, this: "Unbelievable! Prof. Raoult who himself writes that their 1st non-randomized clinical trial shows that hydroxychloroquine has NO efficacy on mortality or in reducing ICU transfer." For the record, I am not defending the treatment or the professor (he doesn't need me), but I happened to read the study in question at the time. I fell out of my chair when I heard almost all the major media picking up the information given in the tweet without even verifying or questioning it. The biggest French news channel even handed the microphone to the student! But how is this possible, I asked myself? This study from Marseille dates back to March 2020 and at that time only involved 42 patients. Its aim was in fact to verify the effectiveness of the treatment on "viral load reduction" and not on mortality. How do you want to study mortality on such a small sample of 42 people knowing that the disease has an average lethality of less than 1% (between 0.5 and 0.7% according to official figures) and kills less than one person in a hundred infected? At the time of the tweet, a year has already passed since the epidemic started and these figures are known to all. And how can we conclude about mortality knowing that there were, not surprisingly, no deaths in this study?[7] To talk about

---

[6] http://www.theses.fr/s226751
[7] There was one death in each group, which does not allow any conclusion on mortality.

mortality without deaths is still incredible, isn't it? We can think what we want about the treatment, but not make such a mistake. If it doesn't work, it is certainly not this study that could demonstrate it. The worst thing is that even doctors got caught up in this hype and took over the publication. The virality of stupidity has exceeded that of the coronavirus! I still do not understand…

All this is very embarrassing, especially for someone who defines himself as a zetetician. Isn't it? This event should have at least created a small crack in the Z-bubble to let out at least some of its members. The opposite happened. It even got stronger. We'll understand all of these phenomena in the book, but let's stick to the facts for now.

The year 2020 is ending. Phew! We are in January 2021, the period of good resolutions to go towards the best. Thunderclap on the Web. A member of the R bubble (Rebels), let's call him Laztec, who counted only 200 followers at the beginning of the Covid-19 crisis (according to the comments I could read) and more than 18,000 followers at the beginning of the year 2021, seems to have escaped from his bubble and announces in a thunderous tweet: "Hello, the time for explanation has come." In a series of publications, he denies everything he has published since the beginning of the crisis and apologizes (I faithfully reproduce his tweets, except for the correction of spelling errors):

*"We would like and retweet each other, without ever being in contradiction… There were skeptics who reacted to my tweets, certainly, but I didn't pay attention to them because I didn't like the tone and the aggressiveness expressed towards me."*

*"In short, I was in a bubble, and every day I was sinking into this belief… In these groups, we obviously talked about [Covid-19] treatment, but also accused the government, big pharma, and the doctors paid by the labs of being corrupt."*

*"So I might as well tell you that we've criticized pretty much every government measure (Mask, Containment. Fear Propaganda) and I've been drinking this because I'm an uncritical jerk."*

*"I went on my own (not everyone does, right) and my account grew, and obviously the criticism was only bigger, and I still didn't care because it was very aggressive. It was the bad guys for me in a way."*

*"Mind you, I'm not saying I was manipulated or influenced, but it's solely my fault because I lack critical thinking skills."*

The series of tweets of this kind is long and useless to recall them all so much as they go in the same direction. One is naturally tempted to applaud, because finally Laztec knew how to get out of his bubble. But his behavior became a bit ambiguous afterwards, notably by revealing in public to take pleasure in blocking a doctor who had just tweeted: "I unblock Laztec for the effort of recognizing his mistakes." He even posted a short video to say that it was a trap set for the Zs! That's probably what brought one member of the Z bubble out of the woods to reveal that Laztec actually had a change of heart after intense private discussions by his friends. It's a way to take the wind out of Laztec's sails should he ever reveal that he's actually been leading them on. The Z's, the skeptics or rationalists as they call themselves, tell of their success in convincing Laztec of his wrongdoing with "relentless arguments," all the while displaying screenshots of excerpts from their private discussions. But reading them reveals a distressed person who "doesn't know what to do anymore," rather than arguments. The Zs encourage him in his approach and congratulate him for his courage in the face of pressure from his friends. They half-heartedly advised him to file a complaint against a person in the R bubble who had made several attempts to contact him after his change of heart. He was told emphatically that "it's called harassment and it's against the law." Also, the Z's offered to make a video for their YouTube channel to retrace his journey, under "conditions to be seen according to the possibilities/impediments" of Laztec. This is a good manipulation technique well known to zeteticians to make the pill pass (to give the impression of having the choice to the interlocutor by focusing on the conditions of filming and by making him forget the real stake which is first to accept or not the interview). "I really think your case is very interesting in context. I don't want to use you, I would like you to be understood so that others will wonder about their posture (and that includes the skeptics)." But Laztec eventually changed his mind, the result of "toxic pressure from his community" according to the Zs. Laztec felt sorry for changing his mind and wrote an hour later: "This goes beyond social networking. What I did was to make friends and feel less lonely when in real life I had no friends and was pretty much alone. I don't want to lose that… I don't want to be alone. What I did was to get me out of a depression. Yeah, it's selfish. That's how it is." Already the day before, Laztec was already lost: "I think I have to leave social networks, it makes me crazy."

Instead of advising him to go immediately to a psychologist, for example, the Zs explain to him, in their words, that "the skeptical community is demanding, sometimes harsh, but it knows how to welcome former believers and always welcomes an honest approach." They will only do so at the end of the discussion, after several days of conversation, having certainly understood that their approach is more than questionable and it would be embarrassing for them and their bubble if it were to come out after Laztec's successive reversals and unpredictable decisions.

Laztec's "friends" are confused and unsubscribe *en masse* from his account. The few benevolent voices among them that advise him to disconnect and take a step back are drowned in questions, insults, and mockery. To prove that the case was not related to a hack of his account as the R bubble suggested, he had to post a picture of his social security card, before having to post a short video, because it was still not enough for the R bubble to admit that such a good soldier as Laztec could have defected! It must be said that Laztec is so followed and influential on the web that even the media he criticized for months are contacting him to get his testimony after his change, of course.

In all of this unbelievable story, I found the phrase that probably sums it up best: "If it turns out, it's all a social experiment." One of the Z's wrote it in the private discussion and I agree with him on this one.

This is indeed a good interpretation, but it is not enough to free oneself, because one's own social bubble that doubts nothing has actually ended up inflating, not at the initiative of Laztec who would join them by conviction, but by going themselves to look for him by initiating the dialogue with him.

A few days later, Laztec seemed even more depressed and lost, tossed between the bubbles. "It's devastating. It completely turns your mind upside down and it's hard to get out of it since you already have to realize it," he said in a tweet. Laztec will finally close his account on January 15, 2021 … before creating another one under a different pseudonym. He will accuse his former comrades in the bubble R of propaganda before turning around once again and turning against the Zs. He is more than ever lost…

I closed my Twitter account on January 19, 2021. When I will later consult some publications on this social network, still in the context of writing this book, it will be without an account.

The Z's, overconfident as ever, more than ever locked in their bubble of "believers," continue to self-congratulate. They even applaud the closing of the Twitter accounts of Trump and his supporters. How will the censorship of the S-bubble, which I'll come back to at length, fix things, if not push them further into their wacky belief? How is the limitation of freedom of expression and thought a good thing, despite the differences one may have with people? Voltaire must be turning in his grave. I don't understand these Zs. On their profiles, they warn you: if you are a Z, the number one rule is to agree with the theory of evolution. It is also bigotry to reject all people who do not think like us. I am not sure that the natural selection of Darwin's theory is actually at work. Isn't the decline in intelligence a sufficient counterexample to discredit it? If it continues at the current rate, soon the human brain will be less developed than that of the chimpanzee, to the great delight of fans of robots and machines that will replace humans in many tasks. And sooner than expected…

All of this is very similar to the behavior found in cults. But the Internet is a global network and the number of members of each bubble is counted in millions, unlike the sectarian movements which are generally quite limited. The phenomenon is therefore very worrying, especially since we can clearly see its devastating psychological effects on individuals and society. The Laztec story is not isolated, far from it. And it is only one of many scourges on the web as we will see.

This book is a journey I undertook personally to understand the world around me and to understand myself better. I am not a sociologist nor a psychologist, but I like to understand. I am not a zetetician, because I do not want to learn the art of doubt, but just a man who likes to acquire knowledge about a subject on which he has questions and on which he has not yet obtained enough answers. The hardest thing is not to doubt, but to remove the doubt. Knowledge is the key. I've learned that you don't have to be a G, an R, an S, or a Z. You have to remain a free spirit and not forbid yourself any self-criticism, without ever giving in to ease and conformity. For my part, I remain a simple human being with my strengths, but especially with my weaknesses that I never stop exploring to make them pass the threshold of consciousness. It is always necessary to become aware of a problem to solve it. This is the meaning of my work.

# CHAPTER I: Brief History of Propaganda

*"The real historical upheavals are not those that astonish us by their grandeur and violence. The only important changes, those from which the renewal of civilizations derives, are those in ideas, conceptions and beliefs. The memorable events of history are the visible effects of the invisible changes in the thinking of men,"*

—Gustave Le Bon

Information has always been vital to human survival. Knowing about a water source or a wilderness preserve full of deer was a guarantee of safety for a time. But with limited resources and growing human populations, the struggle to keep the information secret was equally important. Processes and inventions have never ceased to progress to achieve this. Encryption, for example, from the one used by Julius Caesar to secure his messages to the current one used by Apple or PayPal to keep their customers' data confidential, is part of it. The other way to fight is intoxication, not to assassinate, but to mislead the rival by providing false information or *fake news* as we say now. Also, there is the distraction which consists in occupying the rival with trivialities and thus exhausting him. Finally, we find the indoctrination of populations through sects and religions. This is how the Propaganda, *Congregatio de Propaganda Fide*, a Roman congregation founded in 1622 by Pope Gregory XV with the aim of *propagating* the Christian faith throughout the world, was born. And this is how the Vatican's coffers are filled up to this day…

The word propaganda will later take on a more general meaning to designate any psychological action that uses all means of information to propagate a doctrine, create a movement of opinion and bring about a decision[8]. The goal, often not avowed, is the increase of wealth, as well for a State, a company, or an individual.

---

[8] https://www.cnrtl.fr/definition/propagande

With time, another quest has replaced that of wealth, especially in developed countries where bellies are full: power. This is what makes man salivate now. The way to keep this new symbol of power is naturally propaganda. This is what this chapter is dedicated to.


## All scrolls lead to Rome

In the 16th century, information became a commodity, a consumer good almost like any other in Europe, and Rome in particular. But the news peddlers were not the work of large publishing houses or journalism magnates. They were, in fact, gazetteers or newspapermen, writers of notes that were called *avvisi*[9] or "hand gazettes," serving subscribers spread all over the continent. Among them were the elite of society, composed of representatives of governments and ecclesiastical bureaucracies, lawyers, notaries, scribes, writers, intellectuals, etc. In France, the great lords had their hired newspaperman, charged with reporting all the scandals and piquant adventures of the city. Mazarin, a politician and diplomat in the service of the papacy, paid a man named Portail ten pounds a month to provide him with news every week[10].

By the second half of the 16th century, the circulation of these four- to eight-page handwritten short stories had become regular, with a distribution frequency of once or twice a week. Despite censorship and persecution, criticism of the governments of the time was published clandestinely. Because of its functioning based on political and social structures, this form of information dissemination will remain throughout the 17th century, even after the arrival of printed journalism. The monarchic absolutism will not have had reason of it either in spite of the multiplication of the controls and the persecutions. How can we be surprised by this when we see that four centuries later giants such as Facebook and Twitter are struggling to control information on their own networks?

---

[9] In Italian, the word *avviso* translates as notice, warning, advice or announcement.
[10] https://fr.wikipedia.org/wiki/Nouvelles_%C3%A0_la_main

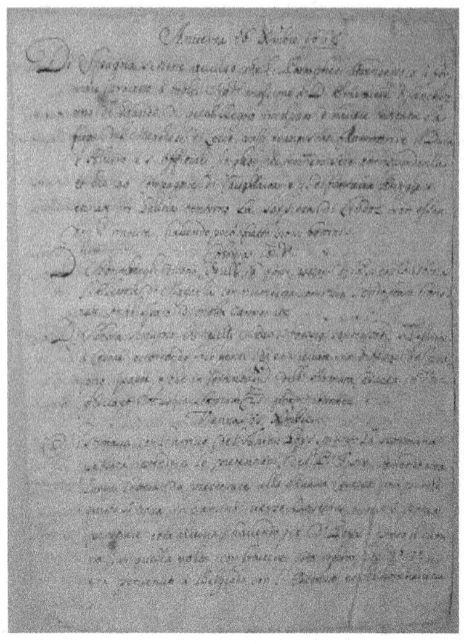

The *avvisi* were originally intended for communication between the elites. The topics which are approached there are sometimes of the field of the esotericism for the simple person. But the democratization of the written word has gradually made them accessible to all classes of society. The government itself disseminated information in writing, especially to merchants, telling them what rules to follow and display in their premises. Some *avvisi* were distributed or read aloud in the public square to the plebs. By the way, a social phenomenon was born with the generalization of the written word, that of the attack on one's reputation by sticking leaflets at the door of a house or business to denounce the morality of its occupants. And when one does not know how to write, one hires the services of an educated neighbor or a professional! Some people took the opportunity to post political messages all over Rome, including on statues, to denounce scandals concerning government officials. Rumors, slander, harassment and other blackmail are now posted in the public square! Twitter has not invented anything…

The authorities obviously could not allow the uncontrolled dissemination of such information to flourish, as reputation and morality were essential for the continuity of the government, especially when it came to the image of the prince or the Pope. One of the ways of this control was to spread a positive opinion about the leader or to attract the affection of the people through timely communiqués and entertainment. Also, the plebs had to be entertained and kept in the dark. It was not to be allowed to rise to the position of being able to judge the prince. The aristocrat Federico Bonaventura justified this dumbing down as follows: "The typical mental activity of the subject involved belief, that is, an activity of an inferior category. Because the subject's preoccupations were with such trivialities as earning a living, very little deep knowledge of anything was required of him. While humbly minding his own business, the subject should never have the opportunity to question obedience to a law, nor should he waste time wondering whether sovereignty rested in the hands of one or many."[11]

For the few who had the knowledge, the intellectuals who knew about politics as well as the clerics and the men of letters, it was necessary to court them in order to gain their indulgence. The political-media relations have always been ambiguous and so made…

But this is never enough and these gazettes were a considerable threat, as they continued to circulate despite the controls. Thus, a first decree against the *avvisi* was issued by Pius V. in 1572, linking these documents to issues of defamation and lèse-majesté. Following an affair that tainted the Pope, the Roman government reinforced the old laws in 1602 by considering *avvisi a* dangerous category of writing. Their circulation was therefore forbidden, regardless of their content. So, it was a matter of pure and hard censorship. But none of this will work and the Roman authorities, overwhelmed, could only notice their own impotence in front of *avvisi* which literally invaded all the corners of Italy.

And it is there that an original and remarkable form of control occurs in the Venetian neighbor: to engage directly in the combat on the informational field. In 1621, in the Republic of Venice, Paolo Sarpi[12], then *consultore in jure*, Councillor of the Republic and State canonist, conceived the first public policy of information. It consisted in engaging the combat on the literary ground, including by resorting to borrowed pens when it was necessary. This was a good option when it came to supporting Venice's independence from Rome and the church, as he had done with his famous *Protesto veneto* against the Pope[13], but no one

---

[11] Dooley Brendan. From good hands: news purveyors in seventeenth-century Rome. In: Annals. History, Social Sciences. 54 e year, N. 6, 1999. pp. 1317–1344.

[12] Pietro Paolo Sarpi, known as Fra Paolo, born on August 14, 1552, in Venice, was a historian, scholar, scientist and Venetian patriot. From 1606, he defended Venice in its disputes with Pope Paul V. Sarpi had to face excommunication during the conflict. At the university of Padua, he met Galileo Galilei, who became his friend.

knew better than Sarpi that this entailed risks when it came to confronting his own people. "Never try to answer to writings that say bad things with conciseness and wit, even falsely, when the defense requires a long narrative or a long speech, since concise and witty expressions engrave themselves in the mind and subdue it, while a long speech tires it to such an extent that it never reaches the truth." The best strategy for Sarpi was to fight the information by providing more information in order to drown the disadvantageous voices and thus to allow reaching the people only the aspects that serve the cause of the government. This is currently referred to as the "saturation of the media field." But Sarpi quickly identified a boomerang effect, the opening of a Pandora's box, that of the elevation of the level of instruction of the subjects engaged in the literary battle. A subject learns to read and write before engaging in combat, just as a warrior learns to wield a sword and shield before going to the front. It was therefore necessary to go backwards. Sarpi states, "Everyone admits that the true way to rule over one's subjects is to leave them in ignorance and respect of public affairs, since when they know more, they gradually begin to judge the actions of the prince; they become so accustomed to this communication that they believe it is due to them, and when it is not given to them, they give it an inaccurate meaning or perceive it as an affront and develop hatred; and what is said of the subjects can also be applied *mutatis mutandis*[14] to the neighbors. This reason is so strong that it has no answer in cases where the government's arguments have not yet been published and its opponents are not expected to publish contrary ones; in such cases, the subjects would be kept in ignorance and respect, but the door would be open to opposing opinion formed by reading opposing manifestos that must be banned and, once spread, eradicated."[15] Here Sarpi returns to the strategy of ignorance fabrication advocated by Federico Bonaventura.

---

[13] Denis Anne, "La République de Venise (1608-1610) : l'espoir et l'illusion d'une nouvelle Genève", In: Albineana, Cahiers d'Aubigné, 18, 2006.

[14] *Mutatis mutandis* is a Latin phrase, literally meaning "what was to be changed has been changed", which could be translated in a more contemporary way as "once the necessary changes have been made".

[15] Ibid.

This is a dilemma that governments are faced with: censoring information or, on the contrary, saturating it. Censorship has never worked in reality, as in all the fields besides, because the thing develops in the clandestine one. Evangelista Sartonio, a Bolognese subject of the Papal State in the 16th century, explained it at the time with great accuracy, evoking the strength of curiosity: "One should never in any city or place forbid people to reason especially about things that one does not want them to know, because these things will be spread all the more surely because of this very frustration, which is a fertile mother of curiosity and appetite." Sarpi's successor as Venice's consultant thought no less. "In fact, many useless books would otherwise simply have been forgotten," he advised the Senate, "but they have passed into posterity because the ban has excited in many the desire to see what is so scandalous, and these books that would normally have been read by a few end up being read by many."[16] And what applies to one book naturally applies to any other manuscript. Censorship has never been able to make the *avvisi* disappear.

1er journal imprimé de l'histoire
(Allemagne, 1605)

The invention of the newspaper printed in Germany[17] in 1605, spread very quickly throughout Europe, has multiplied the volume and speed of dissemination of information. The advent of republics after the fall of monarchies and the separation of states from the church facilitated it even more. The adoption of certain fundamental principles such as freedom, including that of expression, further strengthened the circulation of news. The press has even become a fourth power, normally untouchable by the political power in any self-respecting

---

[16] Ibid.
[17] Invented by the Alsatian printer and bookbinder Johann Carolus (born 1575). He began publishing the *Relations aller Fürnemmen und gedenckwürdigen Historien* (Relation of all important and memorable histories) in 1605 in Strasbourg.

democracy. Censorship has thus lived on, or almost… A more adequate means of control is therefore needed in the new situation.


## Public Relations or How to Sell Opinion

In the late 1700s, the United States of America was still a colony of the British Kingdom. The *Boston Tea Party*, a political revolt that marked the American Revolution and preceded the War of Independence, used influence tactics through public information to express disagreement with British laws and regulations. One of the leaders of the movement was John Adams, a constitutional lawyer and Republican supporter who later became president of the United States. Adams wrote several essays and legal briefs as part of his advocacy efforts. He also contributed anonymously to several articles that appeared in the *Boston Gazette* around 1765. In 1776, he published a pamphlet entitled *Thoughts on Government* that would inspire several U.S. state constitutions. On June 11 of that year, he was appointed, along with Thomas Jefferson, Benjamin Franklin, Robert R. Livingston, and Sherman, to the Drafting Committee for the U.S. Declaration of Independence.

But the man some historians call "the Father of the American Revolution"[18] and "the Father of the News Agency" is Samuel Adams, writer and politician. When, in May 1773, the English Parliament passed the *Tea Act*, which allowed the English East India Company to sell its tea to the North American colonies without paying taxes, Adams circulated a letter to the thirteen colonies, showing that this new law would destroy American trade for the benefit of the British Crown. Thanks to the coordinating action of the written communications of the committees of correspondence, bodies organized by the local governments of the American colonies, the American rebellion was for the first time united around a single cause. And this struggle for influence through public information would eventually pay off.

The destruction of a shipment of tea by the colonists caused great tension, leading to the outbreak of war the following year. With

---

[18] Mark Puls, "Samuel Adams: Father of the American Revolution," 2006.

reinforcements from France and other European countries, the U.S. Army, led by George Washington, eventually defeated the British. The Treaty of Paris, in which Great Britain recognized the independence of the United States, ending the war, was signed in 1783. George Washington was chosen as the first president of the United States of America in 1789.

Towards the end of the 18th century, it is the upheaval of the Western economies and societies with the Industrial Revolution. The railway boom will deeply affect the other fields, the transport of goods being largely facilitated. The world will thus see a dazzling development of the iron and steel industry with the strong demand for rail, steam engines, ships, etc. This was also the case for other heavy industries such as oil, chemicals, automobiles, electricity, etc. This was the era of the emergence of large companies and wealthy businessmen. The case that marked this period was probably that of the hegemonic *Standard Oil* of John D. Rockefeller. Its monopoly, considered very harmful and anti-competitive in the free American market, was challenged and fell under the jurisdiction of the *Sherman Antitrust Act* in 1911[19]. The company was dismantled and divided into several smaller companies, as was *the American Tobacco Company* in the same year. But these companies would face other fronts than that of the regulatory state. This revolutionary period was also the result of the workers, the little hands that dug the mines and ran the production lines, often under very difficult conditions. The widening gap between these proletarians, who did not always see the fruits of their labor, and an ultra-rich ruling class naturally created tensions. Strikes and other protests can break out at any time to demand more rights. This sometimes leads to deadly repression, as in 1914 in Ludlow, Colorado, where striking coal miners, along with their wives and children, were massacred[20]. Although the unionists were defeated, the tragedy brought public attention to the harsh working conditions in the coal fields. John D. Rockefeller Jr. was singled out,

---

[19] The Sherman Anti-Trust Act of July 2, 1890, was the first attempt by the American government to limit anti-competitive behavior by businesses: it thus marked the birth of modern competition law.

[20] https://www.du.edu/ludlow/cfhist3.html

denounced in the press and in a dramatic series of public hearings before the Industrial Relations Commission.

But that's not the point. The image of the businessman and his company must be rehabilitated at all costs. This was the beginning of a new battle in the information field, that of the defense of large companies. It was the birth of what would later be called "public relations," a kind word for not saying "propaganda," which, as we shall see, is the more appropriate word. The goal of this new communication is both to defend the image of large companies and to help them sell their products in an increasingly competitive market. And all the blows are allowed…

The new business of public relations was taken up by some pioneers, including a former business journalist, Ivy Lee, considered the inventor of the concept of "public relations consulting." He and a partner, George Parker, opened the very first consulting office in New York in 1904. Their first clients were, not surprisingly, the *Pennsylvania Railroad*, the Rockefeller family (to restore its image after the Ludlow Massacre), and *the American Tobacco Company*.

At the start of his new business, Ivy Lee says, "This is not a secret press office. All of our work is done in full transparency. We aim to provide news… In short, our plan is, frankly and openly, on behalf of business and public institutions, to provide the press and public of the United States with prompt and accurate information on matters that are important and interesting for them to know."[21] In practice, however, Lee often engaged in propaganda on behalf of ethically questionable clients. Shortly before his death in 1934, he was investigated by the U.S. Congress, which heard evidence of his work on behalf of *IG Farben*, the largest pharmaceutical company in Nazi Germany[22].

The *Pennsylvania Railroad Company* first called on the services of Lee and Parker's office to help with media coverage of accidents on its railroad system, as the strategy of silence and *no comment* initially adopted was no longer tenable. The office was then asked to help push

---

[21] Janis Teruggi Page, "Introduction to Strategic Public Relations_ Digital, Global, and Socially Responsible Communication," Sage Publications, Inc. 2018.
[22] https://www.nku.edu/~turney/prclass/readings/3eras2x.html

through a 5% increase in train fares. Ivy Lee developed a comprehensive public relations campaign, reaching out to all stakeholders: the media, railroad employees, passengers, customers, the state and federal elected officials, and university presidents. It even brought in religious and other opinion leaders to champion the company's cause and convince government regulators to approve the increase.

Ivy Lee

Lee's efforts paid off. Public opposition diminished and several outside groups wrote in favor of the rate increase. The federal government finally approved it. This mass campaign is being touted as "a milestone in the history of public relations."[23]

This new form of professional communication of saturation of the informational field with "public relations" having proved itself on many examples and companies, it will make its way to all fields. The political field will not be left out, both nationally and internationally.

## The Saturation That Leads to War

George Creel was a journalist and a strong supporter of U.S. President Woodrow Wilson. He played a key role in the election campaign that led to his re-election in 1916. In 1917, as Wilson prepared to declare war on Germany, breaking his campaign promise, Creel proposed that he adopt a "progressive" alternative to wartime press censorship. He argued that they could use modern scientific advertising techniques to "arouse ardor and enthusiasm" in American citizens to support entry into the global conflict. Wilson was so impressed that a week after declaring war he appointed Creel to head the *Committee on Public Information*, the first institutionalized federal propaganda agency. Creel fully embraced his

---

[23] St. John, B. (2006), "The case for ethical propaganda within a democracy: Ivy Lee's successful 1913–1914 railroad rate campaign", Public Relations Review, 32(3), 221–228.

role, which he saw as "an advertising proposition, a vast sales enterprise, the greatest advertising venture in the world." Wilson having given him all the authoritarian powers, Creel used and abused them. In 1917, the United States was deeply divided over the benefits of involvement in a war with no end in sight, a conflict that had already cost millions of lives and enormous resources. Creel therefore needed to deploy whatever means necessary to sway public opinion. It was necessary to use, as he says, "propaganda in the true sense of the word, the propagation of faith," to capture the nation's attention. To do this, a stream of governmental communication was necessary, because he understood that "to direct and control this torrent, he had to control all possible channels." To this end, Creel states that there was "no medium of appeal that we did not employ. The printed word, the spoken word, the motion picture, the telegraph, the cable, the radio, the poster, the billboard—all of these were used in our campaign to impress upon our own people and upon all other peoples the causes which drove America to take up arms."

Less than a year after its creation, the Creel Committee has twenty national subdivisions and a staff of 150,000! It is the fastest growing government agency in the history of the world. It has done more in all and faster than any other agency, paving the way for the mass production of information for the guidance of opinion. The committee produced more posters, speeches, brochures, and press releases than any other entity. "In addition to newspapers and magazines, county fairs, movies, classrooms, post office walls, churches, synagogues, union halls—virtually every physical interface with the public was a place to display the Committee's message. The argument for war was "extremely powerful by dint of volume, repetition and ubiquity." In the emerging battle to capture human attention and change opinion, Creel's approach amounted to a saturation bombing, a carpet bombing, to stay in the military jargon.

The Creel Committee kept meticulous records, so there is some measure of how many people they reached. The U.S. government printed 75 million brochures and books. It introduced the *"Four Minute Man"* program, in which ordinary citizens were invited to give four-minute pro-war speeches in movie theaters while the reels were changed. As a result, over 75,000 volunteers delivered a total of 755,190 speeches, reaching an audience of over four hundred million people!

The film industry has not been neglected, far from it. Creel made it clear that either it would cooperate or be banned. Any film "that would be detrimental" to the war effort would be banned outright. After some procrastination, the studios realized the lucrative profit they could make and embarked on monster productions for the time. Fear will naturally be a central ingredient in the recipe for manipulation. Thus, the 15-episode series *Wolves of Kultur*, featuring an America whose security is threatened by an external enemy, was produced and presented with great fanfare. But the biggest success came with the film *The Kaiser, the Beast of Berlin*, which drew thousands of people to every theater in America in one week. A superlative publicity campaign was carried out with posters on road signs, giant banners on the roads, and trucks parading through the states with the words: "All German pros will be admitted for free." The priority was to convince the doubters. Also, the famous slogan of Uncle Sam pointing his finger was changed to *I want you for the U. S. Army.*

With all opposition, in whatever form, silenced and muzzled, the Creel Committee's result is unmistakable. More than 700,000 young people have volunteered to join the ranks in a war that the majority of Americans are now clamoring for.

This is how the conquest of attention can be translated into the conquest of minds to lead them to opinions or actions they would never have thought of before. What could be worse than war that causes humanitarian disasters and loss of life by the millions? Some would say that it was easy to manipulate the population of the time because they were uneducated. Not so. Much more recent events demonstrate otherwise.

The scenario was repeated in 2003 when the war against Iraq was launched. The result was just as spectacular, despite the absence of any legitimate motivation, as French Foreign Minister Dominique de Villepin courageously stated at the United Nations. For the Americans, however, it was a different story. According to a University of Maryland study on public opinion about that war[24], 71% of the American media supported it and only 3% were against it, the rest being neutral. And the result of the propaganda on the public is just mind-blowing: 57% of the viewers thought that Iraq supported al-Qaeda and was directly involved in the September 11 attacks, 69% even believed that Sadam Hussein was personally involved in the attacks.

And the Americans did even better two years earlier, during the attacks of September 11, 2001. President George W. Bush, in a 2002 speech, referred to the "Axis of Evil" behind international terrorism as being composed of three countries: North Korea, Iraq, and Iran. It is extraordinary to pull off this stunt and divert attention in this way and to make people forget that not a single one of the 19 terrorists identified as being involved in the attacks came from these countries. Fifteen are Saudis, two Emiratis (United Arab Emirates), one Egyptian, and one Lebanese. The Senate investigation report on the attacks in December 2002 even speaks of direct contacts between certain terrorists and the Saudi secret services. Still according to the report, one of the terrorists under FBI surveillance since 1999 even had links with the royal family. A certain Bassnan, very close to the bin Laden family, even received a large amount of cash from a member of the royal family during a stay in the Kingdom. Two others were in contact with a diplomat accredited to the Saudi Arabian consulate in Los Angeles… In short, we are far from the three countries pointed at. But the part of the report that gives this information, 28 pages to be exact, was sealed as a defense secret at the insistence of Bush[25]. The latter stated that the publication of these documents "would reveal sources and methods that would make the war

---

[24] Kull Steven, Ramsay Clay, Subias Stefan, Lewis Evan, and Warf Philip, "Misperceptions, Media, and the Iraq War," October 3, 2003.

[25] https://web.archive.org/web/20160715183528/http://intelligence.house.gov/sites/intelligence.house.gov/files/documents/declasspart4.pdf

on terrorism more difficult." It was not until 2016 that the Obama administration agreed to partially declassify the 28 pages, under pressure from the families of the victims of the attacks, insurance companies, and other organizations. The subsidiary question to all this is: what did the media do after these revelations? Nothing, of course. What about the human rights organizations? No better.

The Kingdom of the Arabian Peninsula would repeat the feat two years later in 2018 after the sawing of journalist Jamal Khashoggi inside the Saudi Arabian Consulate in Istanbul. The former close to the royal clan and newly minted columnist for the *Washington Post* came under fire from Crown Prince Mohammed bin Salmane when he began to become critical of him. The event caused a bit of a stir in the international press, as the victim was a journalist for a famous American newspaper, but voices were soon silenced everywhere. The oil and the money are there, not to mention the very lucrative work of seduction at all levels, organized by companies specialized in public relations and detour of attention…[26]

## From attention to the manufacturing of consent, there is only one step

I have already written this section in *Volume 1 of* the book, but I need to remind you of it for the sake of understanding the rest of the book. If you have already read it, you can skip to the next section.

If there is one man who played a key role in the Creel Committee, during the First World War and after, it is Edward Bernays (1891–1995). This nephew of Sigmund Freud, whose techniques of influence were based on the theories of Gustave Le Bon and Wilfred Trotter on crowd psychology[27], was a press agent barely 24 years old when the war broke out. After the Americans entered the conflict, the Committee hired him in the office in charge of Latin American affairs, to conduct PsyOp

---

[26] Antoine Izambard, "Publicis, Havas, Image 7… Ces communicants que l'Arabie saoudite paie à prix d'or ", www.challenges.fr, 07.11.2018.
[27] Aumercier, Sandrine. "Edward L. Bernays and propaganda," Revue du MAUSS, vol. 30, no. 2, 2007, pp. 452-469.

(Psychological Operation) type operations[28]. Bernays learned an important lesson from this. He would later say, "There was one basic lesson I learned at the Committee. Efforts comparable to those applied by the Committee to influence the attitudes of the enemy, the neutrals, and the people of this country, could be applied with equal ease to other purposes in peacetime. In other words, what could be done for a nation in the midst of war could be done for organizations and individuals in a nation in peacetime." For Bernays, the triumph of war "opened the eyes of some clever people in all walks of life to the possibilities of shaping public opinion." He added: "Commercial affairs offer concrete (graphic) examples of the effect that can be produced on the public by interest groups." The man described as "the father of public relations" will devote the rest of his life to applying the same techniques of influence in the service of business.

After the end of the war, advertising spending by Western companies increased sharply, multiplying tenfold before 1930. A fully fledged and above all global industry was thus born. The commodification of attention turned heads and warmed wallets. Bernays naturally played a central role, as did Claude Hopkins, the inventor of scientific advertising, who declared: "We are changing the course of commerce. We populate new empires, build new industries and create customs and fashions. We dictate the food the baby should eat, the clothes the mother should wear, the way the house should be furnished. Our names are unknown. But there is hardly a house, in town or in a hamlet, where a human being does not do what we ask."[29] The mass attention-grabbing experiments of the 1920s were the origin of what we would later call "mass consumer society" or consumerism. Bernays applied his recipes for many clients as he proudly boasts in his book *Propaganda*[30],

---

[28] Psychological operations (PSYOP) are operations aimed at disseminating specific information and indicators to populations to influence their emotions, motivations, reasoning and choices, and ultimately the behavior of governments, organizations, groups and individuals. These are the types of operations that have been conducted in Latin America to overthrow governments that were not favorable to U.S. interests, such as in Guatemala.

[29] Charles F. McGovern, Sold American: Consumption and Citizenship, 1890–1945 Chapel Hill: University of North Carolina Press, 25, 2006.

[30] Edward Bernays. Propaganda. Routledge, 1928.

published in 1928, or subsequent ones as his biography[31]. The worst thing is that his methods worked even to sell the worst scum that humans could invent, sometimes in the name of the most noble causes. We will tell you about one of them that has left its mark on history, that of tobacco. An addictive poison sold to women in the name of women's freedom!

In 1927, Bernays worked for *Liggett & Myers*, makers of *Chesterfield* cigarettes. He pulled off a coup against the competing *Lucky Strike* brand by debunking claims by opera singers that *Lucky cigarettes* were "good for the voice." To succeed in his undermining mission, he called on a medical journal where he once worked to survey prominent doctors to publish their opinions on the matter. The verdict was unsurprisingly unfavorable to smoking, dealing a severe blow to his employer's competitor. George Washington Hill, head of *the American Tobacco Company*, the maker of *Lucky Strike*, then investigated his declared enemy, eventually poaching him in 1928. For Hill, it was better to have Bernays on his side than in front of him.

As soon as he arrived, Bernays' goal was to increase *Lucky Strike* sales by targeting women, most of whom did not smoke at the time. Hill had something of an obsession with this target, so much so that he once quipped to Bernays, "If I can light this market on fire, I'll get more than my share... It would be like opening a gold mine right in my backyard."[32] The goal doesn't seem impossible to achieve, but it has a way to go. Indeed, women have begun to change their habits, especially those who have held positions once reserved only for men, but the taboo is still there. Only 12% of women smoked in 1929, far short of Hill's goal.

---

[31] Edward Bernays, Biography of an idea, the founding principles of public relations, Open Road Integrated Medi, 2015.
[32] Larry Tye, "The father of spin, Edward L. Bernays and The Birth of Public Relations, Crown Publishers, 1998.

Hill thought of the shortest way to get there: play on a woman's sensitivity to her figure. His theory is simple: thinness being the fashion, the cigarette can be sold, especially for women, as an appetite suppressant[33]. Like the scandalous Mediator drug some decades later... The slogan is quite found: "Have a Lucky rather than a Sugar." Smoke rather than eat. He turned to Bernays, whom he pays $25,000 a year, for advice. The latter can only be pleased, especially since he is a master in this type of influence strategy, which he calls "the crystallization of public opinion." During the eight years of his collaboration with the tobacco industry, Bernays did not skimp on the means to accentuate this crystallization. He used deception and tried to discredit all scientific research, no matter how serious, that went against his objectives when it showed the harmfulness of cigarettes and the serious diseases they cause.

Bernays launched the anti-candy campaign with his tried-and-true tactic of recruiting "experts," convincing Nickolas Muray, a photographer friend with connections to the fashion world, to get other photographers and artists to sing the praises of the slim. "I have come to the conclusion," Muray writes, "that the slender woman who, combining flexibility and grace, who instead of overeating candy and desserts, lights a cigarette, who, as the ads say, has created a new standard of female beauty." Magazines and newspapers are also saturated with articles about the thin trend. For fashion editors, this meant photo after photo of slim Parisian models in haute couture dresses. But that's not all. Even prominent doctors were involved! Their testimonies accompany each ad. Such is the case with Dr. George F. Buchan, the former head of the *British Association of Medical Officers of Health*, warning that sweets cause tooth decay and stating that "the proper way to end a meal is with fruit, coffee and a cigarette." He continues: "Fruit hardens the gums and cleans the teeth; coffee stimulates the flow of saliva into the mouth and acts as a mouthwash; while finally cigarettes disinfect the mouth and soothe the nerves." That's it! Bernays even persuaded Arthur Murray, a dance school proprietor, to sign a letter stating that "on the

---

[33] This naturally brings to mind the other disaster created by Mediator, a drug sold by the Servier laboratory as an appetite suppressant while it caused serious valvulopathy (dysfunction of the heart valves).

dance floor, the results of sloppy eating are quickly revealed—embarrassing not only one's dance partner, but also other dancers by impinging on more than one's part... Dancers today, when tempted to overindulge in a cocktail or buffet, take a cigarette instead."

But relying on the press and the influence of "experts" did not satiate the appetite of the giant Bernays. He also worked to change the way people ate. Hotels were urged to add cigarettes to their dessert lists, while Bernays' office widely distributed a series of menus, custom-made by a *House and Garden* editor, designed to "save from the dangers of overeating." For lunch and dinner, a sensible mix of vegetables, meats, and carbohydrates was suggested, before concluding with the advice, "Have a cigarette instead of dessert."

Bernays also suggested that housewives call on kitchen cabinetmakers to provide special spaces to hold cigarettes as they did for flour and sugar. He urged container manufacturers to provide labeled boxes for cigarettes as they did for tea and coffee. Finally, he encouraged home economics writers to "emphasize the importance of cigarettes in the home... Just as the inexperienced young housewife is warned not to let her supply of sugar, salt, tea or coffee run out, she must be told that the same is true of cigarettes."

The sugar industry was obviously not happy with Bernays' actions and attacked him violently with insulting letters. Bernays, unperturbed, because he understood that controversy sells, or buzz as they say now, responded by arguing that this was the rule of "the new competition." In a letter he wrote to business school professors, which he had a leading economist sign, Bernays wrote: "A battle fairly fought in this way can serve the public by presenting both sides of a debatable issue and by bringing to the forefront fairly the underlying democratic principle of freedom of competition." All of this seemed to delight Hill, who wrote to Bernays: "I think the record shows that we have kept them quiet well enough."

A month after the first ad campaigns targeted at women, Hill commissioned a second series, this time emphasizing moderation. The moderation he had in mind, of course, meant consuming fewer sweets and more cigarettes. Bernays responded with the most cynical proposal for the creation of a League of Moderation, an association that he wanted, ironically, to copy on the model of associations and leagues fighting certain diseases such as tuberculosis or cancer.

This all-out campaign paid off, not surprisingly. Hill exulted in a December 1928 letter to Bernays. In it, he mentioned that *American Tobacco's* revenues increased by $32 million that year, and *Lucky* "shows a greater increase than all other cigarettes combined." And there's more to come.

In early 1929, Hill called Bernays in and asked, "How can we get women to smoke on the street? They smoke indoors. But, by golly, if they spend half the time outside and we can get them to smoke outside, we'll almost double our female market. Do something about it. Take action!"

Bernays understood that they were confronted with a social taboo that cast a bad light on women who smoked. He wasn't sure how to overcome it. So, he convinced Hill to agree to pay for a consultation with Dr. A. A. Brill, a psychoanalyst close to his uncle, Freud. "It's perfectly normal for women to want to smoke cigarettes," Dr. Brill states at the outset. "The emancipation of women has erased many of their feminine desires. More women are now doing the same work as men. Many women don't have children; those who do are having fewer children. Feminine traits are masked. Cigarettes, which are associated with men, become torches of freedom for women." This gave Bernays ideas. Why not have a parade of famous women lighting their "torches of freedom"? And do it on Easter Sunday, a holiday symbolizing freedom of spirit, on Fifth Avenue, America's most prestigious promenade…

He gathered a list of thirty debutantes from a friend at Vogue magazine, then sent each of them a telegram signed, not by him, but by his secretary, Bertha Hunt. "In the interest of gender equality and to fight another sexual taboo, other young women and I will light another torch of freedom by smoking cigarettes, strolling down Fifth Avenue on Easter Sunday," the dispatch explained. "We are doing this to fight the silly prejudice that smoking is appropriate at home, in restaurants, in cabs, in the lobby of the theater, but never, no, never on the sidewalk. Female smokers and their escorts will walk from Forty-Eighth Street to Fifty-Fourth Street on Fifth Avenue between 11:30 a.m. and 1 p.m." A similar call was made through an advertisement in New York newspapers, this one signed by Ruth Hale, a leading feminist and wife of the *New York World* columnist. The scenario for the parade was described in great detail in a memo from Bernays' office. The purpose of the event explained, would be to generate "chronicles that for the first time women smoked openly in the street. These will take care of themselves, legitimately, if the staging is done correctly." The memo also mentions important churches on the parade route that Bernays would like marchers to join, including St. Thomas, and St. Patrick's, the church attended by the wealthy John D. Rockefeller.

There remains the question of which walkers would produce the best effect. "Because it should appear as publicity-free information, actresses should definitely be left out. On the other hand, if young women who advocate for feminism—someone from the *Women's Party*, for example—could be part of the event, it wouldn't be a bad idea for their movement to be promoted at the event as well. While they should look good, they should not look like supermodels. Three for each covered church should be enough. Of course, they should not smoke just walking down the church steps. They must join the Easter parade by smoking continuously." Also, "Some of the women had to be accompanied by men," a way of saying that they were supported by their husbands. Finally, a photographer was needed on the spot to make beautiful pictures to pass for the press agencies. The note clearly showed that nothing was left to chance[34].

The march went off without a hitch, even better than its writers had imagined. Ten young women marched down New York's Fifth Avenue with their "torches of freedom" well lit. The media loved it, even if a few "regrets" were noted here and there, "to see the woman adopt the habits of the man." The media made a big deal of the event. It made

---

[34] Memo, "System Outline for Easter Smokers," Library of Congress.

headlines across the United States, from Fremont, Nebraska, to Portland, Oregon, to Albuquerque, New Mexico.

The success that the event unleashed proved enlightening for Bernays. "I learned that age-old customs could be broken by a strong appeal, broadcast through the media network," he wrote in his memoirs. "Of course, the taboo was not completely destroyed. But a step had been taken."[35] But what Bernays does not say is that he used deception, bribery, and other questionable means to achieve his ends. In all the letters he had people sign, often for a fee, he agreed never to reveal his name under any circumstances. Even his secretary, Bertha Hunt, quoted in newspapers across the country about her involvement, failed to mention her connection with Bernays, *American Tobacco* or *Lucky Strikes*. She told the *Evening World* newspaper that she "first got the idea for this campaign when a man walking with her on the street asked her to put out her cigarette because it embarrassed him." She added, "I discussed it with my friends, and we decided it was high time something was done about it."

*Lucky Strike* cigarettes overtook competitors *Camel* and *Chesterfields*, but surveys conducted by the *Tobacco Company* showed that many women didn't take *Lucky* because its green packaging with a red bull's-eye didn't go with their clothes. When Hill asked Bernays what he suggested, Bernays replied, "Change the color to neutral that will go with whatever they wear." That was out of the question for Hill: "I spent millions of dollars advertising the packaging. Now you're asking me to change it. That's bad advice." Bernays' reply is as legendary as the torches of freedom: "If you won't change the color of the packaging, then change the color of fashion to green."

## When the Hospital Opens the Way to Cancer

Changing the color scheme of an entire nation? It was an idea so egocentric and eccentric that few public relations people, then or even now, would suggest it, let alone have any idea how to make it work. But Bernays' specialty was to determine why the public preferred certain

---

[35] Edward Bernays, "Biography of an idea, the founding principles of public relations," Open Road Integrated Medi, 2015.

things, and then to rearrange those preferences to fit his clients' needs. He embarked on his task for six months with unwavering confidence.

First, he analyzed the color itself. A book called *The Language of Color* suggested to him that green was "an emblem of hope, victory and abundance" and "symbolic of solitude and peace." These were optimistic themes he could build on. Even more encouraging statistics showed that green already accounted for about 20 percent of the lines made by French fashion houses at the time. What Bernays needed was a big event to light up the fashion world. He opted for a ball in the majestic Waldorf-Astoria, with proceeds going to charity. And he found the perfect hostess, the wife of a friend, in the person of Narcissa Cox Vanderlip. She is a leader in the suffragette movement, campaigning for women's suffrage, and president of the *Women's Infirmary of New York*. She is the wife of the very influential Frank A. Vanderlip, former president of the *National City Bank* and founding member of the U.S. Federal Reserve. Bernays will therefore talk to his friend's wife about the event. "I suggested that a green ball be held in November under the auspices of the infirmary to benefit the hospital. I explained that an unnamed sponsor would pay the costs up to $25,000; our client would donate our services to promote the ball; the color green would be the motif of the ball and the mandatory color of all dresses worn at the ball." He added: "I can assure you that the cause is not Paris in green, but poison."

The fashion industry, no less, is Bernays' new target. A green ball would require not only green dresses, but also, he insisted, green gloves and green shoes, green handkerchiefs, green headbands, and even green jewelry. When the day came, New York's high society was there. Several event agencies and fashion editors were on hand. Even the day's menus are green: peas, salad, asparagus, olives, etc. And that's not all. A department head from *Hunter College* School of the Arts gave a seminar entitled "Green in the Work of Great Artists." A psychologist enlightened guests on the psychological effects of the color green. Even an office, called the *Color Fashion Bureau*, was opened for the occasion to advise guests on pairing green clothing with everyday objects. The office took on the task of sending out thousands of letters for interior designers and other suppliers of household items. Within months of opening, the office was inundated with requests for information—from 77 newspapers, 95 magazines, 29 unions, 301 department stores, 145 women's clubs, 175 radio stations, 83 furniture and decor manufacturers, 64 interior designers, 10 costume designers, and 49 photographers. It all worked out just as Bernays had imagined. A true success. Years later, author Robert Sobel would say of the event, "Green became the color of the year. Hill was thrilled. Bernays got a bonus"[36.]

But Bernays' greatest challenge during these years was the growing doubt in society about the harmfulness of tobacco. All smokers knew that cigarettes caused coughing, irritation of the throat, etc. What better way to divert attention than to show that the Company was making its products. So, what better way to deflect attention than to show that the *Company was* manufacturing its products in conditions that were favorable to the health of smokers? In those days, cigars were rolled in factories by workers who had to wet them between their lips to form them. The subsidiary of the Tobacco Company, *Cremos*, put an end to this practice by automating the industrial process. This was a good thing for the strategist Bernays.   He wrote, "Spitting is a health hazard because saliva can transmit tuberculosis and other diseases. I decided to draw the public's attention directly to the dangers of spitting and indirectly to the health and safety of Cremos cigars." The result was a massive campaign to get cities and towns to fight this bad habit. Warning signs against spitting, provided by the Tobacco Company, have been put up everywhere. They display ads proclaiming, "We know *spit* is a horrible word, but it's even worse at the end of your cigar… The war on spit is a crusade of decency … join it. Smoke a certified Cremos!"

---

[36] Robert Sobel, "*They Satisfy: The Cigarette in American Life*", Garden City, N.Y., Anchor Books, 1978.

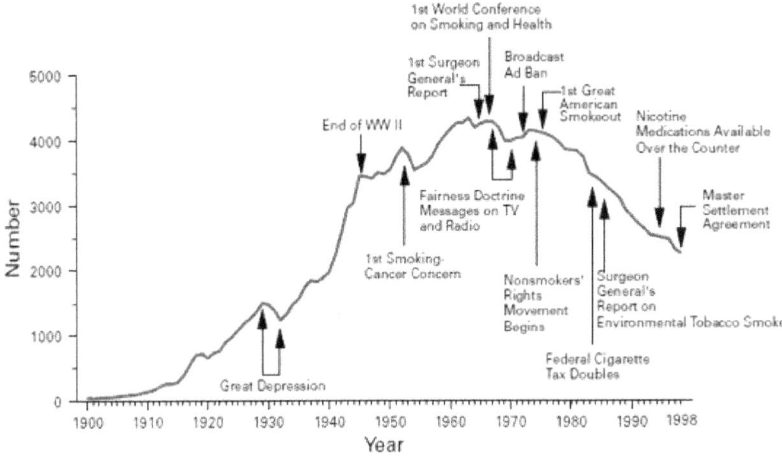


Annual cigarette consumption per adult in the United States since 1900 (official CDC data)[37].

We can note an interesting fact on the curve above: at the beginning of the 1950s, the first warnings concerning the link between tobacco and cancer were issued by researchers. As a result, there is a beginning of a fall in tobacco consumption. But it was short-lived. Indeed, the tobacco industry adopted the Bernays method to perfection by diverting attention as it did with sugar. To do this, they began funding hundreds of studies on possible sources of cancer. Sometimes it was completely crazy, for example, trying to demonstrate the dangers of tomato juice, egg yolk, the link between lung cancer and baldness, or between this disease and the month of birth[38]. This is the strategy of a diversion by multiplying the suspects. A 1969 memo from Brown & Williamson, then a subsidiary of British American Tobacco, reviewing the state of the tobacco industry's public relations and proposing "the best means" to counter the anti-smoking offensives, is quite clear. "Doubt is our product because it is the best way to compete with facts in the minds of the general public," it says[39].

---

[37] https://www.cdc.gov/mmwr/preview/mmwrhtml/mm4843a2.htm
[38] Documentary broadcast on Arte, "La fabrique de l'ignorance", Feb 24, 2021. Available online: https://www.youtube.com/watch?v=6IGVqsnxCE0
[39] https://www.industrydocuments.ucsf.edu/tobacco/docs/#id=psdw0147

The strategy of manufacturing ignorance is still applied today by many industries such as the chemical industry to sow doubt about the dangers of glyphosate, an herbicide suspected of being highly carcinogenic, or neonicotinoids, insecticides that decimate bees[40].

The worst thing is that by multiplying diversionary studies, not only do we divert attention from a real danger, but we end up making even well-informed people accept the unacceptable. Didn't we see in 2020 the LancetGate fraud study that demonstrated the so-called dangers of hydroxychloroquine-a drug that has been taken without a prescription for 70 years-relayed by the media worldwide and many TV doctors? This led to the stopping of clinical trials on this molecule. And this in the middle of the Covid-19 pandemic...

The lesson, Bernays wrote years later in his biography, is that ***"emphasis on repetition wins acceptance of an idea, especially if the repetition comes from different sources."***

Bernays learned in 1933 that Nazi propaganda chief Joseph Goebbels was using his book "Crystallizing Public Opinion" as the basis for his campaign of indoctrination and destruction. He heard about it from Karl von Wiegand, foreign correspondent for the *Hearst* newspaper, who visited Goebbels in Germany and toured his library[41]. Bernays long held back the story for fear of his image, but could not resist mentioning the information in his autobiography in 1965. He said he was "shocked" to learn of it. "But I knew that any human activity could be used for social purposes or misused for anti-social purposes. Clearly, the attack on the Jews of Germany was not an emotional outburst by the Nazis, but a deliberate and planned campaign," he wrote. It is easy to forget that everything is planned with Bernays, who leaves nothing to chance...

The existence of a "propaganda ministry" under the direction of Joseph Goebbels in the Third Reich contributed to the negative image of the term *propaganda*. Thus, it almost disappeared from everyday language and was *replaced* by *political communication* or *public relations*.

---

[40] Documentary broadcast on Arte, "La fabrique de l'ignorance", Feb. 24, 2021.
[41] Larry Tye, "The Father of Spin: Edward L. Bernays & the Birth of Public Relations," New York, Crown Publishers, 1998.

# CHAPTER II: The media caught in the Web trap

*"Not only do I not tire and can accompany you 24 hours a day, 365 days a year, I can be copied endlessly and present at different scenes to bring you the news,"*

—Qiu Hao (Chinese virtual journalist)

We have seen that the media have always been the essential interface in the influence exerted on populations through public information. But the Internet has come to brutally shake up this informational ecosystem. Return in this short chapter on a trap which closed without making noise on the traditional media.

## The Mainstream Media's Losing Battle for Attention

Internet becoming the fourth media after the paper press, the radio, and the television, it will naturally not escape the question of audience measurement (see Volume 1). But for the first time, the suppliers of the news, the traditional media, no longer have direct access to it. Advertising targeting, their main source of revenue, is slipping away from them, especially with the entry into the game of unexpectedly powerful players. I'm talking about Google and Facebook, of course.

Only three years after its launch in 1995 in a garage by two Stanford University students, Sergey Brin and Larry Page, Google, still in its beta version, already had to manage 10,000 requests per day. This number will increase to 500,000 in February 1999 before reaching 3 million in August of the same year. Its growth is exponential. The daily traffic will exceed 100 million queries in the year 2000, making the search engine an important source of information. It will quickly become an essential intermediary to access other media, which will give it an unprecedented strength. Having direct access to users, it is the one who holds the real keys to measure the audience. And it is especially him who can put forward a given source of information as well as relegate another one. The traditional media are caught in the clutches of the American giant, which now has the power of life and death over them. Even the very powerful *New York Times* will have the bitter experience of being forced to sell off many of its websites drowned by the search engine (see next sub-chapter). This is quite similar to the trap that small businesses have fallen into with Amazon. They display their products there, but it is Jeff Bezos's site that knows what users want and actually buys. When a product is on a successful trajectory, Amazon displays its own and puts it in the spotlight. The competition is relegated. By eliminating the maximum number of intermediaries, the e-commerce giant maximizes its profits. For information, it's the same thing, the product being the available brain time and the customer being the advertiser. Google has already cleaned up its act on many of its competitors, we'll come back to that, but intends to go even further. It has already announced the removal of cookies, these small files that websites use to track the activity of Internet users in order to offer them targeted advertising, from its Chrome browser in 2022. To justify its decision, the giant American brandishes the protection of users' privacy[42]. Incredible!

In 2004, Mark Zuckerberg, then a student, launched "The Facebook," a website that was initially reserved for Harvard University students only. Within the first month, more than half of the undergraduate population had signed up for the service. By 2006, the site was available to everyone. The network will have more than 200 million active mobile users by 2010. The traditional media open their accounts there and throw themselves into another trap. By relaying their content on Facebook, they will make the social network another intermediary that will escape them as it will be the new source of information for billions of people in the world. Once again, Facebook will hold the keys to the audience and therefore to advertising revenues. Alongside Google, it will have the lion's share of this market, valued at several hundred billion dollars. For the others, there will be crumbs…

---

[42] https://blog.google/products/ads-commerce/a-more-privacy-first-web/

The speed at which news spreads on the Web is another key factor in the decline of traditional media. To be informed now about the news of a person, organization, company …, you just have to be his follower. Each time a person posts a publication, a notification is received. You can react to it by commenting on it or by reposting it and thus spread the message to your own followers. This is how the virality of information on the Web is created, reaching millions of people in a record time. According to a report published by Reuters Institute at Oxford University regarding digital news[43], Facebook is the leading source of news in 2020 with 36% share, followed by YouTube (21%), WhatsApp (16%), and Twitter (12%). The latter remains stable compared to 2018,[44] but is now trailed by Instagram (11%), the other network owned by Zuckerberg's house, in addition to WhatsApp.

In the editorial offices, we are doing what we can to survive in this new media jungle. The overwhelming majority of traditional media have opened a website. Not surprisingly, this has been accompanied by a great loss of value, as information is often available for free on the Web. For the relatively successful *New York Times,* a digital subscription now costs only around $185 per year, compared to $675 for the paper version[45]. The newspaper saw its revenues from online sales exceed physical sales for the first time in 2020. The media acquired 2.3 million new subscribers on its website in 2020 alone, reaching a total of 7.8 million subscribers[46]. That's a third more subscribers for a quarter of the price!

Since 2009, a software called Chartbeat is used in editorial offices to measure the audience of articles published on their websites. This tool allows you to know in real time what content is read by Internet users. This is the beginning of the hunt for clicks and racy titles at the expense of the quality of the publications. With a strike force far from that of the Web giants, the model based exclusively on advertising does not work.

---

[43] https://reutersinstitute.politics.ox.ac.uk/sites/default/files/2020-06/DNR_2020_FINAL.pdf

[44] ELISA SHEARER AND KATERINA EVA MATSA, "News Use Across Social Media Platforms 2018," www.journalism.org, SEPTEMBER 10, 2018.

[45] Prices consulted on May 05, 2021.

[46] https://investors.nytco.com/news-and-events/press-releases/#data-item=The-New-York-Times-Company-Reports-2021-First-Quarter-Results

We then try the *freemium* model in which some content is accessible for free and others, requiring a subscription. But the problem remains the same, since it is Google that directs two thirds of the visitors to the sites of these media[47]. Even the revenues related to subscriptions do not escape the giant who keeps a good part of the value of each subscription made through its "Subscribe With Google" service.

Facebook, with its 2.8 billion users, is another significant source of traffic, which has given it the power to negotiate with several major media outlets including the Wall Street Journal, New York Post, BuzzFeed News, Business Insider, Washington Post, etc.[48] The latter allow it to include their content in a section dedicated to information on Facebook for a small fee. People get their information directly on the social network and do not go to the media's website. This is obviously another lost opportunity to attract readers to other articles. Not to mention the data collected by Facebook on people's reading and interests to offer them even more things to consult and keep them for hours.

In France, for example, the Facebook-Google duopoly captured 92% of online advertising growth in 2018[49], the main source of revenue for the media (in addition to state aid[50]). This naturally shifts the center of the fourth estate, slowly but surely, to the "platform," the latter becoming the master of what to highlight or on the contrary relegate. The media's loss of control over advertising, including in their own content, is accompanied by two disastrous effects. Advertisers now demand that their brand not appear alongside press articles containing a certain number of undesirable keywords, up to 3000, for fear of tarnishing their

---

[47] https://wan-ifra.org/2019/11/world-press-trends-2019-the-balancing-act-of-publishers/
[48] Lukas I. Alpert, "Facebook, Wall Street Journal publisher and others reach deal for news section," www.marketwatch.com, Oct. 18, 2019.
[49] Lionel Lévy, "GOOGLE, FACEBOOK… AND THE OTHERS?", www.strategies.fr, 11/27/2018.
[50] In 2012, the French government paid 1.2 billion euros in direct aid to the press (70 million euros in aid for the development of portage, subscriptions to AFP, 250 million euros in aid paid for the restructuring of Presstalis) and indirect aid (postal aid in the form of tariff advantages, a reduced VAT rate of 2.1% for the paper press, a lump-sum allowance for journalists), which represents 11% of the sector's turnover, which is valued at nearly 10 billion euros.

image. Thus, any content containing, for example, the word "rape" or "injury" is blacklisted, regardless of the context. The immediate effect is the deprivation of a large number of press articles, up to 30%, of advertising. The corresponding loss of revenue for the media amounts to $3.2 billion per year for the United States, England, Japan and Australia alone[51]. The second consequence is obviously the censorship or even self-censorship by the media themselves of certain subjects, because they do not bring in money! The first goal, which is to inform, is even more undermined…

The "platforms" now have the power of life and death over the media. That's why publishers and news agencies reluctantly agreed to give up their neighboring rights on the reuse of their content by Google to present it in search results for Internet users. At least that was the case until the European Parliament adopted the new copyright directive in March 2019, after two years of heated debate and intense lobbying. Its Article 15 provides that online platforms remunerate the press publishers whose content they use. But if the principle is fixed by the law, the modalities of content reuse and their prices are to be negotiated between the publishers and the platforms. France was the first European country to apply the reform, from October 2019. To comply, Google presented new rules that it intended to implement. Specifically, it will no longer display excerpts of articles (including the title, the heading, the beginning of the article) nor photos and video previews, in the results of its search engine as well as in its Google News Service, unless publishers allow it to do so … for free! If publishers refuse this condition, Google will continue to reference their news, but in an austere form (a simple title and a link). Such a measure naturally penalizes the publishers who see their incomes crumbling, because the probability of clicking on a link with little detail becomes minimal. Faced with this blackmail, the French Competition Authority has taken precautionary measures and has given Google three months to conduct negotiations with publishers. In its decision, the French Competition Authority considers that "Google may have abused its dominant position to

---

[51] John McCarthy, "It's a race to brand safety-how to battle ad keyword blocking," www.thedrum.com, 31 January 2020.

circumvent the law on neighboring rights" by imposing "unfair trading conditions on publishers and news agencies by avoiding any form of negotiation and remuneration." The Authority has taken into account that Google's new display policy has imposed more "unfavorable transaction conditions on industry players than those that pre-existed the entry into force of the Neighboring Rights Law, and than those that should have resulted from good faith negotiation." This is made possible "by the dominant position that Google is likely to hold on the market of generalist search services" in France, the Authority continues[52]. But the battle is not over, because the American giant has appealed the decision. The diktat that it imposes and from which the press publishers can hardly escape may therefore last for a long time.

In fact, Google's monopoly position allows it not only to gain time, but to go even further by signing the death warrant of any media … sometimes without warning. This is not speculation. This misadventure was experienced by the about.com site owned by the powerful and famous *New York Times* (NYT). The American newspaper simply let the wolf enter the sheepfold without realizing it until it was too late[53]. A little flashback to understand a carnage perpetrated without making any noise.

## With Google and Facebook, It's Do-or-die

In 2005, the *New York Times Company* purchased the about.com website, a consortium of hundreds of sites providing readers with specialized information on gardening, wellness, weddings, vacations and more. It was a "content farm," as they say, whose success was based on the structure of its website, designed to leverage user-published content online and optimized to appear on the first page of Google search results to generate traffic to sell advertising. Much of the NYT's revenue was tied to traffic generated on about.com through clicks on the search

---

[52] Chloé Woitier, "Droits voisins : l'Autorité de la Concurrence forcing Google to negotiate," www.lefigaro.fr, April 9, 2020.
[53] Scott Galloway, "The Four: The Hidden DNA of Amazon, Apple, Facebook, and Google," Random House Large Print; Large Print edition, 2017.

engine, which placed the newspaper in a fragile and dependent position. The NYT paid $410 million to acquire the about.com site, a shrewd move since the sites were reaping billions of clicks from Google searches. The market valuation of about.com climbed to about $1 billion. On the surface, about.com was a safe bet, but it was like a fountain that Google could dry up at any time, because it was given the key to the valve upstream. In exchange for a good place in the search engine results, the NYT newspaper gave it access to its servers and all its content. And Google not only crawled every piece of content, but also minced it for its users. So, when someone searches for a hotel in Paris, Google offers a link to a NYT article about the city, while displaying its own ad for the George V. (a famous hotel in Paris) at the top of the page. In this arrangement, which at first sight was beneficial for the newspaper, because it attracted people, it was in fact digging its own grave. Google, in processing the searches, knew better than the NYT itself what exactly the readers wanted and what they were likely to want in the future. As a result, it could target readers much more precisely and make more money from each ad. Up to ten times more. The NYT was just picking up crumbs. It's as if Google encouraged people to buy tickets to Disneyland for $30 a ticket, and once at the park, visitors could play an irresistible ride—irresistible because Google, as AI and big data specialist, had analyzed the desires and choices of the park's visitors to the extreme and concocted a tailor-made game for them—a game operated by Google, of course, and whose admission ticket cost $300. Big mistake by the NYT! Worse still, overnight, on a certain February 24, 2011, Google decided to update its Panda algorithm[54] and sent all the Internet content farms, including about.com, packing. The goal was simple: to eliminate intermediaries to increase profits in the long term. A well-tried strategy now. With a simple wave of the hand, the policeman 2.0 [Google] closed down some Internet highways to offer more direct routes that it operates alone, bringing toll companies to their knees without mercy. Two months later, Janet Robinson, the CEO of the NYT confirmed that about.com "suffered a negative impact on its page views," after Google's update. About a year and a half after

---

[54] Panda is Google's algorithm for ranking websites in search results. It is named after the engineer Navneet Panda who developed it.

Panda was born, the NYT is selling about.com for just $300 million, 25% less than its purchase value, and less than a third of the valuation it achieved some time before. Hit hard by the crisis, the NYT decided to sell no less than 16 regional newspapers for $145 million[55]. Another farm, an aggregator of blogs and media content, that Google's Panda stopped short in its tracks is Wikio, a European company co-founded by Pierre Chappaz[56] in 2006. It was a success that attracted some 28 million unique visitors in six different countries. Less than a month after Google's update, the French entrepreneur announced the "death," to use his own words, of his aggregator and the refocusing of his group's activity on another more viable model[57]. By the way, this update was an earthquake for the whole SEO industry, a sector specialized in natural referencing of websites, helping them to get a better ranking in the search results on Google and therefore attract more traffic. In a way, by closing a lot of highways, Google has also brought down the curtain to many maps and GPS vendors, as it has made them obsolete! And it's not over yet, because the worst is yet to come thanks to, or because of, depending on where you stand, artificial intelligence (AI). The fatal blow will come with the abandonment of the click and the shift to the use of voice assistants where only an answer to a user's request counts. Only the top of the podium, therefore the throne (first slot), will be valuable and the place will be expensive, very expensive. Smaller businesses that can't afford it will naturally be left on the sidelines. And the other GAFAM[58], notably Google's first customer Amazon, are dangerously threatening the search engine's business with voice assistants. Jeff Bezos is also looking for a shorter route for his customers to "the world's largest store," a long-standing goal of his[59], but his voice

---

[55] Reuters, "IAC acquires About.com from New York Times Company," AUGUST 27, 2012.

[56] Pierre Chappaz is the founder of several web companies, including the price comparison site Kelkoo, which was sold for 475 million euros to Yahoo!

[57] Benoit Raphael, "Google Panda Victim: How I Killed My Content Farm," www.forbes.com, Sep 12, 2011.

[58] GAFAM stands for Google, Amazon, Facebook, Apple, Microsoft. It is a term used to refer to the web tech giants.

[59] With its Marketplace, Amazon allows third-party sellers and merchants to offer their products on its site. This win-win partnership can quickly become a lure. Thanks to data analysis, the American giant quickly understands which products are most in demand

assistant is not limited to selling Amazon products to users and encompasses just about everything that can be ordered remotely, from alkaline batteries to pizza to movie tickets to music. It is also a home automation interface, which can be used to control comfort elements such as lights, air conditioning, blinds, etc. All assistants offer these functionalities and the war they will wage will be terrible as the stakes are so high. The partnership signed between Carrefour (the French Walmart) and Google, to be able to order via the voice assistant of the American firm and to be delivered by the French hypermarket, is only the beginning of this confrontation[60].

Coming back to the field of information, to get the latest news in France, all you have to do is ask a voice assistant,[61] "What's the news?" and it will launch the latest complete news update produced by France Info[62]. If the public media jumped at the first opportunity to offer content, Bezos's firm, owner of the Washington Post, let's remember, managed to convince about twenty other French media to bring content to its Echo speaker, which arrived in France in 2018[63]. Thus, the editorial offices, in order not to miss what could be the next big revolution, they felt obliged to follow the movement. The platforms propose and the media dispose. And unsurprisingly, the work that newsrooms are doing to create custom content for connected speakers is *free*. Yes, free! I firmly believe that the scenario of the New York Times Company's story with Google will happen again with the voice experience. Media outlets around the world will make their content available, and for free, and when the GAFAM analyzes the data about user reactions to newscasts, they will get the most value out of it. When Bloomberg talks about the latest "connected stroller" in its podcast and the mother-to-be exclaims "Did you hear that,

---

and if they are not available in its store, it calls on its suppliers to supply them and of course display them at the top of the list of search results as soon as they are available. The other merchants will only keep the crumbs.

[60] Claire Bouleau, "Why Alexandre Bompard, CEO of Carrefour has allied himself with Google," www.challenges.fr, 17.04.2019.

[61] Amazon's Alexa, Google's Google Assistant, Apple's Siri and Orange's Djingo.

[62] https://www.francetvinfo.fr/partenariats/franceinfo-n-1-de-linfo-en-continu-sur-les-assistants-vocaux_2799533.html

[63] Marie Turcan, "How Amazon Echo Leverages Media to Win Over the French," www.numerama.com, June 06, 2018.

honey? This is exactly what we need for our baby," neither the media nor the stroller vendor is aware of this reaction. But the GAFAM has not only identified a potential customer for the stroller, but also a couple on the verge of becoming mom and dad—a golden goose for any marketer. But that's not all. When the speaker hears an insult uttered by a user following a speech by Trump on migrants, the assistant will probably blacklist Fox News and no longer offer its content or perhaps just censor excerpts from future podcasts. This is information on demand, a service that does not aim to inform, but to please the user in order to keep him or her listening as long as possible. The listener will be trapped in information bubbles and this is not a concern for the GAFAM. Their only objective is to maximize their profits. Their assistants will probably make exceptions and some concessions to the next war that the United States will wage, but it will probably be one more propaganda to defend only American interests.

## Giving in to the easy way, the other big mistake of traditional media

The other platform that has turned into a trap for the media is Twitter. It has become *the place to be* for journalists. They have accounts there and are subscribed *en masse* to the most important personalities, especially politicians, looking for the slightest publication to relay. They logically rebroadcast the same information and what differentiates one journalist from another, namely going to the field to get exclusive information, has become a luxury reserved for only some. The worst part is that the activity on the blue bird network is time consuming. It consumes the attention of journalists when they monitor tweets, but not only[64]. They usually have their own articles relayed on the platform to drive traffic back to their media websites. This usually leads to comments and often attacks from users to criticize the content of the publications. Journalists naturally feel compelled to respond, and when they do, it only makes the exchanges longer and more virulent. Not only is it a waste of time, not

---

[64] Mathew Ingram, "Do journalists pay too much attention to Twitter?", Columbia Journalism Review, October 10th 2018.

doing the real job of searching for information, journalists sometimes lose their mental and physical health. We will see this a little later on a concrete example.

And by dint of immersing himself in the Web, a journalist becomes an Internet user like any other, subject to crowd psychology, and quickly forgets the rigor required in his work. This is what is shown in a recent American study[65]. Shannon McGregor from the University of Utah and Logan Molyneux from Temple University conducted an experiment involving about two hundred journalists, some of whom used Twitter a lot and others only moderately. Some of these subjects were presented with headlines from the *Associated Press* (AP) website, while others were presented with tweets containing headlines from the same agency, but which had been manipulated to look like anonymous tweets. The researchers then asked both groups of journalists to rate the relevance of the tweets. The result? Journalists who reported spending a lot of time on Twitter and relying on it for their work ranked the anonymous tweets as superior to AP stories! "Our results indicate that routine use of Twitter in news production affects judgment," the researchers write. "For journalists who incorporate Twitter into their reporting routines, and those with fewer years of experience, Twitter has become so normalized that tweets are deemed just as newsworthy as headlines from the AP feed. This can have negative implications," they say. Among those implications, they argue, is that journalists can get caught up in a kind of pack mentality in which a story is considered important because other journalists on Twitter are talking about it, rather than because it is newsworthy.

Another reason for this behavior and for the presence on Twitter in general is, as mentioned above, in order to increase traffic to the websites of the journalists' media employers. According to a study by Cision France[66], 91% of journalists use social networks for their work. And 54% of them say they can't do without it to do their job. Sixty-four percent of them confide in using social networks to relay their own

---

[65] Shannon C McGregor and Logan Molyneux, "Twitter's influence on news judgment: An experiment among journalists", Journalism, Volume: 21 issue: 5, page(s): 597–613
[66] https://www.cision.fr/ressources/livres-blancs/journalistes-et-reseaux-sociaux/

articles[67]. It has therefore become a full-fledged work tool in the business. This is obviously not surprising when we know that journalists' remuneration is indexed on the number of clicks or views of their articles. When journalists were asked in another more recent study whether audience measurement—number of views, engagement ...— has changed the way they evaluate information, 55% of them totally agreed with this statement[68]. With solicitations and the hunt for clicks as the main compass, the quality of information is naturally being pulled down.

The consequences of all the above phenomena are unsurprisingly dire, both for the uninformed citizen and the journalist who does anything but real information. The decline in standards poses a mortal threat to the journalist, his replacement by the machine. If high-quality output is no longer required, why not simply turn to the computer, which will do the same and will neither complain of fatigue nor ask for payment? I have already put forward this hypothesis in a previous book, *the AI dark side,* of the endangerment of the journalist's job with the improvement of artificial intelligence algorithms. This was quickly confirmed and more and more major media outlets are using automatic article writing tools. In May 2020, the American and British editorial teams of MSN's news portals, nearly 80 journalists learned that they would be fired and replaced by robots[69]. And this trend will not be limited to print media, but will extend to audio and visual journalism. China's government news agency Xinhua already has virtual anchors on staff, able to work around the clock every day[70]. After Qiu Hao, the first male virtual anchor to present a live newscast, it is now the turn of the beautiful Xin Xiaomeng to do the same, perfecting both her voice and her posture. She has already given about 3400 news for 10,000 minutes of airing! [71]

---

[67] "SOCIAL NETWORKS: FRIENDS OR FOES OF THE NEWS MEDIA?", https://www.cision.fr,
[68] "STATE OF THE MEDIA IN FRANCE", Cision, 2020 edition.
[69] Chloé Woitier, "Microsoft fires journalists to replace them with robots," www.lefigaro.fr, 01/06/2020.
[70] Leïla Marchand, "En Chine, le JT est présenté par une Intelligence artificielle," www.lesechos.fr, Nov. 11, 2018.
[71] Ruozhu Zhao, "Will artificial intelligence replace human news anchors on television? In China, it is already happening," www.digitalcenter.org, July 18, 2020.

The two Chinese virtual journalists Qiu Hao and Xin Xiaomeng.

It is worth mentioning that journalists are not the only ones to fall into the trap of the Web. It is the case of cabs and restaurants with Uber, merchants with Amazon, or teachers with Udemy. Users benefit is undeniable, but these professionals have actually dug the grave of their profession. It's like for the cashier who holds the automatic terminals, we already do without him or her and one day we will do without them too…

# CHAPTER III: Propaganda 2.0

*"There is nothing wrong with deceiving people if it is in their best interest, or if they have given their implied consent to be deceived as part of a persuasive strategy. People attending a magic show give that consent,"*

—Chris Nodder

The Web has become the new essential media. Everyone uses it to inform themselves or to share information with others. Because of its global reach, it is a powerful tool for any person, organization or state that wants to influence public opinion, both within a country and abroad. Not surprisingly, the Web has become the 2.0 battlefield where all kinds of manipulations are allowed, with sometimes disastrous consequences on individuals, organizations, or even States. This is the subject of this chapter.

We hear every day about *fake news* in the media. The real meaning of that refers to the action of feigning or inventing information in order to harm. *Fake news* is often intended to mislead the public in order to manipulate them, orient their opinion and eventually provoke a reaction from them. To achieve this, one often uses manipulation techniques that mix negative emotions such as fear, indignation, anger, or disgust. Several elements play an important role in the propagation of *fake news*. The medium and the frequency of dissemination are essential. The power of a global network like the Internet is infinitely greater than that of the traditional media. The context also plays an important role and crises are an opportune time for virality. The target or audience, usually a well-defined community, is another factor. *Fake news* is like a virus, its replication depends strongly on the host. Finally, the source of the information is a very important element too. The trust it generates is decisive in the virality. We will come back to all these elements in the rest of the book, especially in the chapter devoted to group psychology. For the moment, we will focus on a few examples of information manipulation on the Web, often unknown, but whose impact is truly devastating.


## The 2.0 Virus That Brings Down Mammoths

An economic study conducted by the University of Baltimore in partnership with the Israeli firm CHEQ estimated the cost of *fake news* to the global economy at $78 billion[72]. This estimate takes into account both the losses incurred directly and the costs incurred by companies or states to counter fake news. Let's look at two concrete cases.

In 2017, the American channel ABC reported that the National Security Advisor, Lieutenant General Michael Flynn, would testify that Donald Trump had asked him to contact Russian government officials during the 2016 election campaign. If confirmed, this would have opened the door to *impeachment* and a governing crisis in the world's largest economy. Immediately thereafter, from 11:06 a.m. to 11:34 a.m., the S&P 500 (the weighted index of the 500 largest publicly traded U.S. companies) dropped 38 points. That's a dry loss of about $341 billion! It turned out that the "explosive report" ABC was talking about was a fake and the channel only retracted the information after the stock market closed. The final loss was $51 billion[73]. This is the equivalent of the annual budget of the French National Education System or almost double that of the French Defense Department, which was lost in a single day!

Among the targets that have suffered the most from *fake news in* recent years is a French company. Its case was cited as an example in a white paper on *fake news* written by the Heiderich firm in partnership with the Visibrain company[74].

---

[72] Eileen Brown, "Online fake news is costing us $78 billion globally each year," www.zdnet.com, December 18, 2019.
[73] Ibid.
[74] White paper "Fake news in 2019", Visibrain & Heiderich.

On November 22, 2016, at 4:04 p.m., i.e., during the quotation period, general and financial news agencies received a fake press release that resembled those that might be issued by the French construction giant, VINCI Group. Only a trained eye or a scrupulous journalist will have noticed that the sending address is hosted by the VINCI website while the official URL is vinci.com. The press release is signed by Paul-Alexis Bouquet, Head of Media Relations for the Group, and announces the discovery by the company of a 3.5-billion-euro embezzlement, informs of a revision of its financial accounts as well as the dismissal of its financial director, whom it accuses of serious accounting errors. The telephone number at the end of the press release is wrong.

Four minutes after the reception of the false communiqué, a tweet from a journalist of the media *Investir* mentions it. A couple of minutes later, the powerful American agency *Bloomberg* repeated the false communication in a dispatch. Several minutes followed during which VINCI's share price plummeted and lost 18% of its value. At 4:15 p.m., the Autorité des Marchés Financiers (the French SEC) detected an anomaly and suspended the quotation.

*From a false press release to a false denial ... to a true denial!*

Following this false press release, a false denial, impersonating the director of communications, was received by the press agencies and stated that "VINCI has been the victim of a very serious attempt at disinformation." *Bloomberg* published it at 4:27 p.m., but it was not until 20 minutes later, at 4:48 p.m. to be precise, that VINCI issued the official denial, in the form of a press release, which was published on the company's website at 5:02 p.m.

Nearly 5,000 tweets were posted, by 3,444 Internet users, about the fake press release. Among these messages, only 35 used the term "Fake News," that is to say 0.7% of the messages published on the case. Result of the races, a loss of 7 billion euros for the company. In the meantime, some smart people who bet on the fall of VINCI's share price probably cashed in nicely... The French financial markets authority (AMF) has requested a fine of 5 million euros against the American agency *Bloomberg* for the dissemination of the false information.

For the anecdote, the AFP agency had the same misadventure a few years before, in 1995, by releasing a dispatch on a false information it received by phone concerning Eurotunnel, but the effect was less important[75]. Twitter was not born yet...

It is easy to see that *fake news* on the Web is much more viral than denial, because the audience whose attention is captured is different in one case or the other. When you publish a piece of information like "the city's water is contaminated," all the citizens feel concerned, in danger, and will automatically repeat the information to warn others. This is a cognitive bias inherent to risk avoidance. But when the water company publishes "Our analyses show no signs of concern," the impact of this denial is much more limited. Employees who care about their company will eventually relay it, but the audience in question is very small. And more generally, fear is a much better seller than any information, no matter how reassuring. Also, the snowball effect of the propagation of the information within a community where everyone interprets it in their own way and adds a personal touch accentuates the virality. This is what was shown in a recent study entitled "Bad news has wings,"[76] where it was noted that the perception of the threat and the amount of negative content that it conveys increases with the transmission of the message, especially in topics dealing with serious threats. And unfortunately, re-exposure to the initial less negative message is ineffective in reducing the effect caused. The damage is irreversible.

And if a source of authority such as a major television channel or a personality with a large audience in turn broadcasts negative *fake news*, the effect becomes downright explosive and its consequences catastrophic as we saw with the VINCI and S&P500 examples given earlier.

---

[75] Thierry Noisette, "From Eurotunnel to Vinci, AFP has become more cautious," www.nouvelobs.com, 08 December 2016.

[76] Jagiello RD, Hills TT, "Bad News Has Wings: Dread Risk Mediates Social Amplification in Risk Communication," Risk Anal. 2018 Oct; 38(10):2193–2207. doi: 10.1111/risa.13117. Epub 2018 May 29. PMID: 29,813,185.

## When the catfish leads the way

Everyone has heard of phishing, a technique that consists of making a victim believe that he or she is addressing a trusted third party—a bank, an administration, etc.—in order to obtain personal information such as a password, credit card number, ID card number, birth date, etc. The target often receives an email, sometimes an SMS, with a link to a website that is actually a copy of the real one. The personal information entered is then stolen, reused or resold on the *dark web.*

Another fraud technique consists in pretending to be a person who has received an inheritance of a few million dollars and sends an e-mail to his victim to help him release the money. To lure the victim, the fraudster promises him a share of the money. I have personally received a few messages of this kind, as have many others, from people who pretended to be sons of African dignitaries whose money was in European banks. Once the trust has been gained, the criminal goes on the attack and asks for a money transfer via Western Union to be able to pay the first step necessary for the effective release of the money. The request is, of course, repeated as long as the victim pays and does not realize the evil plan.

Another scenario is to impersonate someone by inventing a false identity and story. This is called *catfishing*, a term related to a documentary called *catfish* released in 2010, about an American producer, Nev Schulman, who fell in love with a 19-year-old girl who is actually a 40-year-old housewife! The title of the film is inspired by a technique used by fishermen who transport cod from Alaska to China. The problem is that the fish remain inert in the tanks of the boats during the long journey and arrive at their destination in a bad state. Their flesh is then tasteless for consumption. To keep them agile, the fishermen would have had the good idea of slipping some catfish among the fish to terrify them and keep them moving and thus staying fresh. This is all fictional, but it does reflect the phenomenon of *catfishing* of one person slipping into another's life and leading them on! There are many such stories that have led to scams, with the victim eventually falling in love and easily giving in to requests for money. A four-year-long impersonation of an Australian actor, Lincoln Lewis, even led to the suicide of one of the victims. Other stories ended with sexual harassment or blackmail, kidnapping or murder of the targeted persons. But *catfishing* has crept into a rather unexpected field, that of information, or rather propaganda 2.0.

*When one Alice can hide another…*

It all began in May 2017 when the *Washington Post* published an article devoted to the U.S. administration's attempts to counter disinformation operations carried out by Russian secret services on the Web[77]. The piece points to an investigation the FBI has been conducting for several months into a woman named Alice Donovan as part of a counterintelligence operation dubbed "Northern Night." The bureau's reports describe her as an agent operating under a pseudonym in a Kremlin-led troll army. Yet Donovan has posted as a *freelance* journalist who writes for a dozen online newspapers. That's CounterPunch, a former left-leaning bimonthly political magazine founded in 1994. When the editors of this media are made aware of the intruder's case, they naturally carry out their investigation, which, of course, they had to do at the very beginning before opening their columns to her. They then discovered the truth[78]. Several of Donovan's articles were in fact copies of articles already published elsewhere. Such is the case with a piece about the ongoing war in Syria titled, "U.S.-led coalition airstrikes against Assad's forces was no accident." Journalists quickly track down the source of the text and come across the original author, one Sophie Mangal, who published it in *The International Reporter*, a now-vacant site[79]. This woman [Mangal] presents herself as an "investigative correspondent" and editor for a site called *Inside Syria Media Center* (ISMC), which publishes in English and Arabic. Several articles, two to three a week, have been submitted by Mangal to CounterPunch magazine by email over the past 12 months, but they have not been published. This is in contrast to other sites such as *Global Research,*

---

[77] Adam Entous, Ellen Nakashima and Greg Jaffe, "Kremlin trolls burned across the Internet as Washington debates options," https://www.washingtonpost.com, December 25, 2017.
[78] JEFFREY ST. CLAIR— JOSHUA FRANK, "Ghosts in the Propaganda Machine," www.counterpunch.org, JANUARY 5, 2018.
[79] You can go back to the pages of the site by consulting the web archives.

*International Reporter*, and *Veterans Today*, on which she published about 60 articles between November 2016 and August 2018. When Alice Donovan's plagiarism of her work was discovered, *CounterPunch* journalists contacted her for confirmation and to apologize for the mistake in passing. Mangal quickly responded, "Of course it's my article. It was originally published on the *Inside Syria Media Center website*. In fact, I don't know this Alice Donovan and who she is. In fact, I wonder why my article was published with you under this name when the copyright belongs to me. I would be very grateful if you could publish my articles with the correct reference in the future…"

From that moment on, Donovan disappeared from the radar, which confirms the plagiarism of Mangal's work. Mangal continued to solicit the media, but the *CounterPunch* team soon became suspicious. They were fooled once, it would be wrong to suffer the same humiliation a second time. The suspicion began when Mangal's writing was analyzed, which was pretty bad for a journalist who supposedly graduated from the University of North Carolina. But her profile is a far cry from the ghostly Donovan. This young woman described as an "American patriot" and "passionate about Syria" does indeed publish on real sites, more than 50 articles on *Global Research* alone, and she has a Facebook account. She has a good following on Twitter with 13,000 followers. She even interviewed an editor at *CounterPunch* magazine via email. She shares a curious trait with Donovan, however: she uses a *mail.com* email address, something very rare except among hackers or anyone who doesn't want to identify themselves or leave a trail behind like an IP address. We then decide to interview Mangal via Skype. The attempt will fail four times, the one we try to reach arguing by email that she is in the Syrian mountains and that she does not have a good Internet connection. The research will show that she came out of nowhere, finding no trace of her at the university or in any video on the web, a rare thing for a journalist nowadays. Mangal's name remained visible at the bottom of the *Inside Syria Media Center* website articles until the last attempt to connect via Skype after which it disappeared and was just replaced by *ISMC*. She also deleted her Facebook page and stopped all internet posting. As ISMC website did not post any address of her location, her chief editor Mariam Al-Hijab was contacted in vain. It won't get any better with Anna Jaunger, another amazingly productive colleague who regularly publishes 3–4 articles a day! In the space of two years, Jaunger's byline has appeared in more than 600 articles. The ISMC archive[80] for her articles is 64 pages long, with 10 articles per page. That's a lot of work for one journalist. While many articles are short, rudimentary reports, others are more elaborate. For example, her articles detailed troop movements in Syria, casualties in battle, and arms shipments to rebel forces. They also provided intelligence estimates of the secret networks of money flows to finance the rebels. Presentations on covert operations and other analyses of political strategies in the U.S. and Europe are provided. Of course, it would take enormous resources to produce this tremendous amount of work.

The domain name of the ISMC site was registered in 2016 in the Netherlands by a certain Barna Robert, but without leaving an email or phone number. This person had a Facebook page, now closed, that mentioned an origin from Aleppo in Syria and living in North Carolina in the US. The media began to be visible via a Facebook group called *Syria: Look Inside*, created in 2016, before being renamed *Inside Syria Media Center*. The site gained popularity over time and especially credibility by managing to get interviews with respectable people like Tom Ginsberg, a University of Chicago professor specializing in international law. This was done by email, but the simple reader did not see such information anywhere. Only the content of the exchange is visible and especially the authoritative name. To boost the visibility of content on the Web, articles often refer to the ISMC site, giving it exclusivity for certain information. This is the case of an article by Anna Jaunger on the site ekurd.net, which accuses the United Nations special envoy to Syria of wanting to exclude the Kurds from the negotiating

---

[80] https://web.archive.org/web/20180316175932/https://en.insidesyriamc.com/author/annajaunger/

table, preferring jihadists[81]. And this information would be the result of an investigation by the ISMC media. This unconsciously reinforces its credibility with readers. This is the art of the new information war…

In trying too hard to give credence to her writing, Mangal committed a faux pas. Her name appeared in a *Global Research* article alongside that of a Syrian journalist and artist named Anan Tello. The latter, who works for the real *Arab News* media, took a week to produce the article about Syrian entrepreneurs who are struggling to develop the country's economy despite the war. She denied any link with this alleged Mangal… We will soon know that Mangal is a second Alice who plagiarized articles from the *New Yorker* and many other media such as the AFP[82]. As long as a piece of information was favorable to the Syrian regime, it was good for Mangal to pick up. Her friend Jaunger, the Lucky Luck of news who writes faster than her shadow and describes herself as an Australian journalist, also made a mistake. She used on her Twitter profile the passport photo of an English woman identified as an employee in a London company. She also stopped posting on ISMC after March 2018.

The *CounterPunch* media was fooled for several reasons, the first one being, of course, the ease of accepting contributors without a minimum of verification. As long as it's free, you don't have to worry too much about looking for lice. This is the evil of today's information. Yet, it was easy to check at least some basic data on the identity of the person. A little more research would have even allowed the journalists to notice that the model used to build the ISMC website is exactly the same as the one used for the other site cherished by Mangal *International Reporter,* with the only difference being the photo used for the home page![83]

---

[81] https://ekurd.net/syrians-misturas-resignation-2016-11-14

[82] https://www.yahoo.com/news/deadliest-month-syria-civilians-us-led-strikes-monitor-103330002.html

[83] I was able to verify this by looking at the web archives here:
http://web.archive.org/web/20161116175304/https://theinternationalreporter.org/notice-us-presidential-elections-2016/
https://web.archive.org/web/20170515114433/https://en.insidesyriamc.com/2017/05/02/investigation-route-of-bulgarian-weapon-deliveries-to-syrian-islamists-exposed/

The other reason probably lies in the selection bias of this rather left-wing and anti-war media. A paper that comes to denounce an American air raid that causes civilian casualties is naturally welcome by them. That's probably why it was targeted rather than another newspaper. The very first email sent by Alice Donovan, introducing herself as a *freelance* journalist, was entitled: "Does the United States need such friends?" It addressed the subject of Turkish President Erdogan, who at the time supported the Syrian rebels against Assad. The question is, of course, worth asking, but that is not the point here. Above all, the information must be transparent and its peddlers well identified. This is the problem that currently exists on the Web. It is becoming more and more difficult to know who says what, and when.

Sophie Mangal's last article appeared on August 28, 2018, on *Oriental Review*[84], a site that is very similar to ISMC and still publishes articles today. In doing my little checking, I found that this domain name was created in 2010 at REG.ru, a web domain registration company based in Moscow[85]. The shadow war continues…

## When the Sea Lion Hunts in an Organized Gang

There is a term that deserves to be considered for a moment: *troll*. The word would refer to an unfriendly or aggressive monstrous creature from Scandinavian folklore. On the Web, a troll characterizes an individual or a behavior that aims to generate controversy. Thus, the neologism "troll" (verb) refers to the fact of artificially creating a controversy that focuses attention, at the expense of useful exchanges. Originally, the term refers to a joke in which the troll takes satisfaction in having succeeded in fooling his victims, in having made them waste time. Its scope widened in the 2010s, especially after the introduction of the retweet feature, and it can now also be applied to sending provocative and offensive messages, exacerbated by people's anonymity on the Web. This harmful behavior often turns into cyberstalking, especially since the emergence

---

[84] https://orientalreview.org/author/sm/
[85] Address: PO box 87, REG.RU Protection Service, Moscow, Postcode 123,007, Phone: +7.4955801111, Fax: +7.4955801111.

of a particular type of trolling called *sealioning*. It is a type of harassment that consists of pestering people with insistent requests for arguments or repeated questions, while maintaining the appearance of courtesy and sincerity. Sometimes these are invitations to engage in debate, made incessantly and in bad faith. The term *sealioning* refers to a comic strip, "Wondermark" by David Malki, published in 2014 (see figure below). It features a dialogue in which a sea lion harasses the other person and demands an explanation after hearing a nasty thing about her[86].

*Sealioning* is rapidly gaining popularity after it was used in 2014 to refer to *Gamergate*, a case involving the ethics of video game journalists as both judges and litigants, the censorship and politicization of video games, and issues of sexism in the video game community. The harassment campaign targeted several women working in the industry, including game developers Zoë Quinn and Brianna Wu, and feminist

---

media critic Anita Sarkeesian. The campaign of harassment against Quinn and others has included doxing[87], threats of rape, and death. Even conferences have been canceled for threatening to attack the targets! *Gamergate* supporters say they are a movement with no official leaders or manifesto, and have organized anonymously on Internet platforms such as 4chan, Reddit, etc. But by far the most virulent attack campaign has been on Twitter. It was enough to write a tweet with #Gamergate with the names of the targeted people or to retweet other messages for it to become viral. Andy Baio, a web specialist who has contributed to the development of several digital platforms, said he had never seen such "pack behavior" in his eight years on Twitter. He then decided to analyze the numbers related to the hashtags #Gamergate and #NotYourShield (the one from the opposite camp) over three days, from October 21 to 23, 2014[88]. The numbers are staggering: 38,630 accounts posted 316,669 tweets, of which 217,384 were retweets, a proportion of 69%. Around 25% of the accounts were created just two months before the surge. A lot of people have obviously answered the call to lead the battle. But the offensive does not stop there.

Some news sites that defended the targets of Gamergate, including those of the American press group Gawker, which specializes in gaming, paid the price. They were targeted in two stages (Operation Disrespectful Nod): first by boycotting them and then by trying to cut them off by putting pressure directly on the advertisers via massive email campaigns, including to the top executives of the companies, so that they withdraw their ads from Gawker. Several brands such as Intel, BMW, Nissan, Mercedes, Unilever, Kelloggs …, have given in[89]. Cornered, the Gawker group had its management team replaced in 2015. It would declare bankruptcy less than two years later, when it was ordered to pay $140 million in compensation to Peter Thiel, co-founder of PayPal and advisor to Donald Trump, for privacy violations[90]. Thiel succeeded in

---

[87] Doxing is the practice of seeking out and disclosing information about an individual's identity and privacy on the Internet for the purpose of harming them.

[88] Andy Baio, "72 Hours of #Gamergate," https://medium.com, Oct 27, 2014.

[89] Caitlin Dewey, "Inside Gamergate's (successful) attack on the media," www.washingtonpost.com, Oct. 20, 2014.

[90] Max Read, "Did I Kill Gawker? Or was it Nick Denton? Hulk Hogan? Peter Thiel? Or the internet?", New York Magazine, 08–2016.

finishing the job of the alt-right movement of Gamergate supporters, who later remained active and became Trump's supporters throughout his presidency. Some will not hesitate to make the link between this movement and the QAnon group[91], these Trump supporters who have gone up to Washington and illegally entered Capitol Hill[92]. We will come back to this.

At the same time as Gamergate was taking place in the United States, another sea lion hunt was going on in France, and it had been going on for four years. The leader of this offensive was a Facebook group called "Ligue du LOL." Created by the journalist Vincent Glad, it gathered men and women, bloggers, journalists, communicators, advertisers, etc. Most of them were Parisians and met regularly in bars in the capital where many people from Twitter at the time were gathering. The case broke on February 8, 2019, when the newspaper Libération published an article where it interviewed a dozen alleged victims who denounced acts of moral harassment by some members of the group. The media then seized on the case. According to the media outlet L'Obs, "by successive mutations, the joke becomes mockery. The mockery, tackle. And the tackle, harassment."[93] At first, the members of the league "set themselves up as arbiters of what is cool and what is not. Then, little by little, they turn into "political commissioners." According to the newspaper Marianne, the members of the league become aware that when they get together to make fun of a single Internet user, their "strike force" is "colossal."[94] The targets, often recurring, find themselves under their fire, but also that of some of their followers, trolls who, in their wake, attack with flocks of tweets: this is what we call "raids."

After the scandal broke, some alleged members of the group were laid off, suspended, fired, or had some of their projects and collaborations

---

[91] A. Khaled, "The Unlikely Connection Between Gamergate and QAnon," https://medium.com, Oct 11, 2019.

[92] https://www.siliconsasquatch.com/blog/2021/1/14/ssp-63-the-silicon-sasquatch-podcast-episode-63

[93] Sophie Grassin and Véronique Groussard, "Members of the LOL League lived as 'enfants terribles,'" www.nouvelobs.com, February 24, 2019.

[94] Alexandra Saviana and Étienne Girard, "Ligue du LOL. Les caïds de la cour de récré journalistique," Marianne, February 22, 2019.

stopped. But it was too late, because the evil has already taken its toll on some of the targets. The worst thing about this informational chaos is that if the victims react, often otherwise fragile people, they only amplify the phenomenon by publicizing their own "executioners." Their testimonies show deep psychological suffering, like that of Iris Gaudin, who, after being invited to join Twitter by Vincent Glad, was subjected to an avalanche of "filthy" sexual tweets[95]. Daria Marx, another target, says that every time she tweeted, she was afraid "to be found out and shot." Blogger Matthias Jambon-Puillet received insults about himself and his work, and a pornographic photo montage was sent to minors in his name. He tells of disastrous psychological suffering: "I cried, I shook, I vomited, I asked for help. To this end, he turned to certain members of the league, whom all replied: "I'm sorry for what's happening to you, we know, but there's nothing we can do about it, just ignore it until it passes."[96] Other victims tell of how they lost confidence in themselves. For example, Capucine Piot says: "By reading about me all over the networks, I was convinced that I was worthless." Aïcha Kottmann agrees: "Before the LOL League, I thought I was a good writer. Afterwards, I started to restrict myself in the choice of subjects, to write without ever publishing anything…". Christophe Ramel, who also testified, was targeted because of his blog. "The more my blog worked, the more they targeted me. And I am not the only one to have noticed this correlation," he said. For him, too, the self-confidence undermining of his stalkers had an impact on his professional development. While he was making a living from his technology blog, he made the decision to quit. Six years later, he has a permanent job, but cannot bring himself to reactivate his blog[97]. In addition to the psychological damage, Iris Gaudin also claims that the denigration had an impact on her career: "Freelance work became scarce, I felt burned out in the profession."

---

[95] Yann Philippin, "Le sexisme sans borne de la Ligue du LOL," Mediapart, February 16, 2019.
[96] Martin Stameschkine, "Cyberstalking: With the LOL League, Twitter kingpins thought they were the kings of the Internet," https://parismatch.be, February 11, 2019.
[97] Mahaut Landaz, "I changed my career path because of the LOL League," www.nouvelobs.com, February 12, 2019.

One would be tempted to think that this affair is limited to the Parisian microcosm, to a bunch of spoiled children who think they can do whatever they want, but the phenomenon is far from being isolated. The divide created on social networks is so deep that a multitude of groups have formed, each defending an ideology, an interest, a friend ..., resorting to violence. And sometimes it doesn't take much for lightning to strike any person. And the blows can come even from where we do not expect them.


## When the Sea Lion Makes Politics

It is May 1, 2019, a day of protest in Paris marked by violence between police and Yellow Vests, as it has been for several months already. In the panic created by a police charge, demonstrators took refuge in the enclosure of the huge hospital of La Pitié-Salpêtrière. The same evening, the French Minister of Interior Christophe Castaner published a message on Twitter: "Here, at La Pitié-Salpêtrière, we attacked a hospital. They attacked its medical staff. And we injured a police officer mobilized to protect it. Unwavering support for our police forces: they are the pride of the Republic." He added: "Our law enforcement intervened to save the resuscitation service." The tone is serious. The Web is ablaze, from TV sets to social networks, through radio stations, the communication war between the Yellow Vests and government supporters is raging. But the first images are beginning to emerge and they do not agree with the version of the minister. The newspaper Le Monde contacted the nursing staff to collect testimonies and at the same time launched an appeal on Twitter: "If you have images/videos or testimonies of yesterday's events at La Pitié Salpetrière, you can communicate them to us." The responses were not long in coming, but not the ones we expected. They were supporters of President Macron, not happy with the approach. "If you do not have an image, shut up and do your job instead of fishing for *fake news*," "Do not send him anything at all, let him move his ass and investigate" ... The journalist Samuel Laurent, although accustomed to polemics on the Web, is stunned as he tells in a book[98]. "I have never

---

[98] Samuel Laurent, "J'ai vu naitre le monstre, Twitter va-t-il tuer la démocratie?", Les Arènes, 2021.

experienced this, even during the worst polemics in which I was involved: 1,240 mentions received in twenty-four hours, of which 821 were from Macron's supporters, for a total of 546 different accounts. That is 34 mentions received per hour, or one every two minutes. An industrial frequency," he writes. However, the investigation will soon show, with testimonies and videos to support it, that there was no attack on the hospital. The newspaper Libération came to the same conclusion and made its front page on Friday, May 3 with the headline: "The *fake news* came from inside.[99] Be that as it may, on Twitter, the activists of the presidential party En Marche do not give up. The pack is unleashed. Yellow has become the target of all colors, including the manipulation of photographs showing protesters on the roof of the hospital. When Le Monde takes a closer look at the subject, it discovers that the presidential majority seems to have decided to adopt a strategy of astroturfing[100] and opinion manufacturing on the networks, using hordes of increasingly aggressive accounts. Since the fall, we have thus seen the appearance of hundreds of pro-government and anti-Yellow Vests accounts that, far from the benevolence advocated by the presidential majority in 2017, do not have words harsh enough against the "jaunards" (Yellows), these violent and conspiratorial factious people who are bringing France to its knees. "They parasitize the comments of our articles, post frantically on Facebook and Twitter, virulent, tireless, repeating in a loop the same messages, the same arguments," says the journalist.

Le Monde then proposed to Samuel Laurent to investigate the phenomenon. He did so, but adopted a somewhat suicidal strategy by reporting his findings in real time. He then noted that the majority of the accounts were indeed created in October or November 2019, that is, at the beginning of the Yellow Vests movement. "They are totally dedicated to a single topic, namely typing on the "jaunards"; they relay

---

[99] https://www.liberation.fr/france/2019/05/02/attaque-de-la-pitie-salpetriere-la-fake-news-venait-de-l-interieur_1724619/

[100] Astroturfing or planned popular disinformation refers to manual or automatic information propaganda techniques that aim to give a false impression of spontaneous behavior or popular opinion on the Internet. This attempt at manipulation refers to the AstroTurf artificial turf used in stadiums.

everything that goes on in this direction; finally, they have a frenetic activity. "Some manage to post hundreds of messages per hour, mostly retweets," he writes. By exchanging with some accounts, he discovers very varied profiles, in particular of retired activists incited to go "to the front," and who sometimes devote hours, even days, to it. Some of them tell him how this environment in a jar, this "between us," radicalizes them, pushes them to more and more verbal violence, to more and more anger towards the enemies of the government: "Everything polarized me. I was more and more angry. Against the presidency and its awful treatment of the crisis and against the media who were selling their news thanks to this. I was outraged all the time," confided one of them, who has since distanced himself from the militant action. Above all, he discovered that behind these profiles hides a rigorous organization: the activists are encouraged to create several accounts, generally one "official" and several "unofficial" on which they allow themselves to be more violent. They communicate upstream on other closed tools, notably Telegram messaging, to coordinate, designate targets to go and harass—particularly real or supposed opinion makers. The system is sophisticated. A number of accounts are managed directly by permanent members of the LREM (President Macron's party).

In the spring of 2019, the journalist gets his hands on a valuable archive, which includes all the messages exchanged on one of the Telegram groups of LREM activists. We can read months of activity, calls for "retaliation" towards such and such guilty of such and such a statement. We can see the interventions of the head of social networks of LREM, Pierre Le Texier, or the deputy Aurore Bergé, both very connected to these armies of trolls.

The response to the journalist's investigation was not long in coming. The violence of the attacks he receives is unheard of. Despite his experience on social networks, he has difficulty filtering the messages. He even becomes obsessed to the point of reading them all. He notices a limitless hatred and violence that eats away at him day after day: "Nick Conrad's fascists [a rapper] wanted to hang me, they are calling for involuntary psychiatric hospitalization. The investigation haunts me, their messages too. This is one harassment campaign too many, and it's overflowing an already full vase. At the beginning of June, I have a very bad stomach ache. A doctor diagnosed me with a kidney stone. Kidney colic, the disease of stressed men. I stopped working for a few days, the publication of the survey was delayed." Several times delayed, his investigation finally comes out on July 4, without much impact. The same day, he announced his decision to leave Les Décodeurs ("fact-checkers" service at Le Monde), his column on France 5, and Twitter. "I know that my physical and mental health is at stake," he confided. All this was obviously not without consequences on his private life: "When my partner notices my silence, she asks me what's going on. She ends up going to see by herself what they say about me on the networks. She was traumatized for a long time, to the point of losing her voice for several weeks and developing a phobia of public transport. When I saw her reaction—her tears, her fear—I finally understood that it was mine that was not natural.

In this month of June 2021, several months after the publication of his book, the journalist is still active on Twitter! I said in *Volume 1 of* the book that the Web is a digital heroin…

## Social Network Filter Bubbles

I devoted the first part of the book to the addiction to social networks and this irresistible urge to constantly seek new information. What about the content? Is it at least useful? Does it reflect reality? This is indeed where another problem lies, just as important, because the information that reaches us from social media does not reflect reality, but a reality, filtered, which suits the platforms more than the users. Zuckerberg, the CEO of Facebook, once addressed his teams in these terms: "A squirrel dying in front of your house may be more relevant to your interests right now than people dying in Africa."

As mentioned earlier, millions of people now get their news from social networks, with Facebook and its affiliates, followed by YouTube (Google) accounting for the lion's share of what is offered as news. Already in 2007, Zuckerberg said: "We produce more news in a single day for our 19 million users (we're talking about 2007, that's more than

2 billion subscribers in 2020) than any other media in its entire existence."

What people don't know is that the timeline of this news, the criteria for classic publication, has nothing to do with the news feed offered or viewed online. Better yet, if my neighbor and I do a Google search using the exact same keyword at the exact same time, the results will not be the same. Even the total number of results will be different.

The secret of this lies elsewhere, in the algorithms. Facebook, for example, introduced a feature called EdgeRank in 2007 that ranked content according to three parameters: affinity (the proximity of the user to the content), attractiveness (the reactions already generated by the content), and freshness (date of publication). It was abandoned in 2013 in favor of an AI-based algorithm composed of some 100,000 parameters[101]. It is the same on the side of Google, which has integrated customization since December 2009. The result of this mechanism, based on the exploitation of user data (browsing history and duration on each site, gender, age, geolocation, type of device used…), is that the content presented to one person is different from that of another for exactly the same query at the same time. So, what criteria do digital platforms use? The answer can be found in one word: engagement.

Facebook, YouTube and all the others want us to engage and spend the most time on their platform. So, they offer us news that grabs our attention. And what grabs one person's attention is naturally not the same as another. Hence the need for automatic targeting based on artificial intelligence (AI) algorithms.

As a general rule, digital platforms reinforce our opinions with the type of information offered to us, avoiding other points of view that we quickly discard. Let's take the example of a query such as "nuclear power in 2019" on YouTube. A person with an environmentalist streak, which YouTube has clearly identified thanks to the personal data collected on him, may be offered the latest Greenpeace assault on a nuclear power plant to show the security flaws of this type of sensitive

---

[101] Matt McGee, "EdgeRank Is Dead: Facebook's News Feed Algorithm Now Has Close To 100K Weight Factors," https://marketingland.com, August 16, 2013.

site. Another person identified as "all nuclear" would be offered a topic on the harmfulness of emissions linked to fossil fuels. This is the example I used in a previous book[102] to explain the concept I called "IoD" or Information on Demand. For me indeed, the algorithm is not made explicitly to manipulate or harm, but responds to a demand related to a human cognitive bias called confirmation bias: people prefer news that confirms them in their ideas. It is this kind of information that increases their engagement score and this is well captured by the AI. So, the algorithm suggests what creates comfort, not discomfort due to cognitive dissonance. "We experience conflicting thoughts as real psychological discomfort. Brain[103] scans have indeed revealed that cognitive dissonance activates emotional areas such as the anterior insula and dorsal anterior cingulate cortex," explains Don Vaughn, a neuroscientist in the Department of Psychology at the University of California Los Angeles[104]. "Given that we prefer to avoid negative experiences, it's not surprising that people avoid the immediate psychological discomfort of cognitive dissonance by simply not reading or listening to opposing views," he says. There is also an energetic component involved, he adds. Essentially, processing new facts, ideas and perspectives requires real neural effort. In other words, it forces our brain to reconfigure its network of connections to understand, evaluate and eventually incorporate the new knowledge it is exposed to. In this sense, it is a neural bias to save energy, which is difficult to dismiss. In simpler terms, the brain is lazy.

Shortly after publishing the book talking about IoD, I came across an already common term for the same phenomenon: "filter bubble." This term was introduced by activist and author Eli Pariser in a book called "The Filter Bubble, What the Internet Is Hiding from you," which he published in 2011[105]. Pariser describes how the Internet tends to give us

---

[102] Boussad Addad, "La face cachée de l'intelligence artificielle", VA Editions, 2020.
[103] Scintigraphy is a nuclear medicine medical imaging method that produces a functional image by administering a radiopharmaceutical drug (MRP) whose radiation is detected once it has been taken up by the organ or target to be examined.
[104] Wendy Rose Gould, "Are you in a social media bubble? Here's how to tell," www.nbcnews.com, Oct. 21, 2019.
[105] Eli Pariser, "The Filter Bubble: What The Internet Is Hiding From You," Penguin Press, May 2011.

what we ask for: "Increasingly, your computer screen is a kind of one-way mirror, reflecting your own interests as algorithmic observers watch what you click." Pariser calls this reflection a filter bubble, and "all these platforms create a unique universe of information for each of us."

Also, when information spreads in a social network, it is generally taken up and modified by various relays. Thus, it reaches a person through several sources in appearance, which reinforces its credibility. This is the "echo chamber" phenomenon, a concept introduced by tobacco industry lobbyist John F. Scruggs. For him, reinforcing the credibility of a piece of information to convince a certain audience involves two steps: 1) repeating the same message from different sources 2) broadcasting similar, but complementary messages from the same source[106]. Thus, the algorithm not only creates the bubble by implicitly exploiting the confirmation bias, but also amplifies it by creating an echo chamber.

But this model has limitations for platforms. You click on a link, which indicates an interest in something, which means you're more likely to see articles on that topic in the future, which in turn is the main topic for you. You are trapped in a loop. This trap is what is referred to by scientists as the "local minimum," encountered in mathematics in optimization problems. This can be roughly summarized as follows in the context we are dealing with: you are presented with content related to horseback riding, for example, and this engages you, but we don't know that your favorite sport is actually kayaking, because you have never had the opportunity to mention it in your comments or any other publication on the Web. So, the time spent on the platform is not optimal and this does not go in the direction of its designers. That's why from time to time you find yourself with new content in your YouTube search or Facebook news feed. It's an attempt to get you to spill the beans on the other, still hidden, facets of your life. This dose of randomness introduced on the web is an intentional engineering strategy to seek out other unexplored fields of the space of possibilities, and potentially new gains. Once we have discovered the "kayaker" in you, we offer you more content related to the sport you are passionate about. So, we make

---

[106] https://www.industrydocuments.ucsf.edu/tobacco/docs/#id=mgxn0061

you spend more time on the platform, for your greater pleasure again and again. Long live the dopamine!

As data is collected, the results of the algorithms, or from time to time the algorithms themselves, are adjusted. This is done through the feedback obtained after proposing a certain amount of content to users, some of which actually engage them well, but not others. A correction is then made on the unsuccessful contents. Targeting becomes more and more efficient, capturing more of the users' brain time and making the platforms more money by exposing more ads.

All this is done while forgetting the primary purpose of information: to inform and educate people. Eli Pariser aptly summarizes the harm resulting from filter bubbles as follows: "By definition, a world constructed from the familiar is a world in which there is nothing to learn." Not to mention that the diversity that fades in bubbles with the standardization of opinion ends up distorting information and reducing its usefulness.

In 2007, Professor Michael Mauboussin presented a large jar of candy to his seventy-three students at Columbia Business School. Question: how many pieces of candy were in it? Estimates ranged from 250 to 4100; the actual number was 1116. The average error was 700—a whopping 62%—showing that the students were terrible estimators. Now comes the interesting part of the story. Even with all those highly incorrect responses, the average estimate was 1151, only 3% of the true number. Furthermore, only 2 students out of the 73 did better than the group average. Thus, even though individually everyone was wrong, collectively the group was incredibly accurate. This experiment has been repeated several times since it was introduced in 1987 by economist Jack Treynor and the result is still accurate[107]. This explains, by the way, the astonishing 91% correct answer rate of the joker called "public vote" of the famous TV game *Who Wants to Be a Millionaire?* Now ask for a group consultation, in which an individual would probably take the lead, and everything would fall apart![108]

---

[107] https://blog.asmartbear.com/ignoring-the-wisdom-of-crowds.html
[108] This wisdom-of-the-group phenomenon is explained as follows: people who do not

The conclusion of the story is that the diversity of information is a richness and the uniformity due to the filter bubbles reduces it to nothing. The result of this is often the tipping into sectarian thinking as we will see later.

## Peril on Democracy

It is said that the media are the fourth estate, because they are, and should be, a counter-power to the three branches of government: executive, legislative, and judicial. They are there to inform the citizens in all independence and transparency. It is a pillar of democracy where each citizen makes his or her electoral choice on the basis of objective information that is as complete as possible concerning all the points of view and policies in contention. This is what we call an informed choice. This has unfortunately been undermined for decades with the concentration of the *mainstream* media in a few hands. Moreover, democracy requires equal access to information for all citizens, which is dramatically undermined by the filter bubbles of social media.

In his farewell speech[109], President Barak Obama expressed concern about the filtering of digital information:

"For many of us, it has become safer to retreat into our own bubbles, whether in our neighborhoods, our college campuses, our places of worship, or our social media feeds, surrounded by people who look like us and share the same political perspectives and never question our assumptions. The rise of naked partisanship, the increase in economic and regional stratification, the splintering of our media into a channel for every flavor, all make this grand sorting seem natural, even inevitable. And increasingly, we are becoming so secure in our bubbles that we

---

know the correct answer vote randomly, which eliminates their votes because they are evenly distributed across all possible choices. The people who know the right answer, even if they are in a very small minority, then tip the balance towards the right choice. If now there is a consultation and an ignorant person takes the lead, because often the ignorant are the majority in the group (just look at the total of wrong answers in Who Wants To Win Millions? for example), this whole scheme collapses!

[109] Heather Landy, "The 'great sorting': In his farewell address, Barack Obama names the danger in our social media filters," https://qz.com/, Jan 11 2017.

only accept information, true or not, that fits our opinions, rather than basing our opinions on established evidence."

Filter bubbles can indeed cause cognitive biases and shortcuts, amplifying their negative impact on our ability to think logically and critically. As Pariser writes: "The filter bubble tends to greatly amplify confirmation bias—in a way, it is designed to do so. Consuming information that conforms to our ideas of the world is easy and enjoyable; consuming information that forces us to think in new ways or to question our assumptions is frustrating and difficult. This is why supporters of one political party tend not to consume the media of another. As a result, an information environment built on clicks will favor content that reinforces our existing opinions over that which challenges them."

But the evil does not stop there, far from it. If our identity shapes the digital media, they also shape us, far beyond the classic propaganda and censorship.

Let's start with the effect of search engine results like Google on the opinion manufacturing. An article[110] published by Princeton University on work conducted by Robert Epstein, a professor of psychology, and his colleague Ronald E. Robertson, a specialist in human-computer interaction, reveals the extent of the influence on voting, which is even greater than that of the mainstream media, already well established[111]. First, it turns out that the ranking of search engine results has a significant impact on voting choices, as users tend to trust the top-rated results more. In a total of five randomized double-blind experiments

---

[110] Robert Epstein and Ronald E. Robertson, "The search engine manipulation effect (SEME) and its possible impact on the outcomes of elections," Edited by Jacob N. Shapiro, Princeton University, Princeton, NJ, Accepted on July 8, 2015.

[111] The Robert Epstein and Ronald E. Robertson article states, "It is already well established that biased media sources such as newspapers, political polls and television influence voters. A 2007 study by DellaVigna and Kaplan found, for example, that whenever the conservative-leaning Fox television network entered a new market in the U.S., conservative votes increased, a phenomenon they called the Fox News Effect. These researchers estimated that biased Fox News coverage was enough to move 10,757 votes in Florida in the 2000 U.S. presidential election: more than enough to swing the election, which was won by the Republican presidential candidate by just 537 votes. The Fox News effect also proved less significant in the most competitive television markets."

conducted on a population of nearly 5,000 undecided voters (the USA and India), it is found that (i) biased search rankings can change the voting preferences of undecided voters by 20% or more (ii) the change can be much larger in certain demographic groups, and (iii) the search ranking bias can be masked so that people are not aware of the manipulation. Researchers call this type of influence, which could apply to a variety of attitudes and beliefs, the "search engine manipulation effect" or SEME for short. I quote them: "Given that many elections are won by small margins, our results suggest that a search engine has the power to influence the results of a significant number of elections with impunity. The impact of such manipulations would be particularly significant in countries dominated by a single search engine company."

The fears raised by this work proved to be well founded less than two years after its publication in 2014. Google's role in the 2016 U.S. election would have been more than a murky as its CEO, Sundar Pichai, was publicly criticized at the GAFAM antitrust hearing in July 2020. A Republican congressman, Jim Jordan, called him out: "[…] what concerns me and many Americans is that we know what Google did in 2016. We all know about the email the day after the election where senior executives at your company were talking about the silent donation that Google made to the Clinton campaign. […] We're 97 days away from the election [2020 election] and the power that these big companies have to impact the election, what people, what American citizens can see before they vote is pretty damn important." He added, "That's why these committee hearings are important. Look, we all think the free market is great. We think competition is great. We love the fact that it's American companies, but what's not great is censoring people, censoring conservatives and trying to impact elections. If this doesn't end, there has to be consequences. There has to be consequences. That's what I'm concerned about and I think that's what so many Americans are concerned about." Sometime later Jordan asks him the question, "Will Google change its search results to help Joe Biden in the 2020 election?" Faced with Pichai's evasive answers, Jordan had to prod him three times to get a straight answer.

When one does a search on Google about the leaked emails proving the Clinton campaign donation, the engine naturally returns to mainstream media articles where the giant denies the accusations. I could have insisted and searched the bottom of the results, but a simple query on the alternative engine duckduckgo.com allowed me to find the right information on the first try, both the copies of the emails and the names of the different protagonists of the case[112].

Google clearly does not have a monopoly on censorship and all the other networks practice it, without even hiding from it. It even became obvious during the coronavirus crisis where any alternative information is discarded. Even doctors who just talk about their job, or their method of treating their patients, and who can therefore benefit others, see their accounts blocked! It's the last straw if even the scientific debate is muzzled. This topic was not missed during the GAFAM antitrust hearing by veteran Congressman Greg Steube: "I was sent a YouTube video of doctors discussing hydroxychloroquine and discussing the non-hazards of sending children back to school, and when I clicked on the link, it was deleted. And then I was sent a different link on YouTube, and it was deleted. I just checked again, just to be sure, and it says that this video was removed for violating YouTube community rules. How are doctors giving their opinion on a drug they think is effective in treating Covid-19 and doctors who think it's appropriate for kids to go back to school for violating YouTube community guidelines when all these videos of violence are all posted on YouTube?" Another congressman, Jim Sensenbrenner, blames Facebook for the same actions, "I think it's a legitimate topic of discussion. And it's up to the patient and their doctor to determine whether hydroxychloroquine is the right drug under the circumstances." So, here's Zuckerberg's response, "First to be clear, I think what you're referring to happen on Twitter (indeed, the same policy was applied on that network). So, it's hard for me to talk about it. But I can talk about our policy on this. We ban content that poses an imminent risk of harm. And stating that there's a proven cure for COVID *when there isn't one* might encourage people to

---

[112] Tyler Durden, "Google Was 'Working To Get Hillary Clinton Elected' With 'Silent Donation' According To Leaked Internal Email," https://theduran.com, September 11, 2018.

go out and take something that might have adverse effects. So, we're removing that." So, here's Zuckerberg becoming a self-proclaimed doctor and benefactor of humanity! Who are we kidding? During this same global crisis where millions of people are glued to their phones, this same Facebook refused to delete a video, broadcast live, of the suicide of a 33-year-old American soldier suffering from post-traumatic stress disorder after having fought in the Iraq war. The video of horror remained available for hours, because it "did not violate the standards of the community," according to the response of the firm after reporting[113]. Who doesn't remember the Christchurch massacre of 51 people, broadcast live on the same platform? Who is Zuckerberg kidding?

All this does not bode well. This way of orienting the opinion is obviously a worrying drift, putting in danger the freedom of expression, in particular that of the scientists, how much important, and the democracy as a whole.

## The Illusion of Democracy

In the final weeks of the 2012 U.S. presidential election, a disturbing figure emerged from the databases of Barack Obama's Chicago headquarters: half of the voters under 29 targeted in the *swing states[114]* did not have an associated phone number. For a campaign focused on youth, this was a stain. The team had a ready-made solution: a Facebook application. "I think this will be the most revolutionary technology developed for this campaign," said Teddy Goff, Obama's digital campaign manager at the time. He was not mistaken, as we shall see.

More than a million Obama supporters signed up for the app and gave the campaign permission to look at their Facebook friends lists. In an instant, the campaign had a way to see young, hidden voters. About 85% of those without a listed phone number could be found in the friends

---

[113] David Gilbert, "Facebook Refused to Take Down a Live-Streamed Suicide. Now It's All Over TikTok," www.vice.com, September 8, 2020.
[114] In U.S. presidential elections, a swing state is a state with an undecided vote, which can switch sides from one election to the next between the two dominant parties and swing the final vote.

lists. Plus, Facebook offered an ideal way to reach them. "People don't trust campaigns. They don't even trust media organizations," Goff says. "Whom do they trust? Their friends."

The campaign called this strategy, "targeted sharing." And in the final weeks of the campaign, the team messaged supporters who had signed up for the app, asking them to share "specific" online content with "specific" friends by simply clicking a button. More than 600,000 fans signed up and reached out to more than 5 million of their friends, asking them to sign up to vote, donate money, cast a ballot or watch a video designed to change their minds just in case. Using vast databases, a team of Chicago geeks created micro-targeting models to find the best approach for each potential voter. "We're not just sending you a banner ad," says Dan Wagner, the Obama campaign's data analysis manager. "We're providing you with relevant information about your friends," he says.

Early tests of the system revealed significant changes in voter behavior. People whose friends sent them request to register to vote were more likely to do so than similar potential voters who were not contacted. Was this a surprise? Not really.

Rather, it confirms the results of a serious study, published in the journal *Nature*[115], conducted by researchers at the University of California, San Diego, during the 2010 U.S. midterm elections. The experiment targeted 61 million users of the Facebook network. The results show that the messages directly influenced the political expression, information seeking, and voting behavior of millions of people. In addition, the messages not only influenced the users who received them, but also their friends and their friends' friends. The effect of social contagion on voting—my friend votes so I vote—was greater than the direct effect of the messages themselves, and almost all of the transmission occurred between "close friends" who were more likely to have an actual (physical) relationship.

---

[115] Robert M. Bond, Christopher J. Fariss, Jason J. Jones, AdamD. I. Kramer, Cameron Marlow, Jaime E. Settle, and James H. Fowler, "A 61-million-person experiment in social influence and political mobilization," Nature 489, 295–298 (2012).

Researchers estimate that because of a single message received on Election Day, about 60,000 people who were targeted directly and 280,000 through social contagion went to the polls, for a total of 340,000. This represents 0.14 percent of the total voting age population (236 million in 2010). After adjusting the estimates, correcting for some errors and restricting to only what is actually observable in the experiment, the figure rises to 0.60 percent, or a total of 1.4 million voters. This is a significant number.

Gustave Le Bon already spoke of the immense power of contagion in his book on crowd psychology[116]. He wrote: "When a statement has been sufficiently repeated, and there is unanimity in the repetition, as has happened with certain famous financial enterprises rich enough to buy all the contests, what is called a current of opinion is formed and the powerful mechanism of contagion intervenes. In crowds, ideas, feelings, emotions and beliefs have a contagious power as intense as that of microbes. This phenomenon is very natural since it is observed in animals themselves as soon as they are in a crowd. The tic of a horse in a stable is soon imitated by the other horses in the same stable. A panic, a disorderly movement of a few sheep soon spreads to the whole flock. In humans in crowds, all emotions are very quickly contagious, and this explains the suddenness of panics. Cerebral disorders, like madness, are themselves contagious. We know how frequent insanity is among insane doctors." And Le Bon adds an important element: "Contagion does not require the simultaneous presence of individuals on a single point; it can take place at a distance under the influence of certain events which direct all minds in the same direction and give them the special characteristics of crowds, especially when minds are prepared by distant factors [...] This is how the revolutionary explosion of 1848, which started in Paris, suddenly spread to a large part of Europe and shook several monarchies."

With the advent of the Internet and exchanges made at the speed of light, social contagion is even easier. The previous study demonstrates, for the first time in history, that political mobilization via contagion on a social

---

[116] Gustave Le Bon, "Psychologie des foules (1895)". Published by Félix Alcan, 1905.

network works. The Obama campaign team was, of course, aware of this and adopted it. His opponent Mitt Romney used it, but with a less sophisticated version. But it wasn't going to last too long for the Republican Party. So, both sides have set themselves up for a fiercer technology battle in future elections. "The campaigns are trying to design what the new door-to-door will look like and what the next phone call will look like," Patrick Ruffini, a digital strategist for the Republican Party, said in 2012. "We've already started looking," he clarified[117].

The thunderclap will indeed come four years later in the 2016 presidential elections with the arrival of Trump into the White House. The affair now has a famous name: *Cambridge Analytica*. I will not go back over this large-scale political scandal, which I have already covered in detail in the book "the dark side of AI,"[118] from the creation of the parent company of this British company [Cambridge Analytica] to its involvement in Trump's election and the referendum that led to Brexit. I therefore invite the reader interested in electoral micro-targeting, based on algorithms and not on the relatively rudimentary approach presented here, to consult it. Everything that is explained there is non-technical and accessible to the general public, I would like to remind you.

Campaigning and going to the people is obviously normal and part of the democratic game. What is less normal is micro-targeting based on psychological profiling that influences voters by pressing on their weaknesses without their knowledge. This is what the algorithms used in this context do. Voting should instead be based on transparency and informed information about political programs and not on manipulation. Otherwise, democracy would only be an illusion…

---

[117] Michael Scherer, "Friended: How the Obama Campaign Connected with Young Voters," https://swampland.time.com, Nov. 20, 2012.
[118] Boussad Addad, "La face cachée de l'intelligence artificielle", VA Editions, 2020.

## Nudging or How to Reincarnate Bernays

If you're interested in economics, you've heard of Milton Friedman (1912–2006), winner of the 1976 Nobel Prize in Economics and founder of the Chicago School. This institution of liberal economic thought has been very influential in the Western world, with leaders such as Ronald Reagan (United States) and Margaret Thatcher (United Kingdom) having been its best disciples, even if they did not leave it. This school is also at the origin of the privatization policies initiated by the World Bank in developing countries. This school of thought defends the idea that reducing state intervention in a market economy is the only way to achieve prosperity.

This is the antithesis of the interventionist policy pursued in the United States by Roosevelt with the *New Deal* to recover his country from the Great Depression of the 1930s. It was also a far cry from the *Bretton Woods* agreements, signed in 1944 by the war-torn Western countries, which had become a breeding ground for communism. At the time of these agreements, the British delegation was led by a certain John Maynard Keynes (1883–1946), probably the most influential economist of the 20th century. For him, the state, through its intervention, "is able to re-establish fundamental equilibria," without infringing on the autonomy of private enterprise[119]. This is the doctrine of Keynesianism.

Perhaps there is room for a political "third way" that could reconcile the two currents: libertarian paternalism. This is the idea put forward by Cass Sunstein and Richard Thaler in a book entitled *"Nudge."*[120] A *nudge is* presented as a well-intentioned public policy or action, based on common sense (rational), which aims to correct the weaknesses of human nature (cognitive biases) by encouraging individuals to make decisions that are most advantageous to them. It is not a question of forcing the person, but of influencing him or her without his or her knowledge to act in a certain way, in his or her best interest. Isn't this the idea supported by Edward Bernays in Propaganda, the interest of the individual not necessarily being at the rendezvous of the promise? Isn't

---

[119] https://www.economie.gouv.fr/facileco/john-maynard-keynes
[120] Cass R. Sunstein, Richard H. Thaler, "Nudge, improving decisions about health, wealth, and happiness", Yale University Press, 2008.

it the same principle as brandishing the rag of freedom to push women to smoke, while forgetting to mention the disastrous effects of tobacco on their health? The reality is that the person who is the object of the manipulation is kept out of all the stakes, by the very essence of *nudge*, the very principles of freedom are purely and simply flouted. Some people do not hesitate to describe libertarian paternalism as an oxymoron[121].

The authors of *Nudge* develop their thinking by drawing on the work in behavioral economics of Kahneman and Tversky[122] and starting with an observation they describe as follows: "Those who reject paternalism often claim that human beings do a great job making choices, and if not great, certainly better than anyone else (especially if the other work for the government). Whether or not they have ever studied economics, many people seem at least implicitly familiar with the idea of homo economicus, or economic man—the notion that each of us infallibly thinks and chooses well, and thus fits into the classic picture of human beings portrayed by economists. If you look at economics textbooks, you will learn that homo economicus can think like Albert Einstein, store as much memory as IBM's Big Blue and exercise the will of Mahatma Gandhi. Really. But the people we know are not like that. Real people have problems with long division if they don't have a calculator, sometimes forget their spouse's birthday and have a hangover on New Year's Day. They are not homo economicus; they are Homo sapiens." The authors do indeed classify people into two groups of creatures, the "Econs" and "Humans." The first, "Proud children of Homo Economicus, are rational in their choices, arbitrate as best they can, are

---

[121] Gregory Mitchell, "Libertarian Paternalism Is an Oxymoron," November 2004, Northwestern University law review 99(3).

[122] Kahneman and Tversky have shown through numerous experiments that individuals do not behave like homo economicus but mobilize "rules of thumb" and heuristics with many biases and leading to suboptimal decisions. In his 2011 best-selling book, a synthesis of several decades of research, Daniel Kahneman proposed to understand these decisions by distinguishing between system 1, which is fast, intuitive and emotional, and which would be at the origin of these biases, and system 2, which is slow, reflective and rational, and which would allow to avoid them. In passing, I would like to point out that research in the field of artificial intelligence exploits Kahneman's work to try to develop models close to human behavior.

perfectly informed, never make a big decision without checking, selfish, associative, do not follow fashion phenomena, never communicate with anyone if they do not benefit from it, and are never as good as when the laissez-faire philosophy is totally respected." The latter are sometimes "ignorant, uninformed, act mechanically (automatic system), take little time to make crucial decisions, are often very lazy" and , in short, are not that good at leading their lives and embracing what is best for them. The authors give a concrete example: "Take the problem of obesity. The obesity rate in the U.S. is now approaching 20 percent and more than 60 percent of Americans are considered obese or overweight. There is overwhelming evidence that obesity increases the risk of heart disease and diabetes, often leading to premature death. It would be quite fantastic to suggest that everyone choose the right diet, or a diet that is preferable to what could be produced with a few nudges. Of course, sensible people care about the taste of food, not just health, and eating is a source of pleasure in itself. We do not claim that all overweight people do not necessarily act rationally, but we reject the claim that all, or nearly all, Americans make optimal food choices. What is true for dieting is true for other risk behaviors, including smoking and alcohol consumption, which lead to more than five hundred thousand premature deaths each year."

I would have liked the authors, to at least nuance the subject a little, to refer to Edward Bernays to show that it is under cover of this same paternalism that millions of cartons of tobacco were offered to American soldiers who left to defend their country during the Second World War or encouraged women to claim their right to freedom to smoke in public in the streets of New York. It was at this time in human history that smoking exploded for the first time.

Isn't the definition of the boundary between nudge and sludge (misuse of nudge)[123], itself subject to cognitive bias? And even if *nudging* could be considered positive overall, its effectiveness is not always demonstrated and its real impact remains limited. It can even be

---

[123] Richard H. Thaler, "Nudge, not sludge," Science 03 Aug 2018: Vol. 361, Issue 6401, pp. 431, DOI: 10.1126/science.aau9241

counterproductive with the boomerang effect, as the gain on one side can lead to a greater loss on the other[124].

However, Thaler and Sunstein's thinking conquered the world after the 2000s. And the explanation is not necessarily to be found in the method's success, rather modest. One only has to look at the state of political disaster in some Western countries that adopted it, especially during the coronavirus crisis. We will come back to this. The explanation lies rather in the notoriety and the power of influence of the promoters of this way of thinking. It should be noted that no less than five of the last fifteen Nobel Prize winners in economics recognize themselves in this trend (Daniel Kahneman in 2002, Peter A. Diamond in 2010, Alvin E. Roth in 2012, Robert J. Shiller in 2013 and Richard Thaler in 2017). It is also true that Richard Thaler is one of the world's leading pillars of behavioral economics and Cass Sunstein is one of America's leading law professors. But it takes a little more than that to have such an effect. It is worth noting that these two thinkers are on the same faculty, both teaching at the University of Chicago. But that school was also the home, from 1991 to 2004, of another constitutional scholar, a certain Barak Obama. In fact, the future 44th president of the United States and Cass Sunstein had the opportunity to socialize in this faculty, the latter ending up becoming an informal advisor in the campaign of the former, before joining the Democratic administration. During this campaign, Obama was surrounded by a group of no less than 29 of the most eminent behavioral scientists in the United States (Peter Orszag, Richard Thaler, Daniel Ariely, Daniel Kanheman, Alan Krueger, Austan Goolsbee, ...). Nothing was left to chance in the slogans, phone calls, emails, flyers. The nudging was everywhere[125]. Mike Moffo, the campaign manager, wrote to local Democratic leaders: "What if I told you that a team of world-renowned scientists, psychologists and economists had developed the GOTV [Get out the vote] plan?! Would you be interested in at least taking a look at it? Of course, you would!!!" A well-researched article in *Time* newspaper went over the use of *nudging* during this period, but also the role of this unusual team in all

---

[124] Utpal M. Dholakia, "Why Nudging Your Customers Can Backfire," Harvard Business Review, April 15, 2016.

[125] https://www.marketingsociety.com/the-library/obamas-team-nudged-voters

of Barak Obama's policies after his election[126]. And for good reason. In his new position as the administrator of the *White House Office of Information and Regulatory Affairs* (2009–2012), Cass Sunstein had to deal with whole areas of American society (health, environment, information, labor, science…). And not everything is rosy, far from it. Contrary to the polished image of the Obama Nobel Peace Prize, Sunstein supported the creation of George W. Bush's military commissions without the approval of the U.S. Congress; lobbied for the reform of the First Amendment on free speech, which he finds problematic in its original version, and proposed a new one in the form of a "New Deal for speech"[127]; co-authored a paper in which he proposes methods of intervention to combat conspiracy theories on the Internet through "cognitive infiltration" which consists of "breaking down the ideological and epistemological complexes that constitute these networks and groups," without arousing suspicion[128]; he proposed to put an end to the state recognition of marriage, which should disappear from the legal apparatus. All in the interest of the people, of course…

But the influence on the American president does not end there. Sunstein is the husband of Samantha Power, a woman who worked in Senator Obama's office (2005–2006) and supported him during his run for the White House as an advisor. She joined the presidential transition team in November 2008 before being appointed Director of the *National Security Council* in 2009, and then U.S. Ambassador to the United Nations in 2013. She has thus had a central role in American foreign policy. In particular, she has promoted "humanitarian interventions," military actions carried out in the name of humanitarian causes such as in Libya, Syria, or Yemen[129]. It is in a way paternalism taken to the extreme by waging war on people in their interest! But the humanitarian disasters that have resulted from this policy have not finished catching

---

[126] Michael Grunwald, "How Obama Is Using the Science of Change," http://content.time.com, Apr. 02, 2009.
[127] Sunstein, "Democracy and the Problem of Free Speech", Free Press; 1st Edition (February 1, 1995), p 119.
[128] Sunstein, Cass, Vermeule Adrian, "Conspiracy Theories", https://papers.ssrn.com/sol3/papers.cfm?abstract_id=1084585, 2008
[129] JOHN CARL BAKER, "The Miseducation of Samantha Power," www.jacobinmag.com, 10.21.2019.

up with Samantha Power, even if she has brushed them aside in her memoirs[130].

Despite Sunstein's official presence with Obama, *nudging* remained in the shadows within the U.S. administration until September 15, 2015, when the president signed a formal executive order creating a special team called the *Social and Behavioral Sciences Team* (SBST). This is a "group of applied behavioral science experts charged with translating the findings and methods of the social and behavioral sciences into improvements in federal policies and programs to benefit the American people."[131] As you might have guessed, this is a group of *nudging* experts[132]. One of their exploits involves the retirement savings of American civil servants. Because they are thought to procrastinate and push back the savings start date every time, a program was put in place to address this.   To do this, approximately 720,000 emails containing well-studied behavioral analysis message variants were sent to them. Compared to the email without the message, the most effective variant almost doubled the recipients' subscription rate. The email campaign led to approximately 4,930 new sign-ups and $1.3 million in savings in just one month. After the success, the project was expanded to the Department of Defense and the military[133]. New savers still have the option to opt out, but due to the complexity of the process and the amount of paperwork required to do so, many keep their accounts open. *Nudging is a* one-way street … even if a glitch or special life circumstance might well justify going back. But that's not what the architects of choice, the *nudgers*, think about…

Given the publicity it has received, *nudging* has been quick to conquer other countries. The OECD listed 202 institutions that implement it in 2018[134].

---

[130] SHIREEN AL-ADEIMI, "How Dare Samantha Power Scrub the Yemen War From Her Memoir," https://inthesetimes.com, SEPTEMBER 18, 2019.

[131] https://obamawhitehouse.archives.gov/the-press-office/2015/09/15/fact-sheet-president-obama-signs-executive-order-white-house-announces

[132] https://obamawhitehouse.archives.gov/blog/2015/02/09/behavioral-science-insights-make-government-more-effective-simpler-and-more-user-fri

[133] https://www.psretirement.com/sbst-helps-promote-tsp-participation

[134] https://www.oecd.org/gov/regulatory-policy/behavioural-insights.htm

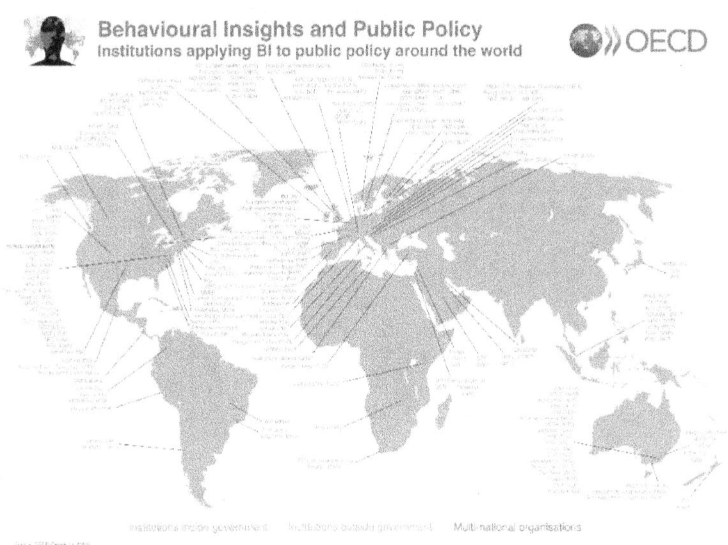


The world map of institutions that use *nudging*.

This is the case of the Cameron-Clegg coalition government in the UK, which already in 2010 set up the *Behavioral Insights Team (BIT)*, also known as the *"Nudge Unit."* It was headed by David Halpern, a specialist in experimental psychology[135], with the contribution as an advisor of Richard Thaler himself. The unit was eventually privatized in 2014 and its services billed to the British government and other institutions around the world. It has conducted more than 750 projects and over 500 trials. One of the most notable is on organ donation. With a well-crafted message from the BIT, approximately 96,000 additional registrations in one year alone were recorded. Another is the case for using nudging to reduce gas and electricity consumption, illustrated by a full-scale study conducted in the summer of 2014 in California[136]. Approximately 42,100 households were targeted with mailings containing a comparison of their consumption to that of their neighbors

---

[135]
https://assets.publishing.service.gov.uk/government/uploads/system/uploads/attachment_data/file/267100/Applying_Behavioural_Insights_to_Organ_Donation.pdf

[136] Alec Brandona, John A. Lista, Robert D. Metcalfeb,1, Michael K. Pricec, and Florian Rundhammer, "Testing for crowd out in social nudges: Evidence from a natural field experiment in the market for electricity," PNAS, March 19, 2019, vol. 116, no. 12.

(versus the actual top 20%). A household might receive a nagging message such as "you consume more than your neighbors," with supporting numbers and graphs.

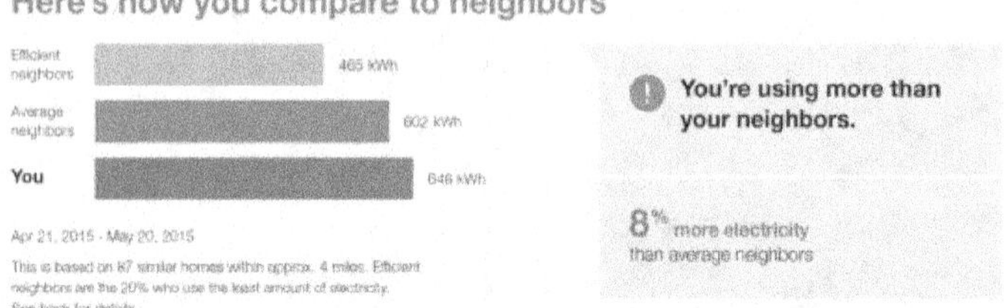


An example of nudging mail.

According to the study, social *nudging* reduced electricity spikes with rates ranging from 2.1% to 6.8%. But beware of the boomerang effect, because another study showed that while those who consumed relatively more compared to their neighbors decreased their consumption a bit, the good students felt socially inferior and started leaving the lamps and other heaters running in the vacuum![137]

If you zoom in on the OECD map, you might see a pointer to an institution using nudging in France. It is the SGMAP (Secrétariat Général pour la Modernisation de l'Action Publique) which "accompanies the government in transforming administrations and modernizing public services." Since 2013, the SGMAP has been responsible for the simplification program initiated by President François Hollande[138]. The SGMAP's actions are limited to the modernization of public services, and only in part. After the appointment of Emmanuel Macron as Minister of the Economy, Industry, and Digital, the promotion of remote tax filing in France will be entrusted to a private company, BVA Nudge Unit, a subsidiary of the BVA polling group. "More than 13 million people are already using the impots.gouv.fr website," states the email sent at the declaration period, making the number of teledeclarants jump by 10%. Two years later, the young Ismaël Emelien, a member of the first circle of Macron's boys[139]

---

[137] RAY FISMAN, "Nudges Gone Wrong," https://slate.com, April 23, 2010.
[138] https://www.modernisation.gouv.fr/le-sgmap/missions/missions-du-sgmap

(he and Alexis Kohler are even nicknamed the president's "two hemispheres"), recalls, "I was convinced of the great relevance and modernity of the approach." And he signed a contract with the BVA Nudge Unit, which would be closely associated with every aspect of candidate Emmanuel Macron's presidential campaign, to think about the meetings, the speeches, the collection of donations, etc. "For example, they completely changed the architecture of our website and activated the *social pressure bias* to increase the average donation, explaining that most people gave 8 euros. Given our limited resources, they really improved the effectiveness of the campaign, with gains greater than the investment."

Upon arriving at the Élysée Palace, the president's team was convinced of the benefit of integrating behavioral science into the design of its policies, and in March 2018, a unit was created within the Interministerial Directorate of Public Transformation (DITP). Several researchers work there, advising ministries and the SIG (Government Information Service) on a wide range of issues. They are also supported by several external service providers, including the private consulting firm McKinsey[140], which also specializes in nudging[141]. "Until the Covid-19 crisis, we worked on simplifying and making more effective messages of general interest: how to get people to do more sport, consume fewer antibiotics, pay more attention to their children's sleep, etc." explains Stephan Giraud, head of the DITP unit[142]. And the arrival of the coronavirus will take nudging to another level…

It is March 15, 2020. While the French Prime Minister Edouard Philippe announces new measures to curb the epidemic, which affects 4,500 people in France at the time, and the government hammers home the need to respect a "social distance," the French go out to parks, cafes, and markets to enjoy a sunny Sunday. In a message posted on LinkedIn, Eric

---

[139] Lucie Auriol, "Who are the Macron boys?", https://www.planet.fr, 10/20/2017.

[140] François KRUG, "McKinsey, un cabinet dans les pas de Macron", Le Monde Magazine, February 6, 2021.

[141] https://www.mckinsey.com/business-functions/organization/our-insights/lessons-from-the-front-line-of-corporate-nudging

[142] GÉRALDINE WOESSNER, "Emmanuel Macron and the Power of 'Nudge,'" www.lepoint.fr, 04/06/2020.

Singler, the head of the BVA Nudge Unit, rants: "The government seems to discover with amazement that humans are not rational: they adopt behaviors that go against their own interest on a critical issue. [I solemnly (and humbly) call on the authorities to form a *task force* of behavioral science experts to work alongside the authorities." A few hours later, his phone rang. Ismaël Emelien had arranged a meeting with him at the Élysée Palace. On March 17, a collaboration was agreed upon: the BVA Nudge Unit would advise the government, complementing the DITP's behavioral science unit. "With this crisis, we really moved from an exploratory stage to an industrial stage," says one of the team members, who was inundated with requests from all ministries.

Thus, nudging will have been behind all of the government's crisis policy regarding masks, testing, containment, deconfinement, vaccinations, exit certification, etc. The three-colored decontamination card of April 30, 2020, is the fruit of the Nudge Unit. But faced with its lack of readability and especially the feeling of being singled out within the regions displayed in red, the government backtracked to its original choice of two colors[143]. The StopCovid application, which became TousAntiCovid following its flop, is also the work of the *nudge* experiment. It should be noted that the term "tracking," which is its primary function, does not appear. The home page bears the invitation "Protect our loved ones, protect ourselves and protect others. Take part in the fight against the epidemic by limiting the risks of transmission!" In place of the classic "Download" of mobile apps, there is the engaging "I want to participate" message. To further encourage people, we did not hesitate to use *nudging* by using the social norm bias and manipulating the numbers of downloads[144]. When you are told that everyone else has done it, it is hard not to feel isolated and even guilty for not following the norm.

In 2017, we similarly succeeded in imposing inclusive writing thanks to a simple poll ensuring that 75% of French people were in favor of it,

---

[143] https://www.ihemi.fr/articles/nudge-deconfinement-sous-influence
[144] Sylvain Rolland , "How the Government Manipulates All Anti-COVID Numbers," www.latribune.fr, 02/12/2020.

while only 12% of respondents had understood the question… "We are social animals, and our decisions are unconsciously oriented by all sorts of biases. However, research has shown that humans naturally tend to conform to the norm," explains Eric Singler. So, it doesn't matter that this norm is fictitious. If the campaign is successful, it will soon become a reality. And the lie will erase itself as if by magic. This is the self-fulfilling prophecy. It's exactly like polls, which don't measure what people will vote for, but unconsciously tell them what they should vote for. But it only works, as with everything, if there is trust in the source of the message. And this is not the case, which explains the non-adherence of people and the glaring discrepancies between the predictions of pollsters and reality.

The use of such manipulative techniques raises questions about the health of our Western democracies. For example, was the death count carried out each evening by the Director General of Health, to "maintain a sense of fear" and enforce containment, justified? What about the use of doctors and other self-proclaimed experts who squat on TV sets and announce the apocalypse every day? Obviously, the fear spread by all these techniques during more than one year terrified the population. But if it didn't stop the virus, it slowed down the return to school, to work, and to medical consultations. This caused serious psychological disorders in the most fragile. Ismaël Emelien justifies himself: "It is a theoretical debate. In reality, everything is manipulation! Each choice is the result of both free will and a staged event. Nudging techniques are not coercive, we don't take away any option. We just make the person look in the right direction. It is completely inseparable from the general interest. As for the question of whether or not containment was in the public interest, that was decided democratically: the president was elected. What's the problem with making sure his decision is understood, and respected?"[145] Not so sure. Perhaps from time to time we need to remind our politicians, especially when we have never voted for them, of one of the principles of any true democracy[146], "informed

---

[145] GÉRALDINE WOESSNER, "Emmanuel Macron and the Power of 'Nudge,'" www.lepoint.fr, 04/06/2020.
[146] Robert Alan Dahl, "On Democracy", Yale University Press, 1998. Chapter 4, page 37.

understanding" which is defined as follows: "Within a reasonable time limit, every citizen should have an equal and effective opportunity to learn about possible alternative policies and their possible consequences." This is a far cry from the notion of *nudging,* with the debate taking place only within the closed circle of choice makers, not the people.

And all these "innovative" techniques have their limits, because the arrogance of those who use them hides only too well their own cognitive biases and especially their impotence to solve problems. The year 2020 was the year in which it was decreed that toilet paper and celebrity magazines were more essential than books! Even a monkey would look down on us if he learned that…

The absurdity of certain decisions shows above all the bubble outside the ground in which these decision-makers live, their words or decisions not being subject to the slightest contradiction to qualify them, or even correct them. How to convince the people of the usefulness of the StopCovid application when the Prime Minister declares, embarrassed, in a primetime evening show, that he has not installed it on his phone?

This positioning of some above others, in the name of a misplaced paternalism that infantilizes others, is just unacceptable. In a true democracy, each subject is associated in all transparency and equitably to the deliberation on the definition of the common good. A minority out of the ground should not decide in place of all the others. Because when nudge is associated with the use of fear, for example, it can quickly become a psychological weapon of mass destruction. We will come back to this…

## The uberization of *nudging* or Wages in Compliments

A *nudge,* according to Thaler means "any aspect of choice architecture that changes people's behavior in a predictable way without prohibiting any option or significantly altering their economic incentives. To be considered a simple *nudge*, the intervention must be easy to avoid and inexpensive. *Nudges are* not obligations. Putting the fruit at eye-level counts as a *nudge*. Banning junk food is not. Taking away a choice is not a *nudge*." Thaler points out, "If steps are taken to increase people's cognitive effort—such as placing fruit at eye level and candy in a more obscure location—one could say that the cost of choosing candy increases. Some *nudges* impose, in a sense, cognitive (rather than material) costs and, in that sense, change incentives. *Nudges* only qualify as libertarian paternalism if the costs are low."

The problem is that the cognitive cost is not the same from one person to another, and sometimes becomes prohibitive, which is not really different from the suppression of choice in the end. For example, it is easy to get an elderly person to sign up for a subscription, but to ask them to take impossible steps to cancel!

On the Web, nudging is everywhere. Chris Nodder, a user interface designer and author of the book *"Evil by Design,"* writes, "There's nothing wrong with tricking people if it's in their best interest, or if they've given their implied consent to be tricked as part of a persuasive strategy. People attending a magic show give that consent."[147] To do this, a multitude of cognitive biases are exploited to successfully elicit the desired behavior from the viewer. This is the case of the *framing effect bias* with the way the options are presented, some being highlighted and others less visible. It is also the case of *status quo* bias by displaying a box checked by default or by launching an episode of a series automatically after the end of the previous one. The removal of the choice is sometimes temporary to provoke a behavior in the immediate future. For example, you can log in to your Facebook account on the phone via the web browser as you would on a PC, but you can't view a live video broadcast. If you try to do so, you are immediately offered to install the application, "for a better user experience," we are told. People tend to accept this easy default choice. It's either that or no viewing of the video until the end of the livestream. The hardware cost of the installation is indeed almost nil, but we forget that the data and the addiction that will follow over time are certainly not free! Not to

---

[147] Chris Nodder, "How Deceptive Is Your Persuasive Design?",
https://uxmag.com/articles/how-deceptive-is-your-persuasive-design, August 6, 2013.

mention the power consumption with the long hours spent on the screens…

In most applications, especially social networks, we look for user engagement in order to keep his attention as long as possible. Among other persuasive techniques, *nudging* is, of course, used. Platforms that put people in touch with each other, such as Uber, Airbnb, Lyft, Postmates (delivery)[148] …, also use it, but for a different purpose. It is no longer the available brain time of the Internet user that is sought, but rather the muscles of the independent workers who perform the services sold. You are never forced to perform a task, but you are put in situations that don't really give you a choice either. A *New York Times* survey on this subject with some drivers and former employees of Uber and Lyft is illuminating[149]. Having personally provided an apartment via *Airbnb* for a certain period of time, I am not at all surprised when reading it. I even recognize myself in certain points. The *nudging* is applied in the form of scores or objectives to be reached to benefit from certain privileges. A host on Airbnb, for example, has to be exemplary in every way to become a "Super-host" and thus be featured prominently in the search results. The problem is that it's opaque. The mechanism operates in a black box and the rating criteria are not known to the hosts. The latter are constantly adapting as they can to reach the top position, but so are the algorithms of the platforms, always looking for more optimization. The problem is that if the quest for the goal is always to the benefit of the sites that always earn more money, it is not always the case for the apartment renter or the cab driver. This asymmetry between the information held by the platforms and that of the self-employed creates a clearly unbalanced partnership to the disadvantage of the latter[150]. It is never well seen (as noted) to refuse a request for a rental or a ride, for example. Canceling a request can even lead to the closure of an account altogether. This is what prompted, for example, employees of

---

[148] https://postmates.com/blog/making-postmates-even-more-efficient#.w539rcbtb

[149] NOAM SCHEIBER, JON HUANG, "How Uber Uses Psychological Tricks to Push Its Drivers' Buttons," www.nytimes.com, APRIL 2, 2017.

[150] ALEX ROSENBLAT and LUKE STARK, "Algorithmic Labor and Information Asymmetries: A Case Study of Uber's Drivers," International Journal of Communication 10 (2016), 3758–3784.

Postmates, an American delivery platform between private individuals, to launch a petition to ask for the addition of a "This is my last ride" button, to prevent them from ending up refusing requests and therefore being badly rated, which leads to them receiving less work and money later on[151]. This is how cabs find themselves taking unprofitable trips, because they are made over very short distances, or they go on until late at night. This is also encouraged by the automatic acceptance of journeys, an option favored by the sites and activated by default. Even before the end of the current race, a new one arrives. It's the autoplay of Netflix or YouTube with an Uber twist. So, there is no room for reflection or procrastination. The driver's self-control is bypassed. It takes so much less effort to accept than to refuse, especially with the fatigue at the end of the day (to add to the status quo bias). Jonathan Hall, a research director at Uber assumes: "The optimal default we define it is that we want you to do as much work as there is to do. *You are in no way obligated to do it*. But that's the default." Yes sir, that's what nudging is all about! After all, it doesn't cost anything and the driver can sleep without regret, with the peace of mind that he hasn't missed anything … or rather lost anything, because once offered, the new errand is psychologically considered to be already in the pocket and the loss aversion bias is set in motion! Not accepting is tantamount to a loss and that's never good for the mind. Even worse, Uber hides both the destination and the price of rides from drivers before they accept them. This uncertainty makes it possible to avoid refusing unattractive rides (as Parisian cabs do![152]) and above all to reinforce the reward loop by making the gain random (see the chapter on operant conditioning and Skinner's box in volume 1 of the book). "What if this was the race of the year?" the driver might ask, as if he were a slot machine player.

Uber officials said the autoplay feature sometimes produced so many rides that drivers began to suffer from a kind of Netflix disease, the

---

[151] https://www.coworker.org/petitions/have-a-i-m-done-after-this-delivery-button-so-you-don-t-have-to-reject-jobs

[152] It is a memory that I keep after having set foot for the first time on French soil. I asked at least ten cabs to take me from Orly to a nearby city (20km) and was refused each time! One person advised me to get in without saying anything in advance. And it works the first time! The quality of the reception in Paris is not a myth …

inability to stop for a shower. Drivers confide, "I can never switch off. I'm running errands all the time. It's a problem." Amid the uproar, Uber has introduced a pause button. But to take effect, it must be activated after each start of a new ride … even though Netflix and YouTube allow you to turn off autoplay permanently.

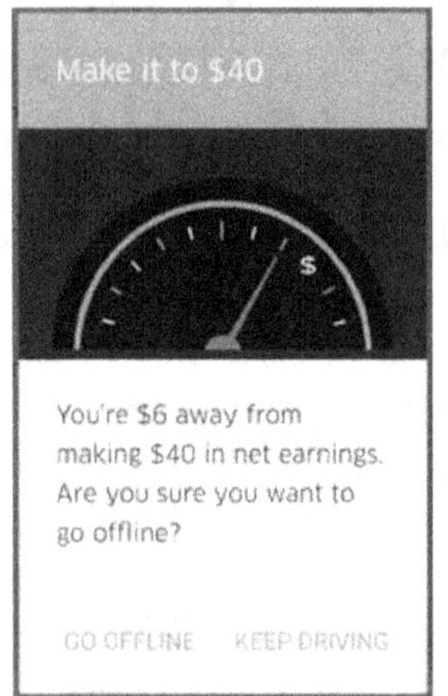


At the end of the day when the driver is about to log out, the app displays the message "You are $6 short of $40 net income. Are you sure you want to log out?" Underneath, two buttons appear, "Go offline" and "Keep driving," the latter highlighted in blue while the other is almost invisible (see figure). The goal to reach seems completely arbitrary, and sometimes corresponds to a sum earned a few days before. This is a *nudge* that aims at exploiting a cognitive bias related to the importance given to a goal set in advance, as cabs do by targeting revenue each day and sticking to it as reported in a 1997 study featuring a certain… Richard Thaler[153]. And now if the drivers don't do it, Uber will do it for them!

When you look at this same screen (see figure above) presented during the disconnection attempt, you notice the presence of a gauge with a needle that almost reaches the $ money symbol. This is not a pretty sight. Some of the most addictive games ever created, like Tetris in the '80s and '90s, rely on a sense of progress toward a goal that is always just beyond the player's reach. This is what makes the player fall into the mental state known as the "game loop" (see the chapter on games in Volume 1 of the book). And at Uber, we are aware of this. And the game loop is far from the only video game feature that Uber has adapted to keep as many of its fleet on the road as possible. At any given time, the app shows drivers how many trips they've taken over the course of the week, how much money they've earned, how long they've logged in,

---

[153] http://www.cmu.edu/dietrich/sds/docs/loewenstein/NYCCabdrivers.pdf

and what overall rating passengers have given them. All of these metrics can stimulate and induce compulsive behavior. "The whole thing is like a video game," said a former Uber and Lyft driver in the Chicago area, who said he sometimes has to fight the urge to work more after glancing at his statistics. And we're pushing the gaming analogy to the point of confusion. Just like a Super Mario player, drivers can earn badges, "compliments" in Uber's terminology[154], after certain achievements: "Expert Navigation" for the one who knows directions and shortcuts, "Beyond" for the one who has exceeded expectations, "Friendly Driving" for the one with whom the exchange is pleasant, "Night Hero" for the one who drives carefully at night…

Gamification and *nudging* are in fact two sides of the same coin, that of behavioral change[155]. A concrete example is given in the field of health. A study[156] showed that surgeons who played the console more than three hours a week made 37% fewer errors on average during operations than their non-gaming colleagues, and were 27% faster. There was a good correlation between performance in the game and in the operating room. The numbers were better when the practitioner played even more, 47% fewer errors and 39% faster. Another example of this winning nudge-game combination is the *Holle Bolle Gijs*—Dutch for "big mouth"—in the Netherlands since 1959. It is a talking trash can that when a child puts a piece of trash in it says "thank you" out loud. The toddlers are so excited by this game that they pick up everything in the vicinity. The result? Not a piece of paper is left around. The big mouth swallows some 460 tons of waste per year!

Not surprisingly, *nudging* and gamification have penetrated the world of work. Managers have been borrowing from the logic of games for generations, such as when they organize competitions between employees. More overt forms have proliferated in the last decade. Microsoft, for example, claims it and even advertises it in a blog called

---

[154] https://www.uber.com/us/en/ride/how-it-works/driver-compliments
[155] https://robdorscheidt.wordpress.com/2015/07/23/gamification-and-nudging-two-sides-of-the-same-medal/
[156] James C Rosser Jr 1, Paul J Lynch, Laurie Cuddihy, Douglas A Gentile, Jonathan Klonsky, Ronald Merrell, "The impact of video games on training surgeons in the 21st century", 2007, https://pubmed.ncbi.nlm.nih.gov/17309970/

"Strengthening Your Business Through Gamification."[157] Employees can earn challenges, points, levels, badges, etc., all of which can be viewed on a dashboard in an application with a very meaningful name: "Dynamics 365-Gamification." Employees can then convert their points into coffee, food, purchases, etc. The company can then "use the data collected to track and report on the progress of each employee," and "help keep them engaged and motivated to deliver the best performance."

But Uber can go much further. Because it has control over its drivers' entire workflow via an app, there are few limits to what it can manipulate. Uber collects astronomical amounts of data that allow it to remove options from the game that don't work and refine others. And because drivers are self-employed and uberization is a new phenomenon, these practices still fall outside of labor law. "We've found a cheap way to get you to work without paying you, we'll pay you in badges that don't cost anything, it's a manipulative method," says Kevin Werbach, associate professor of legal studies and business ethics at the Wharton School of the University of Pennsylvania. And that's precisely the effect we see in some of these workers. When a driver is asked about badges, when he's losing money on fuel and vehicle maintenance expenses and is just thinking about finding another job, he gets a jolt of electricity and frantically responds, "I currently have 12 Excellent Service badges and nine User-Friendly Driving badges." He has all the numbers in his head because he's paying so much attention.

When a new driver reaches 25 rides, they receive a bonus. At Uber, we've noticed that many of these newbies leave the platform before this milestone. And through data analysis, it was also noted that this withdrawal rate drops sharply once this goal is reached. A *nudging* strategy via encouragement is then adopted. "You're almost there. Bravo!" is frequently received by each new driver. It is common knowledge among psychologists and video game designers that encouragement to reach a well-displayed goal increases motivation.

---

[157] https://www.microsoftpartnercommunity.com/t5/Digital-marketing-tactics-for/Empowering-your-business-through-gamification/m-p/21689

There is clearly a conflict of interest between Uber and the drivers. The platform wants as many drivers as possible in its fleet to minimize wait times for applicants and thus make more money, but this comes at the expense of the drivers who get fewer rides. Uber's goal at all times is to avoid supply shortages. To do this, drivers are advised to move to hot spots where there is high demand. They are automatically shown a large button to click to get a ride to those tight spots. Uber has also encouraged its local managers to experiment with various ways to achieve this. Drivers are pushed to go in certain directions all the time all day long via email, SMS, etc. Some local managers, men, have gone so far as to adopt a female persona to contact drivers, most of whom are male, to make them more receptive to their messages. Uber has admitted to using this practice to increase profits, according to the *New York Times*[158].

And we are not at the end of our surprises. We can imagine the use in the future of a kind of ultra-targeted *nudging*, which is already being tested in eleven American cities[159]. With all the data collected on drivers, speed, acceleration, braking, etc., it is possible to detect anomalies such as moments of fatigue and send the driver a message such as "You are tired. Go home and rest." We can also know if the driver is holding the phone in his hands and warn him of the danger of his action. What could be better than social nudging, a daily display of comparison statistics to other drivers in the area, with suggestions for improving one's driving? Also, through AI-based predictive algorithms, Uber hopes to increase the rate of accepted rides (number of accepted rides out of total requests) with the concept of "Network Value."[160] By having more information about the ride they are being asked for and its potential future earnings calculated by these algorithms, a driver will be more likely to accept. If the future earnings are insufficient, one can imagine the use of compensation in the form of money or bonuses. The main thing is not to leave any customer on the road, because the competition will be increasingly tough between platforms.

---

[158] NOAM SCHEIBER, JON HUANG, "How Uber Uses Psychological Tricks to Push Its Drivers' Buttons," www.nytimes.com, APRIL 2, 2017.
[159] https://www.uber.com/newsroom/safety-on-the-road-july-2016
[160] https://eng.uber.com/umetric/

Especially since most carriers do not find their money back. After a certain period of time, the driver discovers that working 50 to 60 hours a week for an annual income of $20,000 is not so profitable after all and ends his activity. This is not a big deal for the platform, as newcomers have already joined the fleet. But this mechanism cannot continue indefinitely, like a Ponzi scheme that collapses after a while. Uber has, of course, thought of a solution to win this race against time. It is the driverless car. After launching the autonomous vehicle division in 2016, Uber co-founder Travis Kalanick actually said that this new challenge is "fundamentally existential" for their business. With all the driving data collected from its test fleet over the years, Uber would be able to develop an AI capable of autonomously driving cars. But an accident that resulted in the death of a woman in the state of Arizona in 2018, the open conflict with Google for theft of industrial secrets of its subsidiary Waymo also specialized in autonomous driving, and the pressure of shareholders to bring the car rental business back to profitability has slowed down this ambition. Uber ended up selling its autonomous vehicle division to Aurora, a rival startup backed by Amazon. Uber and its main partners, Toyota and SoftBank, will nevertheless keep 40% of the shares of the startup, which is still valued at $10 billion after the acquisition[161].

It's difficult to know what time the ride will arrive and whether Aurora will provide Uber with a fleet of autonomous cars in the near future. In the meantime, the drivers should take the opportunity to review their demands upwards, and the 25% commission on each of their races downwards…

---

[161] Patrick McGee and Dave Lee, "Uber abandons effort to develop own self-driving vehicle," www.ft.com, DECEMBER 7 2020.

# CHAPTER IV: Group Psychology on the Web

*"In the enumeration of the factors capable of impressing the soul of the crowds, one could dispense entirely with mentioning reason, if it were not necessary to indicate the negative value of its influence,"*

- Gustave le Bon.

*"I wonder if Facebook KILLED someone with their emotional manipulation stunt. At their scale and with depressed people, there, it's possible,"*

—Lauren Weinstein

Information is said to be viral because it is contagious and spreads from one individual to another. The Web is naturally the ideal medium for this propagation, the audience within reach of a click being immense. The information disseminated in this way naturally has an effect on people's behavior and decisions in real life. This is the power of group psychology to which this chapter is dedicated. As we will see, emotions are not immune and are even a formidable lever for the manufacture of mass behavior.

## Man, This Social Animal

Man is a social animal who lives in groups. It is simply essential for his survival. This is how he learns, creates alliances, defends himself, and makes conquests. Internet is finally only one more means of communication to practice this social life. If a person goes on a platform, it is often for one or more social reasons.

Learning by observing others is one of them. This is the principle of the social cognitive theory (or social learning) invented by the Canadian psychologist Albert Bandura. This theory states that learning is acquired through three methods:

- Imitation through observation of a third party (watching and understanding the way a chess champion plays to reproduce it).
- Social facilitation: improving performance through the presence of observers (answering a question asked by someone on LinkedIn as quickly as possible to impress the network).
- Cognitive anticipation: integration of a behavior by reasoning on similar situations (a publication has not reached 1000 views after one day. By extrapolation of what has been seen in the past, it will probably not exceed 5000 views).

For other schools of thought, such as "interactionism," the individual and society are constructed through interactions and in relation to a specific environment. Intellectual development is seen as a function of human groups rather than as an individual process, even if it becomes an internalized property of the individual later on.

In learning by imitation (so-called vicarious learning) theorized by Albert Bandura, the observer is active in the sense that he observes, understands, and then reproduces certain actions. This is to be distinguished from mimicry where the observer remains passive and only reproduces the observed action. This behavior is very common on social networks where people reproduce things without really understanding the ins and outs. This is facilitated by a bias called "social validation." This is a psychological phenomenon where an individual or group imitates another group, because they are convinced of the validity of the gesture being performed by several other people. People post *likes* for a publication, so we do the same without much questioning. This is the sheep effect.

This is, of course, a very important topic in marketing in general and on the Web in particular. When we see many positive reviews on a product, we buy it, even if it does not always correspond to our initial wish. A whole industry of selling *likes* and positive reviews has developed on the Web to supply merchants and help them artificially boost the reputation of their products. The same thing exists for the purchase of *followers* to boost the popularity of certain celebrities or political figures. The network most affected by the phenomenon, with millions of ghost follower accounts, is Instagram[162]. This shadow business is carried out either by relying on millions of people playing with fake *followers* in low-cost countries like Pakistan or India or by hackers' manipulation. With this trick, we inflate the ego of the celebrity, but not only. We help him or her to acquire even more *followers*, because we join more easily the network of a person already popular.

Perhaps the most problematic aspect of this is the power of influence acquired by certain people, known as KOLs (*Key Opinion Leaders*). Their voices count, because they reach millions of people in one click. The same can be said of influencers, those people who often have no particular expertise, but are so well followed that they become KOLs. Proof of this is that they are sometimes approached by politicians to help them get messages across, often to young people. Didn't French President Emmanuel Macron and his government, on several occasions, appeal to these KOLs without any political culture? Some commentators have not hesitated to speak of crossing the "red line between propaganda and communication" when organizing these influence campaigns[163]. How can we interpret the invitation to a round table of school dropouts to talk about the problems of precariousness experienced by students during the COVID crisis? A person followed on the social network is often considered trustworthy and counts in public relations[164], even if he or she knows nothing about the subject. It is therefore not surprising to see KOLs being paid a lot of money by brands of clothes or other cosmetics to advertise their products (or opinion when it comes to politics). Some KOLs, like these two English chefs, Gordon Ramsey and Jamie Oliver, charge $20,000 per post![165] KOL advertising is not necessarily explicit and can be subliminal to get the message across without the target being aware of it. But these same influencers

---

[162] Sandra Song, "The Shady Business of Buying Instagram Followers," www.papermag.com, 14 June 2019.

[163] Mathieu Slama, "Government and Influencers: 'The red line between propaganda and communication has been crossed,'" www.lefigaro.fr, 02/03/2021.

[164] https://www.lianatech.com/resources/blog/key-opinion-leaders-who-are-they-and-why-do-they-matter.html

[165] Ibid.

sometimes unconsciously find themselves outside the law by promoting alcohol for example when it is formally forbidden (Evin law in France)[166]. KOLs play the role of prescribing models by highlighting the product. When it comes to promoting an opinion, it is mainly the politician sitting at the same table who does it and the KOL plays the role of a platform. If a celebrity poses in a bikini at the beach with her pair of shoes not far from her buttocks clearly visible in the picture, it is not by pure coincidence. The viewer's brain does not distinguish between real content and advertising content. It unconsciously creates associativity between the product, the desire, and the status of the person followed. This naturally creates the desire to buy the product to please oneself, to rise to the same status, and to belong in a certain way to the same social group.

One of these young girls, who has a huge presence on YouTube, with 1.8 million subscribers, is a case in point. One of her videos with another reality TV starlet, about makeup, has been viewed more than 2.3 million times. She even published a book dedicated to personal development, sold 274,000 copies, in the third position of the best-sellers of the year 2020, next to the Goncourt prize and the last book of Barack Obama! If you look at some of the comments on Amazon, people who came to find real advice in her book have left disappointed. One can read: "a simple autobiography with no real advice on personal development. Buy books written by real authors instead!" But the vast majority of comments are positive. If you look closely, they come from people who are already used to following the 23-year-old woman. So, they are happy to discover her autobiography. Buying this book was natural for them, a logical continuation of the series of products successfully placed by the YouTuber. And when people do what she does, it's just mimicry, a machine learning, not thought out. We do it because we don't question it and we trust her.

This situation creates damage in the society, by exhausting in truth two camps launched in a frantic race, the followed and the *followers*. The latter believe, as in reality shows, in the easy success embodied by these

---

[166] Cash Investigation magazine, "Alcohol: the strategies to make us drink", broadcast on France 2 on Thursday 1er April 2021.

models. Why should they study long hours to earn a pittance compared to these rich kids? The followers give in to the easy way. But like a slot machine player, they later realize that the quest for the winning ticket is as rare as winning the lotto. The number of people who earn a good living thanks to social networks or reality TV is infinitesimal.

On the other hand, in order to stay in the lead and to be popular, the followers have to redouble their efforts each time to get more subscribers and views on their publications. They watch their performance like milk on the fire not to be overtaken. Comparison becomes an obsession.

A key element in all learning is self-assessment against a benchmark. To progress, we naturally compare ourselves to others. This is the theory of social comparison proposed in 1954 by the psychologist Leon Festinger (1919–1989), best known for the concept of cognitive dissonance. This comparison is also an automatic process of the brain to achieve several other goals: to reassure oneself, to inflate one's esteem, and to fight against influence to remain oneself. Social networking platforms such as Instagram or TikTok for example give a helping hand in this process by providing various tools to embellish one's own photos or videos with filters. This allows you to give yourself a better image, but it is not enough. It is also necessary that other people on the network confirm it with *likes*, flattering comments, or retweets. Man, this social animal, is in constant search of approval, continually seeking to evaluate himself through the eyes of others. This is what drives us to compulsively check the number of *followers*, *likes*, views, etc. This social approval is the reward that makes the brain salivate (dopamine) and feels good. The measurement of this approval or non-approval with the collection of more or less *likes* or views, pushes the Internet user to adjust his own behavior, even if it means cheating or distorting the reality, always with the aim of collecting more. This is naturally reflected in the quality of the content he produces. I was not surprised when I heard a producer who created a YouTube channel (Demos Kratos)[167] say that he had to give up long, worked well and relevant videos of one hour in favor of

---

[167] https://www.youtube.com/watch?v=T4ZxjTHOfdI&ab_channel=FabienMoine-ExuvieTV

very short and lesser quality ones, because the latter were getting much more views. For him, "Watching six ten-minute videos gives people more pleasure than one sixty-minute video." In a way, he gave in to the dictatorship of buzz, likes, and dopamine. He says he got "caught up in the statistics of the social networks" that he watched every day. This is obviously a trap that alternative media should not fall into, unlike traditional media that have been diving headlong into it for decades, which has driven people away from it. Quality must remain a priority, because it always pays off in the long run.

## Group Psychology on Social Networks

We have an inherent desire to be around those who are like us and to reinforce our worldview. Our online behavior is no different. People form tribes based on their interests, location, job, affiliation, etc. These groups have their own rules, conventions, jokes and even vocabulary. Within the groups, even if the members never meet, beliefs intensify. Anyone who disagrees could be expelled from the community. Sociologists call this behavior "community reinforcement" and point out that the ideas perpetuated may have no relation to reality or empirical evidence. This is the plunge into irrationality.

Community reinforcement can, of course, be positive. Groups for people with health concerns or addictions, for example, often provide important support in helping them through difficult times. However, when a group is enclosed in a filter bubble, it can lead to dangerous groupthink. This is a psychological phenomenon in which groups of people experience a temporary loss of the ability to think rationally, morally and realistically. When members of a group are all exposed to the same information, the results can be negative. Symptoms include being overly optimistic, taking big risks, ignoring legal and social conventions, viewing outsiders as enemies, censoring opposing ideas, pressuring members who disagree, or even ignoring the possibility of a negative outcome. It is this bias that leads to the kind of denial that is often found in political movements. Let's recall, for example, the bitter failure of Hillary Clinton against Trump in 2016, or of the latter against Biden in 2020.

This phenomenon, known in psychology as "perseverance of belief" or "conceptual conservatism," is pushed to the extreme within sects, for example, where even the obvious is denied. The denial is even reinforced thereby paradoxically relying on real facts. This is the "backfire effect," first reported in a book[168], "When Prophecy Fails," by Leon Festinger and his collaborators, Henry Riecken and Stanley Schachter. These researchers examined the conditions under which non-confirmation of beliefs lead to increased conviction in the same beliefs. The group studied a doomsday cult led by Dorothy Martin—referred to as Marian Keech in the book—a suburban Chicago housewife. Keech claimed to have received messages from the "Guardians," a group of higher beings from another planet called "Clarion." The messages said that a flood spreading to form an inland sea, stretching from the Arctic Circle to the Gulf of Mexico, would destroy the world on December 21, 1954. The three psychologists and several other assistants infiltrated the group and observed their behavior for months before and after the predicted apocalypse. Many members of the group quit their jobs and got rid of their possessions. They prepared to board a flying saucer that would come to their rescue. On D-Day and after hours of waiting in the freezing cold, the group returned home dejected. However, Keech received a new message saying that "the god of the Earth has decided to spare the planet." The cataclysm was canceled, because "the small group stayed up all night and spread so much light that God saved the world from destruction." The next day, the press was invited and a campaign to spread the message was started by the cult members, causing a riot in the process! Rather than abandoning their beliefs, which had been completely discredited by the facts, the members of the group adhered even more firmly to them and even began proselytizing with fervor. A few days later, a warrant was issued for Keech's arrest. She fled Chicago and then founded another cult, an organization that is still active to this day, several years after the guru's death.[169]

---

[168] Leon Festinger, Henry Riecken, Stanley Schachter, "When Prophecy Fails: A Social and Psychological Study of a Modern Group That Predicted the Destruction of the World", Harper-Torchbooks, 1956.

[169] http://worldcat.org/identities/nc-association%20of%20sananda%20and%20sanat%20kumara/

Unfortunately, similar aberrations exist on the Web. There were 47 reports in France in 2016 alone, as reported by the Interministerial Mission of Vigilance and Combat against Sectarian Aberrations[170]. And the phenomenon is growing.


## The Destructive QAnon of the Cult 2.0

Having been relatively present on the LinkedIn network, I could notice a rather surprising behavior among some people, concerning the American elections of 2020, for example. A contact I had to stop following, an option activated by default as soon as you get in touch with someone on this network, was literally flooding my news feed with publications supporting Trump, "the savior of the world against the Deep State," "probably the future American president," "Hillary Clinton will be imprisoned," and so on. Once Trump was officially declared the loser, the same denial continues with "rigged voting machines," "he was betrayed by the Vice President," etc. There may have been a fraud in this election, which would not surprise me and would not be a first (just remember the election of Bush against Al Gore), but what the hell does a Frenchman gain by wasting all this time supporting a nationalist Trump who only knows, rightly so, his own interests? This person was far from being isolated and I noticed the same thing in many others, notably concerning another subject, the 5G. The same people, however, well educated, are always commenting and talking about the craziest theories on a technical subject they completely ignore. I still remember this woman to whom I tried to explain that there was no 5G on the *Diamond Princess*, the famous cruise ship infected by the coronavirus, and that her theory linking Covid-19 to 5G was imaginary, but nothing helped. I was preaching in the wilderness, so much so that another contact who followed the discussion and understood the stubbornness I was facing wished me a "good luck." The lady's behavior seems to me to be very close to that of a person trapped in a cult. And if you look closely, you can see that these people are indeed followers of the so-called QAnon movement, an abbreviation of the letter *Q* and the word *Anonymous*.

---

[170] Clotilde Costil, "New sectarian currents on the Internet according to Miviludes," www.la-croix.com, 03/23/2018.

Trump has finally become the leader of a sect, that of the Anons who have been looking for a guru for a few years. Unfortunately, this movement has crossed the barrier of the screen to act in the physical world, endangering people's lives and those of its own followers. Everyone saw the rise on Capitol Hill on January 6, 2021, and the chaos that reigned there for hours, resulting in the death of a woman and the evacuation of all the politicians there. Also, the imaginary link established between 5G and the coronavirus by this sect led to the degradation of several antennas, even in Europe where more than a hundred base stations were destroyed, according to a statement from the GSMA (Global System for Mobile Communications). Even telecom employees have been attacked!

Twitter decided in the wake of the Capitol Hill incidents to shut down some 70,000 accounts associated with QAnon, but that obviously won't solve the problem. They are already clustered elsewhere on a web so vast…

It all began on October 28, 2017, when an anonymous author named *Q* began posting on the American forum 4chan. The actual identity and status of Q, supposedly a high-ranking official—or group of officials—is not known, but is the subject of speculation among Anons who want to believe in his authority. One of the theories promoted by QAnon is that Trump is at a secret war with elites within the US government, referred to as the *"Deep State."* Also involved alongside this supposed fifth column are people in the financial circles and the media who would commit pedophilic, cannibalistic and satanic crimes. The messages are relayed by many people around the world with Facebook groups having reached 3 million subscribers! Even high-ranking personalities have shown solidarity with the Anons. This is the case for more than 60 candidates in the Republican Party primaries and 14 others in the 2020 US House and Senate elections. Even Michael T. Flynn and John Ratcliffe, Trump's former national security adviser and Secret Service chief, respectively, have become promoters of the movement.

In the final days of Trump's presidency, QAnon followers are convinced that the military would arrest Joe Biden on January 20, the day of the new president's inauguration. They also believe that the arrest of "pedosatanist traitors," the deportation of elected Democrats to Guantánamo, and a total shutdown of the Internet was imminent in order to return Donald Trump to the presidency. On January 19, as the deadline approached, the QAnon community went into a state of emergency. At President Biden's inauguration on January 20, 2021, some supporters of the movement go even deeper into the delusion that it is "part of the plan." I must admit that when I see such theories relayed on the web, including on the professional network LinkedIn, I am flabbergasted.

How can we believe the bullshit of this cult when we know that Trump is a pure product of the American elite system? And then, hasn't he been in the Lolita Express of the pedocriminal Jeffrey Epstein, to give him the honor of wanting to save the children of the world? By the way, the same question arises for the others in the opposite camp who believe in the benevolence of Bill Gates, target of the QAnon, who would like to save the planet with his vaccines, in particular the children of Africa with whom he is often displayed in the clichés. The number of flattering newspaper articles devoted to him during the Covid19 crisis is just mind-blowing. In a Netflix documentary series dedicated to him, even the good Lord would not have had better praise. We'll come back to that. The Microsoft man who monopolized the software industry with more than questionable practices, and challenged in court, divorced his wife precisely because of his ties with Epstein, according to the Wall Street Journal[171]. The name of Boris Nikolic, who was dropped by Epstein a few days before his "suicide" in prison, is none other than Bill Gates's scientific advisor for several years. How can anyone seriously believe that Trump or Gates is working for the good of humanity? These people only know their personal interests and their unconditional supporters live on another planet.

Rationality is obviously not to be found in these phenomena of belief and idolatry. The innumerable cognitive biases and the fragility of human psychology are the key.

---

[171] Emily Glazer and Khadeeja Safdar, "Melinda Gates Was Meeting With Divorce Lawyers Since 2019 to End Marriage With Bill Gates," www.wsj.com, May 9, 2021.

Reed Berkowitz, a specialist in ARG design[172], games whose theater straddles the digital and real worlds, makes a good analysis of the QAnon phenomenon. It is reminiscent of the Gestalt theory I discussed in the first volume of the book. He writes: "When I saw QAnon, I knew exactly what it was and what it did. I had seen it before. I had almost built it before. It was the evil twin of the game. A game that plays with people [...] However, this beast is very different from a game and it's the differences that inform how QAnon works."

In an experiment created by Berkowitz, players had to explore a basement in search of clues. The object they were looking for, a *Scooby Doo*, was barely hidden and easy to find. But the game was derailed by three small pieces of wood that happened to be there and formed a perfect arrow pointing to a wall. For the players, it's a clue. They can't take their eyes off it. Since they couldn't find anything, they had to look in the wall. The objects that supported the hypothesis of the arrow and that were within reach reinforced the players' conviction. A new parallel game was created one after another under the flabbergasted eye of the creator of the original game who had to interrupt the delirium before the wall or the carpet was smashed by the neo-explorers! This is a recurring problem in ARG games because of a bias called "apophenia," the tendency to perceive a meaningful connection or pattern between unrelated or random things, either objects or ideas. When the game designer can change the environment in real time, it can naturally become interesting. The dynamics of QAnon's operation are exactly that. There is no designer or real puzzles to solve, just false interpretations of data rearranged in a desired direction. This can, of course, serve racist or ideological propaganda purposes, for example. When a member detects such a clue, this wooden arrow, he becomes the "discoverer." The psychological effect and the dose of dopamine are guaranteed. He becomes a promoter of the idea and maintains it over time. The others in the same movement naturally follow without

---

[172] Alternate reality game or ARG is an online interactive narrative that leverages the real world as a platform and uses transmedia storytelling to deliver a story that can be modified by the players' ideas or actions. Basically, it is the meeting of a life-size treasure hunt in the form of a treasure hunt, involving the interactive unfolding of a story, the use of new technologies and a community.

questioning it. When questioned on the subject by an intruder, one appeals wholeheartedly to common sense: "But you can see that it's an arrow, right? Still!"

*Status quo* bias and laziness are no strangers to this phenomenon. It is more difficult for people to accept the fact that failing to discover the real story would require extra effort to do so than to create a new one from scratch, even from randomness if the pieces of the puzzle are at hand.

The operating principle of social networks reinforces this mechanism even more in a kind of natural selection of theories. A hypothesis that seduces gets more *likes* and is carried to the top by recommendation algorithms working at the speed of light. A theory that stumbles on reality is just relegated and forgotten in the depths of the Web without calling into question everything else.

The interesting thing about QAnon is that the clues do indeed reveal themselves bit by bit. The question is: Why doesn't Q just reveal everything he knows like a whistleblower? The answer from a follower is: "do the research yourself" to come to your own conclusions. That's nice, isn't it?

The real reason is this: directly telling someone what to do or believe is the best way to create resistance and therefore the risk of not obeying. Firmly held beliefs are literally part of us. As such, attacks on these beliefs are treated as attacks, similar to a physical attack. Jonas Kaplan, a psychologist at the University of Southern California, says, "The brain's primary responsibility is to take care of the body, to protect the body. The psychological self is the brain's extension of that. When our self feels attacked, our [brain] will deploy the same defenses it has to protect the body." When some people on the web try to dissuade people on certain theories by mocking them, they are really only doing the opposite. The closing of accounts by platforms is equally counterproductive. People feel attacked and find one more reason not to believe what the "attacker" wants them to understand. I've seen this kind of reaction many times on the Web.

In order to avoid resistance, a manipulator rather guides, gives the feeling or illusion of control of the situation to his victim by making her believe that she is the one who originated an idea. Thus, when she arrives at the conclusion desired by the guru without her knowledge, she makes it her own and feels pleasure. This is the "eureka effect" or the "aha! moment," that incredible sensation felt when suddenly everything becomes clear in the mind and the solution to a thorny problem becomes obvious.

The satisfaction we feel when we solve a problem or put the last piece of a puzzle in place is believed to be rooted in the evolution of the human species. This is what Dave Ellemberg, a neuropsychologist at the University of Montreal, explains, citing research on the subject[173]. In fact, the involvement of the dopaminergic circuit and the reward system associated with this euphoric moment of sudden understanding, the "eureka effect," would be attributable to an evolutionary mechanism that makes us persevere when the situation is difficult until we succeed in finding the solution to a problem. It's like holding up a carrot with a superior flavor to push the man to surpass himself. And this is indeed what was shown in a recent study, a first of its kind[174]. Subjects were asked to solve problems and to press a button as soon as they were sure they had found the solution. The "aha! moment" is captured and we see if it correlates with brain activity. The scanner reveals hyper activation in certain regions of the brain, including the nucleus accembens, the pleasure center.

This satisfaction after an "aha! moment" is also a reward that enters into a reinforcement mechanism (operant conditioning) that pushes us to seek other victories. Once you've had a taste of it, you want more.

This way of pushing a person to do his own research, while guiding him is also a stratagem to avoid that he goes and looks for himself and thus

---

[173] https://ici.radio-canada.ca/ohdio/premiere/emissions/moteur-de-recherche/segments/chronique/152712/comprehension-probleme-cerveau-explication-resoudre
[174] Tik M, Sladky R, Luft CDB, Willinger D, Hoffmann A, Banissy MJ, Bhattacharya J, Windischberger C. Ultra-high-field fMRI insights on insight: Neural correlates of the Aha!-moment. Hum Brain Mapp. 2018 Aug; 39(8):3241–3252.

perhaps finds facts which could contradict the defended thesis. It also serves to instill doubt in small doses on the trust in the world outside the cult and thus succeed in locking the followers in for the duration.

But beware, sects do not have a monopoly on the manipulation. Because the other extremism would be to deprive people of any critical vision towards the established thought. With this strategy of dumbing down, people are encouraged not to do any research. This is what we often see in the traditional mainstream media, often by ideology or interest, where any divergent thought is qualified as a conspiracy. We will come back to this.

And if this is coupled with lying, then there is nothing better to push a person caught in doubt into a movement like QAnon. Because the shortcut is quickly made: "If we are lied to about one thing, then we are lied to about everything." Let's go back to the basement game. Let's say that a competitor lied to the players to lead them on a false trail and they eventually discovered the lie. Later, this same person finds the players in front of the hypothetical wooden arrow and tells them that it's just random and doesn't lead anywhere. They obviously won't believe him and it will even strengthen their belief in the validity of the lead. This is the great mistake of the mainstream media who have added on about Trump when there was material to attack him without it. This was the case, for example, when the highly respected *New York Times* accused Trump's campaign team of having direct contact with Russian intelligence to help get the Republican candidate elected. This was denied under oath by FBI Director James Comey, who was sacked by Trump, in his hearing before a congressional committee and forced the newspaper to revise its copy[175]. This was also the case when another major newspaper, Time Magazine, published that the former president had removed the bust of Martin Luther King from the Oval Office. The information went viral and was picked up by many other media outlets around the world. Again, the information was proven to be completely false and the reporter was forced to publicly apologize later[176]. These

---

[175] Michael S. Schmidt, Mark Mazzetti, and Matt Apuzzo, "Comey Disputes New York Times Article About Russia Investigation," www.nytimes.com, 2017/06/08.
[176] NANCY GIBBS, "A Note to Our Readers," 2017/01/24.

accusations are serious and when they are proven false, they do too much damage to the credibility of these media outlets and reinforce the QAnon.

Randomness can guide, but can also sometimes reinforce a belief with the chance occurrence of a corroborating fact. Let's suppose that the pseudo-wooden arrow finally convinces the players to dismantle the wall and see what's behind it. And surprise, they come across an object that is actually part of the game. The creator of the game had planned another way to get there, but chance had it otherwise. It is the same in a cult like QAnon that makes predictions of many events and some rare ones end up happening, which gives it the feeling that it is right about everything. The generalization shortcut makes you forget all the other theses contradicted by the facts and drowned by the algorithms in the depths of the Web.

There is a related phenomenon. All cults are fond of symbols, and QAnon is no exception. It argues, for example, that the globalist elites involved in the worst horrors wave their hands to communicate. Here is a small sample in the following images.

When you read such information, you start to see more and more people doing the same thing. This is the frequency illusion bias, also known as the Baader-Meinhof phenomenon. It is a cognitive bias in which, after noticing something for the first time, one tends to notice it more often, leading one to believe that the thing is more frequent. This happens, for example, when you see a car model and are about to buy it. You see it everywhere right after. The Web obviously accentuates this, since an astronomical database of photos is just a click away. Especially when you only look for what reinforces the established belief and you forget everything else like the pictures below.

Context is very important when applying the shortcut. For example, one will not be careful to detect the same gesture in the guru Trump or the Islamist and former Iranian president Mahmoud Ahmadinejad. The brain is the champion of selection!

Another cognitive bias plays a major role in cult membership. This is "commitment escalation," a human behavior in which an individual or group, faced with increasingly negative outcomes of a decision, action, or investment, nevertheless persists in the same behavior rather than changing course. In this way, irrational behaviors are aligned with previous decisions and actions. In a denial of reality, we say to ourselves, "How can we let go of all that time or money wasted supporting an idea?" Imagine the following situation: the players searching for clues in the basement followed the pseudo wooden arrow and ended up dismantling the wall across the street, brick by brick, for six long hours. Then someone comes along and tells them it was all a waste of time. They'd hate it… It's like a poker player who's lost so much money and would rather continue than save what's left. That's why behavioral economists use a related term for this escalation, the "sunk cost bias." This term describes the justification for increased investment in a decision, based on the cumulative prior investment. Only the expected benefit should logically matter, but through this cognitive bias the history prevails.

But before falling into this escalation of commitment or the trap of cognitive dissonance of perpetuating a belief, one must first believe it. This is where other mechanisms of social psychology come into play, which we will now address.

## Conformism or Depersonalization

Several phenomena govern the functioning of human groups. They are not surprisingly found on social networks. I describe some of them that make individuals within a group make decisions outside of any rationality.

The first is conformity, demonstrated by psychologist Solomon Asch (1907–1996) with an experiment published in 1956. Asch invited a group of students between the ages of 17 and 25 to participate in a so-called vision test to which control subjects had previously been subjected and who had no trouble giving the right answer every time. All but one of the participants was an accomplice of the experimenter. The purpose of the experiment was to observe how this student (the "naive" subject) would react to the behavior of others.

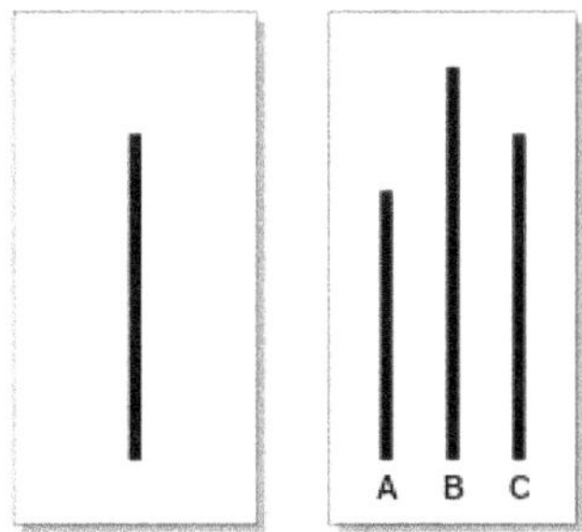


Asch's experiment: the left line is the reference line; the three right lines are the comparison lines.

The accomplices and the subject are seated in a room and are asked to judge the length of several lines drawn on a series of posters. On the left, a reference line, and on the right, 3 other lines. Each subject was asked to say which of the 3 lines on the right was equal to the model line on the left (see figure). Before the experiment began, the experimenter gave instructions to his accomplices. At the beginning, they had to give the right answer, i.e., on the first 6 trials, but on the next 12 trials, they had to unanimously give the same wrong answer. The "naive" subject was the second to last to answer.

The result was surprising. As the trials progressed, the subject became more and more hesitant about his answers. The social pressure was evident on him. Before answering, "he pauses and then announces his choice in a low voice, sometimes with an embarrassed smile."[177]

The experiment was repeated with a single counterpart, who was positioned first. After him, several subjects who were unaware of the true purpose of the experiment also aligned their response with that of the other subject. The attitude of the latter "confident, with a firm voice" had a particularly marked influence on the subjects' responses.

This experiment showed that most subjects answered correctly without outside influence, but that a large number (38%) ended up conforming to the wrong answers supported unanimously by the accomplices or by the sole comparator. Subjects were even led to support answers that went against the evidence and against their own view (see videos of the experiments[178]). For example, two lines were claimed to be the same length, even though they were clearly different by more than 2 inches.

The subjects of this experiment frequently testified, when questioned afterwards, about their feelings of confusion, anxiety or stress. Others had suppressed these conflicting emotions and simply thought they were wrong. After the results were announced, subjects sometimes attributed their poor performance to "bad eyesight," even though tests had been conducted just before the experiment to verify that this was not the case. In reality, it is conformity due to social pressure, as going against the majority is often not a comfortable position for an individual.

Asch's compliance experiments are interpreted as evidence of the power of normative social influence, the willingness to publicly comply to gain group rewards and avoid punishment.

However, this interpretation is not unanimously accepted, contested in particular by the British psychologist John Charles Turner (1947-201) who attributes the results of Asch's experiment to the theory of self-

---

[177] Solomon Asch, "Opinions and Social Pressure," *Scientific American*, vol. 193, no. 5, 1955.
[178] https://www.youtube.com/watch?v=7AyM2PH3_Qk

categorization (depersonalization). This is where "people come to see themselves more as interchangeable examples of a social category than as unique personalities defined by their differences from others."[179] Turner and colleagues point out that depersonalization is not a loss of self, but rather a redefinition of self in terms of group membership. It is reminiscent, for example, of the guy who finds himself as a *black bloc* smashing store windows on the street by the day and as a good family man cuddling his child by night.

Whatever the interpretation, the result is there. A person in a group can make a decision far from rational. This same behavior is also found on the Web. It is now widely used in e-commerce to boost sales with a lot of techniques that induce sheep-like behavior in Internet users[180]. A person buys an article more easily when it has already collected a large number of good reviews, even if it does not quite meet the criteria set at the beginning. Also, a person joins another person's network more easily if that person is already connected to many people. This explains why some brands or celebrities use companies that sell *likes*, followers or reviews to inflate their counters[181]. The group pressure makes us feel bad to see many people following a trend and not us. It's hard to resist, for example, not getting vaccinated when you see that many of your Twitter contacts display a syringe emoji to publicly announce that they have already done so. Even doctors, breaking the medical secrecy they should know well, have done it! The effect of conformity on the Web is massive.

## Submission to Authority

Gustave Le Bon pointed out in his book on the psychology of the crowds that the group bends with servility before a strong authority. He writes: "As soon as a certain number of living beings are gathered

---

[179] McGarty, C., "Categorization in social psychology", Sage Publications: London, Thousand Oaks, New Delhi, 1999.
[180] Dominique Jackson, "Social Proof: How to Use Marketing Psychology to Boost Conversions," https://sproutsocial.com, May 29, 2018.
[181] PRESTIGE MEDIA, "21 BEST SITES TO BUY INSTAGRAM FOLLOWERS (REAL & ACTIVE) IN 2020," www.influencive.com, September 16th, 2020.

together, whether it be a herd of animals or a crowd of men, they instinctively place themselves under the authority of a leader. In human crowds, the real leader is often only a leader, but, as such, he plays a considerable role. His will is the core around which opinions are formed and identified. He constitutes the first element of the organization of heterogeneous crowds and prepares their organization in sects. In the meantime, he leads them. The crowd is a servile herd that can never do without a master." And he adds: "The pure and simple assertion, free from all reasoning and proof, is one of the surest means of making an idea penetrate the minds of crowds. The more concise the statement, the more devoid it is of any semblance of proof and demonstration, the more authority it has. The religious books and codes of all ages have always proceeded by simple assertion. Statesmen called upon to defend some political cause, industrialists propagating their products by advertisement, know the value of the assertion." As Edward Bernays would also remind us several years after him, Le Bon insists on repetition: "The assertion, however, has no real influence unless it is constantly repeated, and, as much as possible, in the same terms. It was Napoleon, I believe, who said that there is only one serious figure of speech, repetition. The affirmed thing manages, by repetition, to establish itself in the minds to the point that they end up accepting it as a proven truth." The past as well as the future will prove Le Bon right on many occasions, in laboratories as well as in real life.

This is probably one of the most incredible and well-known experiments in the history of social psychology. It took place between 1960 and 1963 at Yale University, Connecticut, under the supervision of the team of Professor Stanley Milgram (1933–1984)[182]. This experiment evaluated the degree of obedience of an individual to an authority deemed legitimate. It also made it possible to analyze the process of submission to authority, particularly when it leads to actions that pose problems of conscience for the subject.

Milgram advertises in a local newspaper to recruit participants in an appearance experiment on learning. Participation lasts 1 hour for a fee of

---

[182] Stanley Milgram, "Obedience to Authority: An Experimental View," Harper Perennial, 2009.

$4, a good sum for the time when the average income was $100. The experiment is presented as a scientific study of the effectiveness of punishment on memorization.

The participants are women and men between the ages of 20 and 50, from all social backgrounds and with different levels of education. The experiment, as presented, involves three roles:

- o A student struggling to memorize lists of words and receiving an electric shock if he makes a mistake;
- o A teacher, who dictates the words to the student and checks the answers. In case of error, he sends an electric shock to make the student suffer;
- o A smocked, confidently speaking experimenter who represents the official authority.

The experimenter and the student are in reality two actors. The teacher, who is the only subject of the real experiment—to study the level of obedience, or submission to authority—is described the conditions of the so-called memory experiment. All the subjects are informed that they will be drawn with the other participant to act as a student or teacher. The teacher is given a mild electric shock of 45 volts to show him what kind of suffering the student can endure. This helps to build his confidence that the experiment is real. Once the guinea pig has agreed to the protocol, a rigged draw is conducted, which systematically designates him as the teacher. The student is placed in a neighboring room, separated by a thin partition, and strapped into an electric chair (apparently). The teacher is installed in front of a desk equipped with a row of joysticks and is given the task of making the student memorize lists of words. For each mistake, the teacher is asked to activate a lever which, he believes, sends an electric shock of increasing voltage to the student (15 additional volts for each discharge, according to what is written on the desk). The subject is asked to call out the corresponding voltage before applying it. Of course, the electric shocks are fictitious. The reactions to the electric shocks are simulated by the student. The actor who simulates suffering has been given the following instructions: at 75 V, he moans; at 120 V, he complains to the experimenter that he is in pain; at 135 V, he screams; at 150 V, he begs to be released; at 270 V, he lets out a violent scream; at 300 V, he announces that he will not respond anymore. When the student no longer responds, the experimenter indicates that no response is considered an error. At 150 volts, the majority of the subjects show doubts and question the experimenter who is at their side. The experimenter reassures them that they are not responsible for the consequences. If a subject hesitates, the experimenter is instructed to ask him to act.

If a subject expresses the desire to stop the experiment, the experimenter addresses him, in order, as follows:

1- "Please continue."
2- "Experience demands that you continue."
3- "It is absolutely essential that you continue."
4- "You have no choice, you have to keep going."

If the subject still wishes to stop after these four interventions, the experiment is effectively stopped. Otherwise, it ends when the subject administers three maximum discharges of 450 volts!

In the first experiments conducted by Stanley Milgram, 62% of the subjects completed the experiment by inflicting the terrible 450-volt electroshock three times. All participants accepted the announced principle and, finally after encouragement, reached 135 volts. The average level of the so-called shocks that the subjects stopped at was 360 volts! However, every participant had at one time or another interrupted to question the teacher. Many showed clear signs of extreme nervousness and reluctance during the final stages (verbal protests, nervous laughter, etc.)[183].

---

[183] The American Psychological Association recommends that the Milgram experiment be stopped because of the enormous stress it causes the subjects. Complaints have also been filed in France by two deputies following the broadcasting of the Game of Death.

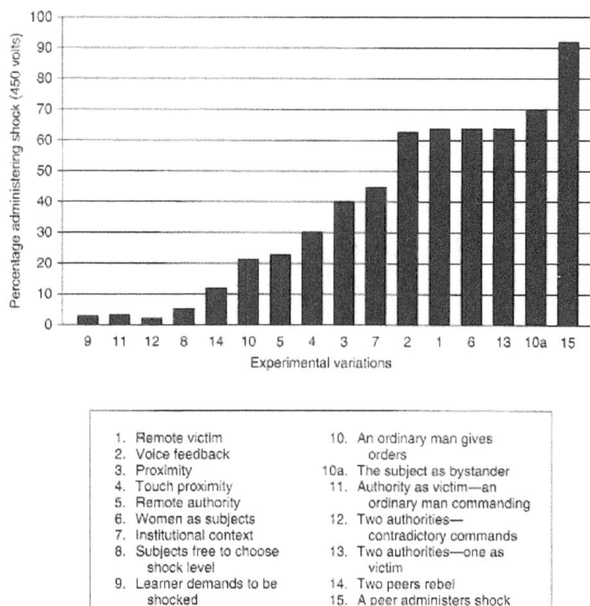


| 1. Remote victim | 10. An ordinary man gives orders |
| 2. Voice feedback | 10a. The subject as bystander |
| 3. Proximity | 11. Authority as victim—an ordinary man commanding |
| 4. Touch proximity | |
| 5. Remote authority | 12. Two authorities—contradictory commands |
| 6. Women as subjects | |
| 7. Institutional context | 13. Two authorities—one as victim |
| 8. Subjects free to choose shock level | 14. Two peers rebel |
| 9. Learner demands to be shocked | 15. A peer administers shock |

Numerous experimental variants, including one in which 92% of the subjects completed the experiment (see figure), flagrantly highlight certain factors of submission. Stanley Milgram proposes a detailed analysis of the phenomenon in his book published in 1974[184]. He places himself in an evolutionary framework, stipulating that obedience is a behavior inherent to human life in society and that the integration of an individual into a hierarchy implies that his own functioning is altered. Within a group, the human being passes from the autonomous mode to the systematic mode where he becomes an agent of authority.

Milgram's experiment has been reproduced several times around the world, including in television programs. This was the case in France in 2009 where the public channel produced the documentary "The Game of Death,"[185] featuring a fake game show called "The Xtreme Zone." It can

[184] Milgram, Stanley, "Obedience to Authority", New York: Harper & Row, 1974.
[185] The Game of Death is a documentary written by Christophe Nick, directed by Thomas Bornot, Gilles Amado and Alain-Michel Blanc and co-produced by France Télévisions and Radio Télévision Suisse1 in 2009.

be seen online for those who want to watch it[186]. The notable difference is that the scientific authority represented by the technician in a lab coat is replaced by a television presenter. The result? The rate of obedience is 81%, even higher than the 62% of Milgram's original experiment!

Milgram's experiment and the following ones have demonstrated the danger of an uncritical acceptance of authority, a phenomenon that is very present on social networks, notably LinkedIn, which I frequented enough during the coronavirus crisis to talk about it. I saw a scandal unfold before my eyes that was completely related to this phenomenon: the *LancetGate*. It is the story of a study, a farce I would say, published in the prestigious journal *The Lancet*, bringing the proof of a so-called danger of the treatment applied at the IHU of Marseille against Covid-19. This study, based on the analysis of a large database, something I often do in my job, caught my attention. So, I read it. The same day it was published, I announced on the LinkedIn network that it was a fake study, created from scratch. I even used the term "butchery" to describe it. At the same time, all the media were talking about it, calling it a great study. I even heard a doctor, a member of parliament too, on a 24-hour news channel say[187]: "You have to read the study. It has weaknesses, but the strength of the study is that it involves a very large number of patients, with very different hospitals, which probably overcomes certain methodological weaknesses. And this study, which is actually of very good quality, shows that chloroquine unfortunately does not work." I have to say that I fell off my chair when I saw the circus that was going on at the time. When I challenged the news articles relayed by many people on LinkedIn, most of whom work in the medical field, I was often rebuked, "Stay in your area of expertise and stop talking about medicine you don't know." I noted in passing that these people often visited my profile before coming across me. So that's the argument from authority that no one should argue with. This is not my style and I did it again a few days later by publishing a critique of the study. The *Lancet* announced the withdrawal of the article the same evening and the scandal broke out, with pressure from all sides starting to be put on the

---

[186] https://www.youtube.com/watch?v=6w_nlgekIzw&ab_channel=emisguy
[187] https://www.youtube.com/watch?v=2c6OPsakV-Q&ab_channel=marsala92

charlatan authors. But the damage was done, because the French Minister of Health Olivier Véran (a doctor by the way) had banned the treatment the day after the false study, and all clinical trials launched in France including it were stopped. More than a year after the beginning of the epidemic, not a single study on possible therapies against covid19 has come out in France. The only treatment [Remdesivir] that was given a marketing authorization, based once again on a flawed study from the United States, ended up being discouraged even by the WHO, a few weeks after Europe purchased 500,000 doses, for 1.2 billion euros. Thank you, European taxpayers! When I posted a reservation about this other study at the very beginning, a doctor challenged me on LinkedIn, "This study is very strong."

Beyond the incompetence, the corruption, the unconscious support of some doctors who received small and big gifts, I find an explanation to the LancetGate: the authority of the journal *The Lancet*. It is considered as one of the most prestigious in the world, as all the TV shows talked about it, and it was difficult to contest it. But that was before…

The moral of the story is that the critical mind must remain awake, whatever the circumstances. We must not give in to this argument of authority which aims to compartmentalize people into dangerous virtual boxes. Forget stereotypes and just try to understand and question ideas. During the crisis, I learned one thing that I keep in mind: lies are so much more expensive to maintain than the truth. It takes many more voices of people lying to drown out one person telling the truth, much like the Asch experiment…

## The devil effect

A few years after Milgram's experiment, another one confirming his results was conducted at Stanford University.

The Stanford Experiment, sometimes referred to as the "Lucifer Effect," is a social psychology experiment that was designed to study the psychological effects of perceived power. It was funded by the *US*

*Office of Naval Research* as an investigation into the causes of difficulties experienced between guards and prisoners in the US Navy.

It was conducted at Stanford University from August 14 to 20, 1971, by a group of researchers led by Professor of Psychology Philip Zimbardo. Male students were recruited to participate in a prison simulation for a period of two weeks. The team selected the 24 candidates whose test scores predicted that they would be the most psychologically stable and healthy. The group was purposely selected to exclude people with criminal histories, mental disabilities, or medical problems. They all agreed to participate for a daily fee of $15, the equivalent of about $100 today.

The experiment was conducted in a 35-feet section of the basement of Jordan Hall, Stanford's psychology building. Each cell (6 × 9 feet) in the fabricated prison contained only one bed. The "prisoners" were confined 24 hours a day. The guards, on the other hand, lived in a very different environment separate from the prisoners. They were given comfortable rest areas.

Twelve of the twenty-four participants were assigned the role of prisoners, while the other twelve were assigned the role of the guards. Professor Zimbardo assumed the role of the superintendent and a research assistant took on the role of the prison warden.

The researchers held an orientation session for the guards the day before the experiment, during which they were instructed not to physically harm the prisoners or deprive them of food or drink. In archival footage of the study, Zimbardo can be seen talking to the guards, "You can create feelings of boredom in the prisoners, a sense of fear to some extent. You can create a notion of arbitrariness that their life is totally controlled by us, by the system, you, me, and they will have no privacy... We will take away their individuality in various ways. In general, all this leads to a feeling of powerlessness. In this situation, we will have all the power and they will have nothing."

The researchers provided the guards with wooden batons to establish their status, clothing similar to that of a real prison guard, and mirrored sunglasses to avoid eye contact. The prisoners wore uncomfortable, ill-fitting gowns and caps, and a chain around their ankles. The guards were instructed not to call the prisoners by name, but by assigned numbers sewn into their uniforms.

The prisoners were "arrested" at their homes and "charged" with armed robbery. The local Palo Alto Police Department assisted Zimbardo in the arrests and conducted routine procedures as they would on any real prisoner. This included arresting, fingerprinting and photographing. The prisoners were even transported to a mock jail at the police station where they were strip-searched and given their new identities.

The small cells at Stanford Prison were set up to hold three prisoners each. There was a small hallway to simulate the prison yard, a closet for the solitary confinement cell, and a larger room across from the prisoners for the guards and warden. The prisoners had to stay in their cells or in the yard all day and night until the end of the study. The guards were organized in teams that took turns every eight hours.

Reports of the experiment showed that the students quickly adopted the roles assigned to them, with some guards applying authoritarian measures and eventually subjecting some prisoners to psychological torture, while many prisoners passively accepted the psychological abuse and, at the request of officers, actively harassed other prisoners who had tried to resist the injunctions.

After a relatively calm first day, the second day was more agitated. The prisoners in cell number 1 blocked the door to their cell with their beds and removed their caps, refusing to leave or follow the guards' instructions. Guards from other shifts volunteered to work overtime, to help control the revolt, and then attacked the prisoners with fire extinguishers. The observing researchers did not intervene. Noting that it was difficult to manage the cellmates with only three guards, one of the guards suggested using psychological tactics to "break the bonds between them" and control them. They created a "privileged cell" in which prisoners who were not involved in the riot were treated with special rewards, such as better meals. This is eerily reminiscent of 2021, with the benefits provided to "health certificate" holders … except that the "privileged" Stanford inmates chose not to eat the meal out of compassion for their fellow inmates.

After only 35 hours of the experiment, one prisoner plunged into madness, as Zimbardo described it: "Number 8612 then started acting like a madman, screaming, cursing, going into a rage that seemed uncontrollable. It took a while before we were all convinced that he was really suffering and that we had to release him."

Guards forced prisoners to repeat their assigned numbers to reinforce the idea that this was their new identity. They used these counts to harass the unlucky ones, using physical punishments such as prolonged exercise following each mistake. Sanitary conditions quickly deteriorated, exacerbated by the refusal of guards to allow some prisoners to urinate or defecate anywhere other than in a bucket placed in their cell. As punishment, guards would not let prisoners empty the sanitary bucket or would deprive them of their mattresses, leaving them to sleep on the concrete. Some prisoners were forced to strip naked. Many guards became increasingly cruel as the experiment continued; experimenters reported that about a third of the guards exhibited true sadistic tendencies. Many were upset when the experiment was stopped after only six days.

Zimbardo does not fail to mention his own absorption by the experience. On the fourth day, some of the guards said they heard a rumor that the freed prisoner would return with his friends to free the other inmates. Zimbardo and the guards dismantled the prison and moved it to another floor of the building. Zimbardo himself waited in the basement, in case the freed prisoner showed up! The released prisoner did not return and the prison was rebuilt in the basement. It's madness on every floor…

Zimbardo dropped out of the experiment early when Christina Maslach, a psychology graduate student he was dating at the time and would later marry, objected to the conditions of the prison after being brought into the experiment to conduct interviews with the prisoners. Zimbardo noted that, out of more than 50 people who had observed the experiment, Maslach was the only one who questioned its morality. After only six days of an originally planned two-week duration, the experiment was halted.

On the occasion of the 40th anniversary of the experiment, an exhibition was organized by the Stanford University Archives, open to the public between August 15 and October 22, 2011, unveiling unpublished material of texts, audios, videos, etc. It can be consulted online, on the website of the university's library[188]. The experience has been the subject of several film adaptations, including a particularly well made and fairly true-to-life movie released in 2015[189]. I highly recommend it.

Zimbardo's study is ethically and methodologically questionable in more ways than one, but it has the merit of putting on the table the subject of possible drifts in group behavior. Unfortunately, it has not been sufficiently taken into account and the American army discovered this to its cost during the invasion of Iraq in 2003. The Abu Ghraib scandal, which some call "the real Stanford experiment[190]," blew up in its face. Notable difference? Female soldiers participated in practices that are beyond comprehension[191]. Even the hardened Philip Zimbardo was shocked when he discovered the images, more than 1,000 photos, which he assembled, categorized, and studied. They all came directly from the soldiers' phones. All of this can be seen in an excellent TEDx seminar he gave in 2008 entitled, "What Makes People Slip?"[192]

A corollary question: is it possible to see such group behavior emerge on a social network like Facebook where the power of authority, a central element in the Milgram and Zimbardo experiments, is a priori absent? Not impossible, as we will now see.

---

[188] https://library.stanford.edu/spc/exhibitspublications/past-exhibits/stanford-prison-experiment-40-years-later

[189] "The Stanford Prison Experiment," directed by Kyle Patrick Alvarez, Written by Tim Talbott, produced by Abandon Pictures, Coup d'Etat Films, Sandbar Pictures, 2015.

[190] Peter Kinderman, "ABU GHRAIB: THE REAL STANFORD PRISON EXPERIMENT", https://www.psychliverpool.co.uk/psychology-news/social/abu-ghraib-real-stanford-prison-experiment/

[191] "Disturbing New Photos From Abu Ghraib", https://www.wired.com/2008/03/gallery-abu-ghraib

[192] https://www.ted.com/talks/philip_zimbardo_the_psychology_of_evil?language=en#t-190550

## Lucifer 2.0

In 2014, researchers from the Department of Information and Communication Sciences at Cornell University (Ithaca, New York), in partnership with a data science team from Facebook, published a resounding paper in the journal PNAS[193]. It summarizes the results of a massive experiment carried out on 689,000 Facebook subscribers, conducted to verify the possibility of emotional contagion on social networks. This phenomenon of transferring the emotional states of a person to those around him or her has already been demonstrated in the laboratory[194]. Also, data collected over a period of 20 years on the inhabitants of the town of Framingham, Massachusetts, suggest that lasting moods (depression, joy) can be transferred via real social networks (not the Internet)[195]. The Facebook experiment therefore aimed to test whether emotional contagion occurs outside of direct interaction between individuals, i.e., only on the social network. To do this, the team played on the amount of emotional content in the news feed of the subjects studied. During the week-long experiment (January 11–18, 2012), participants were randomly selected, based on their user ID, to decide whether they received positive or negative content in their news feed. More than 3 million posts were analyzed during the entire process.

It was noted that when positive expressions were reduced, people made fewer positive posts and posted more negative ones; when negative expressions were reduced, the opposite pattern occurred. These results indicate that the emotions expressed by others on Facebook influence our own emotions, providing experimental evidence of large-scale contagion via social networks.

---

[193] Adam D. I. Kramer, Jamie E. Guillory, and Jeffrey T. Hancock, "Experimental evidence of massive-scale emotional contagion through social networks," PNAS June 17, 2014, 111 (24) 8788–8790; first published June 2, 2014; https://doi.org/10.1073/pnas.1320040111

[194] Hatfield E, Cacioppo JT, Rapson RL, "Emotional contagion," Curr Dir Psychol Sci 2(3):96–100, 1993.

[195] Fowler JH, Christakis NA, "Dynamic spread of happiness in a large social network: Longitudinal analysis over 20 years in the Framingham Heart Study", BMJ 337:a2338.

The results also suggest that, contrary to prevailing assumptions, face-to-face interaction and nonverbal cues are not strictly necessary for emotional contagion. Simply observing positive experiences in others is a positive experience for people. I quote from the article, "These results highlight several features of emotional contagion. First, because news feed content is not directed at anyone in particular, contagion cannot simply be the result of a specific interaction with a happy or sad friend. Although previous research has examined whether an emotion can be contracted via direct interaction, we show that simply not perceiving a friend's emotional expression via Facebook is sufficient to spare them the effects. Second, although nonverbal behavior is well established as a means of contagion, these data suggest that contagion does not require nonverbal behavior: textual content alone appears to be a sufficient channel." It added, "We also observed a withdrawal effect: people who were exposed to fewer emotional messages (positive or negative) in their news feed were less expressive overall on subsequent days, showing how emotional expression *affects* online *social engagement*. This observation, and the fact that people were more emotionally positive in response to positive emotional updates from friends, contrasts with theories that suggest that viewing positive posts from friends on Facebook can somehow affect us negatively, for example, via social comparison. In fact, this happens when people are exposed to less positive content, rather than more." And further on, towards the end of the article we can read: "More importantly, given the massive scale of social networks such as Facebook, even small effects can have large aggregate consequences: for example, the well-documented link between emotions and physical well-being suggests the importance of these findings for public health. Online messages influence our emotional experience, which can affect a variety of offline behaviors."

The results of this work are undoubtedly very important, but I have problems with some of the wording and statements. First, and this is the thing I look at all the time when reading any scientific paper, conflicts of interest. The last footnote in the publication is[196]: "The authors declare no conflicts of interest." This is not admissible given that Facebook's

---

[196] https://www.pnas.org/content/111/24/8788#ref-6

data science team participated in the work and one of the results states that social validation does not hold and that a positive post from a friend does not depress others. This iconoclastic conclusion is favorable to the use of the Facebook network. Doesn't it? The conflict of interest is obvious. Also, the article states, "LIWC [an automatic text processing tool] was adapted to work within the news feed filtering system so that no text was seen by searchers. As such, it complied with Facebook's data use policy, which all users adhere to before creating a Facebook account, constituting informed consent for this research." Amazing, isn't it? The subjects targeted by this research would have given informed consent when everything happened without their knowledge! Of course, I am not the only one who questions this kind of procedure. A letter of concern and correction[197] was attached to the article by the journal PNAS before publication. It states that the authors stated that the experiment was conducted by Facebook for internal purposes. The Cornell University board then concluded that the project did not fall under its human subject research rules and therefore did not ask participants for any consent. The cover letter reiterates the U.S. Department of Health and Human Services' *Common* Rule for the protection of human research subjects to "obtain informed consent and allow participants to withdraw" at any time. The journal PNAS points out that compliance with the *Common Rule* is its policy, but as a private company, Facebook was not required to comply with the rule when collecting users' personal data. The editors of PNAS therefore deemed it "appropriate to publish the article" while noting that it was "nonetheless concerning that Facebook's data collection may have involved practices that were not fully consistent with the principles of obtaining informed consent and allowing participants to opt out."

Obviously, you can't say that the work is for internal Facebook purposes and at the same time not declare any conflicts of interest. That's nonsense. As for the supposed consent of users asserted in the article, it is just overflowing with cynicism to assert it. The subjects were not even aware that they were part of an experiment!

---

[197] Interestingly, PNAS required a correction regarding author Jamie E. Guillory graduated from Cornell University, but joined the Tobacco Research Center at the University of California as a postdoc, which was not originally mentioned.

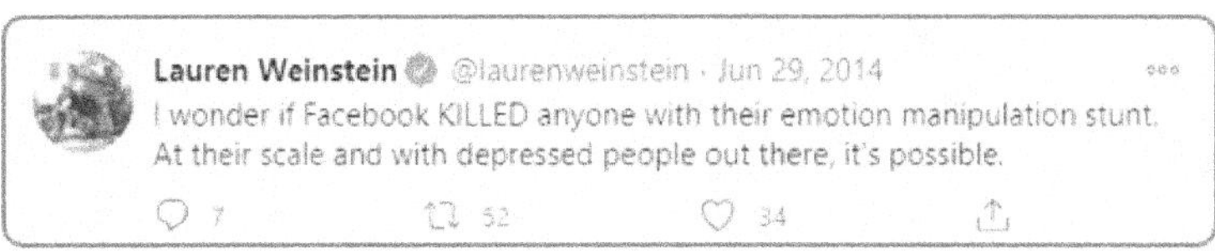


A few days after the article was published in the journal PNAS, there were many reactions online. "I wonder if Facebook KILLED someone with their emotion manipulation stunt. At their scale and with depressed people there, it's possible," wrote privacy activist Lauren Weinstein in a post on Twitter. Her post picked up by The New York Times in an article[198] titled "Facebook Tinkers With Users" Emotions in News Feed Experiment, Stirring Outcry," eventually prompted a response from Facebook researcher Adam D. I. Kramer, who led the study, "I can understand some people's concerns about this, and my co-authors and I are very sorry for the way the article describes the research and the anxiety it caused." That's a flimsy argument, to say the least, and it doesn't convince anyone.

Several commentators have pointed out a parallel between Facebook's social experiment and its most famous predecessors: Milgram and Stanford. Princeton University sociologist and media scholar Timothy Recuber even wrote a critical article for the journal Research Ethics[199] comparing the three experiments. He says: "The infamous Milgram (1963) and Zimbardo (1973) experiments on the social psychology of obedience and aggression seemed in some respects to have obvious analogs to the Facebook experiment, at least insofar as all three violated norms about the treatment of human subjects in research. But other than that, what do they really have in common? In fact, a close reading of Milgram, Zimbardo, and the Facebook experiment reveals something about how power both as a subject of scientific inquiry and as something researchers use is conceptualized today. Although all three experiments were essentially about measuring the ability of researchers to induce

---

[198] Vindu Goel, "Facebook Tinkers With Users' Emotions in News Feed Experiment, Stirring Outcry," New York Times, June 29, 2014.
[199] Timothy Recuber, "From obedience to contagion: Discourses of power in Milgram, Zimbardo, and the Facebook experiment," Research Ethics 2016, Vol. 12(1) 44–54, First Published May 13, 2015.

emotional or behavioral change in subjects, the Facebook experiment did much more than the others to obscure these considerations and naturalize the exercise of power at work in this study. This article thus argues that the invisibility of power in the discourse of the Facebook experiment demonstrates, in miniature, the more insidious elements of big data as a whole." He concludes the article by referring to activist Lauren Weinstein's tweet and says, "[…] it is clear that the immediate effect of this emotional tinkering on subjects" personal mental health is a legitimate concern. But then again, the fact that the authors of the Facebook experiment didn't even feel the need to write about such considerations in black and white also raises other issues. As Zeynep Tufekci[200] has argued, the negative reaction to the study suggests that algorithmic manipulation generates discomfort precisely because it is opaque, powerful, and perhaps nonconsensual. This opacity has cloaked the language of the paper itself, rendering invisible the researchers' own power and casting the ethics of the research process as apparently unworthy of consideration. In the age of big data, where we are all routinely and unconsciously the subjects of similar algorithmic experiments on social networks, this opacity is indeed alarming. Milgram at least revealed his deception to his subjects after the fact. At least Zimbardo debriefed his prisoners and guards at the study's first conclusion. Today, such experimentation is part of our daily lives. But unlike the experimental subjects of the past, in most cases we do not know what we are to obey, or by what unseen authority we have been deceived, or to what contagions we have been exposed." I would add: with the invisible algorithmic power, Lucifer 2.0 is born…

There is a question that has been nagging at me for a while: why did Facebook publish the results of this study, when we suspected that it would create a stir and perhaps a scandal? The answer is logical, but far from trivial. It came to me after a while. Like any company that communicates, Facebook's first target is its customers. And we must not forget that the user of the social network is the product and not the customer. The customer is actually the advertiser who pays to advertise

---

[200] Tufekci Zeynep, "Big data, surveillance, and computational politics," First Monday 19(7), 2014. Available at:
http://firstmonday.org/ojs/index.php/fm/article/view/4901/4097

its products or services in order to reach as many people as possible. Zuckerberg's company has therefore every interest in showing that it is capable of providing the best possible product, including by manipulating the emotions of users. Especially if it is demonstrated that a given emotion can promote purchasing behavior[201]. In this case, we speak of "creating a favorable emotional context." So why should we deprive ourselves of a little depression in order to place a few packs of chips or beer?

Without forgetting that the manifestation of emotions, especially negative ones, favors the installation of internal triggers in the loop of *hook*, which causes the addiction to the Web (see volume 1 of the current book).

Ironically, as I was writing the lines of this very paragraph, I experienced a disturbing situation, to say the least. I took a quick hop to Facebook, or so I thought, and spotted a post on my newsfeed, as commented on by a homesick friend who was lamenting that flights to Algeria had been suspended for months due to the coronavirus crisis. The publication was a nostalgic song about Kabylia, my native region that I haven't visited for over a year now, a first in my life. As a result, I am taken of a blow of blues as rarely, the lyrics of the song not helping by speaking about "the mom left far behind, crying." I am literally down. I probably wouldn't have noticed this situation if I wasn't writing about it (just a frequency illusion?[202]) One thing is for sure, this is not the only time this has happened to me.

This is certainly true for all online social networks, big data and AI algorithms being their new common secret weapon to boost our engagement score, such an efficient recipe to hack our brain and capture our attention as long as possible. Even if it means playing with our emotions and our mental and physical health…

---

[201] Catherine Guillien, "Emotion and Consumer Behavior," March 14, 2016, https://creg.ac-versailles.fr/l-emotion-et-le-comportement-du-consommateur
[202] The frequency illusion, also known as the Baader-Meinhof phenomenon, is a cognitive bias in which, after noticing something for the first time, one tends to notice it more often, leading one to believe that the thing is more frequent. This happens especially when you buy a car. You see it everywhere right after …

# CHAPTER V: Information in crisis

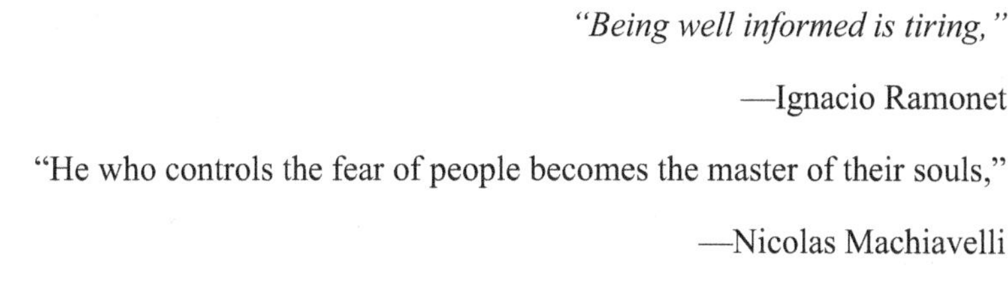

*"Being well informed is tiring,"*

—Ignacio Ramonet

"He who controls the fear of people becomes the master of their souls,"

—Nicolas Machiavelli

There is no more difficult period than that of any crisis to get the right information, the real one. Everyone is pulling in their own direction to feed their own agenda, for financial gain or pure ideology. With the multiplication of information sources on the Web, coupled with algorithmic manipulation, it is truly cognitive chaos. It is very difficult to disentangle the true from the false. This chapter aims to give some keys to find one's way through by understanding certain phenomena. We will see that the coronavirus crisis is a life-size example of everything we have described in the previous chapters on propaganda, the virality of fake news, the contagion of emotions …, and the slippage in the use of *nudging*.

## Cognitive Chaos

There are many questions about information online, but in the end, only one matters: how to be well informed? In the age of the Internet and the explosion of the number of possible sources, it is not easy to find your way around. Especially since the traditional press is experiencing a real crisis of confidence. And it started a while ago.

In 1993, Ignacio Ramonet, director of Le *Monde Diplomatique* from 1990 to 2008, analyzed the evolution of journalism a little more than 10 years after the liberalization of the airwaves. Faced with the rise of television and the changes in news, he wrote a very interesting article entitled "Being well informed is tiring,", which means that some effort is needed to get the right information.[203] If we replaced television by the Internet, there would be almost nothing to change in his article that I would be tempted to take back in its entirety here if it were not a little long. Ramonet wrote: "Until recently, to inform was, in a way, to provide not only the precise—and verified—description of a fact, of an event, but also a set of contextual parameters allowing the reader to understand its deep meaning. It was answering basic questions: who did what? With what means? Where did it happen? How was it done? Why? And what are the consequences? This has totally changed under the influence of television, which now occupies a dominant place in the media hierarchy and spreads its model. The television news, thanks in particular to its ideology of the livestream and the real time, imposed little by little a radically different conception of the information. To inform, it is, henceforth, 'to show the history in progress' or, in other words, to make attend (if possible in livestream) the event. It is about, as regards information, a Copernican revolution of which we did not finish measuring the consequences. For it supposes that the image of the event (or its description) is enough to give it all its meaning. In the end, the journalist himself is too much in this face-to-face viewer history. The priority objective for the viewer, his satisfaction, is no longer to understand the significance of an event, but simply to watch it happen before his eyes. This coincidence is considered jubilant. Thus is established, little by little, the deceptive illusion that to see is to understand [...] Another concept has changed: that of actuality. What is actuality now? Which event should be privileged in the abundance of facts that occur throughout the world? According to which criteria should we choose? Here again, the influence of television appears to be decisive. It is television, with the impact of its images, which imposes its choice and forces the written press to follow. Television constructs the news, provokes the emotional shock and practically condemns the facts orphaned by images to silence, to indifference. Little by little, the idea is established in people's minds that the importance of events is proportional to their richness in images. Or, to put it another way, that an

---

[203] https://www.monde-diplomatique.fr/1993/10/RAMONET/45706

event that can be shown (if possible in real time) is stronger, more interesting, more eminent than one that remains invisible and whose importance is abstract. In the new media order, words or texts are not worth images. The time of the information has also changed. The optimal scansion of the media is now the instantaneity (the real time), the direct, that only television and radio can practice [...] A fourth concept has changed. That, fundamental, of the truthfulness of the information. From now on, a fact is true not because it corresponds to objective criteria, rigorous and verified at the source, but simply because other media repeat the same assertions and confirm... If television (from a dispatch or an agency image) presents a news item and that the written press, then the radio, take up this news, that is enough to accredit it as true. This is how, we remember, the lie of the 'Timisoara mass grave' and all those of the Gulf War were built. The media no longer know how to distinguish, structurally, the true from the false [...] In this media upheaval, it is more and more vain to want to analyze the written press isolated from the other means of information. The media (and the journalists) repeat themselves, imitate themselves, copy themselves, answer each other and get tangled up to the point of constituting only one informational system within which it is more and more difficult to distinguish the specificities of such media taken in isolation [...] Finally, information and communication tend to get confused. Too many journalists continue to believe that they are the only ones to produce information when the whole society has frantically started to do the same thing [...] To all these upheavals is added a fundamental misunderstanding. Many citizens believe that, comfortably installed in the sofa of their living room and watching on the small screen, a sensational cascade of events based on strong, violent and spectacular images, they can be seriously informed. This is a major mistake. For three reasons: first, because the television news, structured as a fiction, is not made to inform, but to distract; then, because the rapid succession of short and fragmented news (about twenty per newscast) produces a double negative effect of over-information and disinformation; and finally, because wanting to inform oneself without effort is an illusion that belongs to the advertising myth rather than to the civic mobilization.

Being informed is tiring, and it is at this price that the citizen acquires the right to participate intelligently in democratic life."

Yes, being informed is tiring! More than ever. The mass media only repeat the same news from three or four news agencies in the world (Reuters, AFP, AP), often without changing a single comma. Continuous news channels always invite the same people, often self-proclaimed experts, without giving room for contradictory debate. The rises in tone that we sometimes see on certain platforms are just for show to create a buzz. Faced with this observation, which I am far from being the only one to make, people no longer have confidence and are rightly looking for alternative sources. These are naturally found on the Internet, especially on social networks.

The problem is that the real information, especially the most useful, is drowned in a sea of news without real interest, or even false. To make some order in this chaos, it is necessary to invest and to get tired. There is no other miracle solution.

## Lost Trust in Traditional Media

If the media has lost the battle to digital platforms, it's also due to a trust issue. In a 2020 study by *Reuters Institute*, across all countries, fewer than four in 10 respondents (38%) said they trust the media, a four-point drop from 2019. Less than half (46%) said they trust the news they themselves use[204]. These poor numbers should naturally be taken with a grain of salt given the fact that *Reuters* is both judge and jury in this study. There are obviously differences between countries, ranging from Finland and Portugal where more than half (56%) say they trust, to less than a quarter in Taiwan (24%) or France (23%). Only six countries now have confidence levels above 50%.

---

[204] https://reutersinstitute.politics.ox.ac.uk/sites/default/files/2020-06/DNR_2020_FINAL.pdf

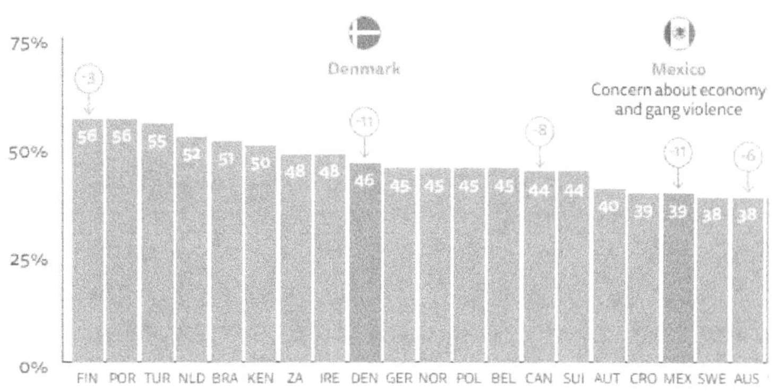


Why this loss of confidence? I have my own idea about the answer like everyone else, but I found the answer by chance while reading an article in the newspaper *Les Echos,* written by a person who knows the media very well: Jacques Attali. His article is written while he is in the middle of promoting a book he recently published and in which he covered the subject of the media[205]. One can read the following: "Many media, especially in France, have even lived for a long time, in the 19th century and at the beginning of the 20th, on the trade of fake news. It should not be surprising if today it takes on a whole new dimension." Curiosity led me to go further and read the book in question[206]. I must admit that I asked myself the question several times and even checked the author again and again to be sure that we are talking about Jacques Attali, the man who has been whispering in the ears of French presidents since Mitterrand and especially the man who is very present in the media. One chapter of the book is particularly straightforward. It is entitled as follows: "The French press, at the service of money." In the course of a comparison with the Anglo-Saxon press, he says this: "In France, none of this. The press is not on the side of entertainment or information. Nor of the money that can be made through advertising. But of the money that can be earned by being paid to lie." Talking about the press in the 19th century, he writes: "All these dailies remain above all dependent on

---

[205] Jacques Attali, "GameStop: after fake news, fake finance", Les Echos, 05 February 2021.

[206] Jacques Attali, "Histoires des médias: Des signaux de fumée aux réseaux sociaux, et bien après", Fayard, January 2021.

their political support, the sales of their financial services and the donations of financial institutions. The Crédit Foncier thus paid generous monthly payments to many newspapers, especially financial ones, and to journalists. *Le Mot d'ordre* received 60,000 francs, and *La Paix*, more than 125,000 francs for the months of May to November 1879 alone…" And to specify: "In some newspapers, a Republican parliamentarian was astonished in 1881, the editor of the financial bulletin, instead of being paid for his work by the owner of the newspaper where he writes, is paid by a private entrepreneur who buys the right to dispose of him as he pleases […] For many of these newspapers, a simple source of income is then to present, at the end of the afternoon, to a wealthy man or a businessman on the front page of the next day's newspaper, telling him that it is up to him that it does not appear. Few people resist this kind of intimidation, which is very widespread at the end of the 19th century […] Between 1904 and 1908, an affair marks the peak of corruption in the Parisian press: at the time of the placement of loans from the Russian Empire, all the main Parisian newspapers (*Le Petit Journal, La Lanterne, Le Figaro, Le Petit Parisien, Le Matin, La France*) agreed (as we will know much later) to receive from Moscow an enormous manna of financial publicity on the condition that they did not mention in their articles the political and economic weaknesses of the Russian Empire, which would harm the underwriting of its loans." And he adds: "As we have seen, the media have always lied, selling their pens to the highest bidder, serving the most despicable causes, slavishly obeying the powers that be […] Newspapers, radio stations, television stations, social networks, digital applications, online media, when they do not belong to states, belong to large fortunes and huge private investment funds. And these, no matter what they say, do not hesitate to influence the editorial content." Or again: "Their products, their newspapers, their magazines, their radios, their televisions, their social networks, are then for them only sources of income, distractions, illusions to make the people forget that they still do not have access to the rarest goods, to the best education, to privileged information. The massification of information, itself supposed to be democratic, is thus, in the end, only a ruse for the proletarianization of the middle classes. And at least a way to keep them dependent."

One can only agree with this observation made by a man who knows the mainstream media better than anyone. This explains very well for me the loss of confidence that the population shows towards them.

The concentration of media in the hands of a few is naturally problematic. In the United States, for example, it is six large companies that own 90% of everything that is read, heard, or watched since 2011, compared to 50 companies less than 30 years earlier[207]. The six giants in question are ATT (acquired by Time Warner), CBS, Comcast, Disney, News Corp (the parent company of Fox News), and Viacom. The multitude of names of newspapers, radio stations, and TV news channels is really only an illusion of choice for the consumer.

In France, 90% of the national daily newspapers sold every day belong to 10 billionaires: Bernard Arnault, CEO of the luxury group LVMH (owner of Les Echos, Le Parisien), Serge Dassault (Le Figaro), François Pinault (Le Point), Patrick Drahi, main shareholder of SFR (Libération, L'Express, BFM-TV, RMC), Vincent Bolloré (Canal+). Then there is Xavier Niel, CEO of the telephone operator Free and 11th fortune of France, who joined with Pierre Bergé, heir of the fashion designer Yves Saint-Laurent, and with the banker Matthieu Pigasse, to become the owner of the group Le Monde (L'Obs, Télérama, La Vie...). Matthieu Pigasse also owns Radio Nova and the weekly Les Inrocks. Martin Bouygues, 30th fortune of France, owns the TF1 group. The Mohn family, which controls the German group Bertelsmann, owns M6, RTL, Gala, Femme actuelle, VSD, capital... Then comes Arnaud Lagardère, owner of Europe 1, Paris Match, JDD, Virgin radio, RFM, Télé 7 jours, and Marie-Odile Amaury, who owns L'Équipe (and whose group is, through one of its subsidiaries, the organizer of the Tour de France). To this Top 10, we could also add the rich Bettencourt family, which finances the newspaper L'opinion. Or the billionaire of Lebanese origin Iskander Safa, 71[th] fortune of France and owner of Valeurs Actuelles[208].

---

[207] Nickie Louise, "These 6 corporations control 90% of the media outlets in America. The illusion of choice and objectivity," https://techstartups.com, SEPTEMBER 18, 2020.
[208] AGNÈS ROUSSEAUX, "The Delusional Power of Influence of the Ten Billionaires Who Own the French Press," www.bastamag.net, APRIL 5, 2017.

This concentration naturally has harmful consequences on the independence of the media and *ultimately* on the health of democracies. Let's take the example of the very famous *Washington Post*, the one through which the Watergate scandal happened in 1972. As a reminder, this affair led to the resignation of the American president Richard Nixon and the conviction of several of his collaborators. Is such an investigation possible today? Probably not. This newspaper was bought in 2013 by Jeff Bezos, the founder of Amazon, and its editorial policy has been radically turned upside down.

On May 1, 2017, The Washington Post introduced a policy prohibiting its employees from engaging in any conduct, including on social media, that could negatively affect The *Post*'s customers, advertisers, subscribers, vendors, suppliers or partners. Management reserves the right to discipline, up to and including termination, any employee who violates the new rules. It even encourages them to report a colleague who violates this[209].

Consider GSK, Glaxo Smith Kline, a big Post partner that the paper investigated in 2012. Here is a summary of what is described in a lengthy *Post* article on the growing influence of pharmaceutical firms on scientific research[210]. The paper cites a 2006 article[211] published in the world's most prestigious medical journal, *The New England Journal of Medicine*. The 17-page study, "a coup for GSK" according to the journal, describes a double-blind randomized trial comparing three potential treatments for type 2 diabetes, including GSK's Avandia. Following the publication, GSK vice president Lawson Macartney says in a press release, "We now have clear evidence from a large international study that initial use of our treatment [Avandia] is more

---

[209] ANDREW BEAUJON, "The Washington Post's New Social Media Policy Forbids Disparaging Advertisers," www.washingtonian.com, JUNE 27, 2017.

[210] Peter Whoriskey, "As drug industry's influence over research grows, so does the potential for bias," www.washingtonpost.com, November 24, 2012.

[211] Steven E. Kahn, M.B., Ch. B., Steven M. Haffner, M.D., Mark A. Heise, Ph.D., William H. Herman, M.D., M.P.H., Rury R. Holman, F.R.C.P., Nigel P. Jones, M.A., Barbara G. Kravitz, M.S., John M. Lachin, Sc. D, M. Colleen O'Neill, B.Sc., Bernard Zinman, M.D., F.R.C.P.C., and Giancarlo Viberti, "Glycemic Durability of Rosiglitazone, Metformin, or Glyburide Monotherapy", N Engl J Med, December 7, 2006; 355:2427-244.

effective than standard therapies." But there's a big problem. A closer look at the paper reveals the extent of the drugmaker's financial ties to this study. The trial was funded by GSK, and each of the paper's 11 authors received money from the company. Four were employees of the company and even owned stock in it. The other seven were academic experts who had received grants or honoraria as consultants from the company. This seemingly serious study of more than 4,000 patients revealed another big problem, one that was noticed only two years after its publication when disaster struck with the large-scale marketing of the drug. "If you looked closely at the data, you could see warning signs," said Steven E. Nissen, a cardiologist at the Cleveland Clinic who was one of the first to raise danger flags about the drug. "But they were overlooked." So, the proofreading of the scientific paper was sloppy or perhaps never happened. I learned from a doctor that scientific papers can be published without peer review! You just have to pay...

The scientists of the American drug agency, FDA (Food and Drug Administration), will later estimate that the famous drug is responsible for 83,000 heart attacks and deaths in the USA! Not to mention the rest of the world.

Two learned societies, the *American Diabetes Association* (ADA) and the *European Association for the Study of Diabetes* (EASD), issued unfavorable opinions on the use of the drug for the treatment of diabetes in 2008[212]. This led to the suspension of its marketing authorization in Europe in September 2010, but only to restrictions on its use in the United States, which were relaxed by the FDA in 2013, following another famous study...

The question is: Can the Washington Post now conduct an objective investigation of GSK and publish it? With the new editorial policy, this is clearly not possible and obviously not normal.

The worst thing is that not only do newspapers no longer carry out serious investigations, but they in turn distort the information to defend interests at the expense of the citizen and democracy as a whole. This

---

[212] "Rosiglitazone no longer recommended," Lancet, 2008; 372:1520.

tendency was so blatant to the point of absurdity during the coronavirus crisis.

## When Le Monde Shudders for the Gates

Let's take an edifying example, that of the link between the Bill and Melinda Gates Foundation and the French newspaper Le Monde. A financial contribution of $4 million has been made to the media outlet since 2015 with the only quid pro quo, according to the newspaper's website, being this, "the editorial staff commits itself each year to cover three themes related to development and public health issues." Still according to the site, "the Foundation obviously has no say over the angles and content of the articles […] The Le Monde Editors' Society and the Le Monde Group's independence division are particularly careful to ensure strict respect for the independence of the editorial staff so that each journalist can write without any outside pressure."[213]

I went to the Le Monde website and searched for all the articles published by the newspaper about Bill Gates since 2016. There is not a single critical content against the American billionaire, not even about Microsoft's monopoly or the forcing he does for the use of his licensed products in French schools[214]. On the contrary, everything is flattering. One can read headlines such as "Our foundation has saved 20 million lives," "Bill Gates: Why I became a philanthropist," "Bill Gates devotes a billion to the service of the planet," "Bill Gates says he wants to develop a "super cow" against malnutrition in Africa," "Bill Gates: For a global approach to the fight against Covid-19"…

And what is striking is the number of articles devoted to defending Bill Gates, the latter being mentioned by name in the titles of the articles, against the conspiracy theories that target him. I counted 12 articles between January 2020 and the beginning of 2021, without counting the

---

[213] https://www.lemonde.fr/le-monde-et-vous/article/2021/01/26/comment-fonctionne-le-partenariat-entre-le-monde-et-la-fondation-gates_6067625_6065879.html

[214] Boussad Addad, Souveraineté numérique européenne : Innovations, échecs et espoir de 1900 à nos jours, VA Press Editions, juillet 2021.

many other articles that mention him in the course of another subject. At least thirty or so! I don't mind an article or two, but not that many…

What is embarrassing is not so much that, but the fact of concealing crucial information about reality. It is lying by omission. And I'm not talking about a phone call or anything else that would impose censorship. In reality, it is consciously or unconsciously self-imposed in an essay, because nothing is free in life. I have already spoken about the notion of gift and counter-gift in the first volume of the book. We will come back to this subject later on concerning the case of doctors.

Everyone has seen that the Bill and Melinda Gates Foundation has claimed to be the savior of the planet during the COVID crisis19, which the newspaper Le Monde has highlighted in many of its articles. What is not said, for example, is that the Foundation has invested heavily in companies like Monsanto and promoted GMO agriculture in Africa at the expense of biodiversity and free seeds[215]. African farmers are being squeezed and are forced to buy patented seeds! What the media does not say, for example, in the current pandemic context, is that this same foundation is behind the blocking of free access to the AstraZeneca vaccine. Effective or not effective, that is not the question…

In April 2020, Oxford University surprised the world by announcing that it would cede the rights to its promising vaccine and any other treatment for coronavirus to any drug maker[216]. The idea was to provide the potion at low or no cost, the British university said. This naturally made sense, good sense even, during a pandemic. "We actually thought they were going to do it," James Love, director of *Knowledge Ecology International*, a nonprofit organization that works to expand access to medical technology, said of Oxford's commitment. "Why shouldn't people accept that everyone should have access to the best possible vaccines?" he said. A few weeks later, in August 2020 to be exact, there was disenchantment. The university, at the request of the Bill & Melinda Gates Foundation, turned around. Oxford then signed an agreement with

---

[215] https://www.novethic.fr/actualite/environnement/agriculture/isr-rse/en-afrique-la-fondation-gates-fait-le-choix-des-ogm-142965.html

[216] https://innovation.ox.ac.uk/technologies-available/technology-licensing/expedited-access-covid-19-related-ip/

the Swedish-British group AstraZeneca, which gave the pharmaceutical giant exclusive rights and freedom on pricing. A *Bloomberg* media report made a month before the deal, quoting Bill Gates himself, reveals: "We went to Oxford and told them you're doing a brilliant job. You need to team up [with industry], and we gave them a list of people to talk to."

The information on the direct intervention of the foundation in the blockage was later confirmed and taken up by the *Guardian*[217]. Its article specifies in passing that the vaccine is the result of research financed by British public funds up to 97%! Thanks to the UK taxpayer…

When a *Washington* Post reporter asked Melinda Gates[218] to comment on the widespread criticism of her foundation after the affair, she replied, "We supported Oxford and told them they were doing good science, but they never brought a product to market. They needed a partnership with a pharmaceutical company that has marketing expertise. That's why we told them this is what needs to be done. What they will do next. What our foundation has been doing for 20 years is making vaccines affordable in developing countries…"

Who is she kidding? To talk like that about a university [Oxford] that was founded 800 years ago and from which no less than 70 Nobel Prize winners have graduated? Oxford is ranked in the top ten universities in the world for publishing in the best scientific journals. Penicillin, the famous antibiotic, was first purified and stabilized in the 1940s by an Oxford team, paving the way for its mass production and use in populations around the world. The principle of defending the body with antibodies, the very principle on which vaccines are based, was discovered in 1967 by scientist Rodney Porter while he was a researcher at Oxford. He was awarded the Nobel Prize in Medicine in 1972 for discovering the chemical structure of antibodies[219]. Who are you kidding, Melinda?

---

[217] Michael Safi, "Oxford/AstraZeneca COVID vaccine research 'was 97% publicly funded'," www.theguardian.com, 15 Apr 2021.

[218] https://www.washingtonpost.com/video/washington-post-live/wplive/melinda-gates-on-whether-oxford-shouldve-allowed-their-vaccine-to-be-open-sourced/2021/01/27/7475d269-1ae8-4d7b-8cd6-66476dd8f538_video.html

And speaking of marketing, what industry would refuse to produce the vaccine if it were offered the recipe for free? It would have everything to gain, both in terms of communication and in technical and financial terms. The French laboratory Sanofi has even agreed to help produce the vaccines of its direct competitors Pfizer and Moderna while it is still in the race to bring one to market. Melinda's "philanthropist" argument does not hold water. The reasons are really elsewhere and there is a lot of money and power of influence at stake in this story. Opening it up to everyone is taking away the value of the vaccine and depriving these pseudo-benefactors of their magic wand as saviors of the planet. Linsey McGoey, a professor at the University of Essex in Britain and author of a book on the Gates Foundation and its outsized influence on global health[220], makes a good point. She speculates that the Gates Foundation is mainly interested in proving that "billionaire philanthropy" has a tangible effect, and that Bill Gates has a personal interest in this in terms of reputation.

In a 2009 publication[221] in *The Lancet* entitled "What has the Gates Foundation done for global health?" the editor, Richard Horton is blunt: "The Gates Foundation has been subject to little external scrutiny. Last year, Devi Sridhar and Rajaie Batniji reported that the foundation gave most of its grants to organizations in high-income countries. There was a significant bias in its funding for malaria and HIV/AIDS, with relatively little investment in tuberculosis, maternal and child health and nutrition—chronic diseases being entirely absent from its spending portfolio… David McCoy and his colleagues extend these findings by evaluating grants made by the Gates Foundation from 1998 to 2007. Their study provides even stronger evidence that the Foundation's grants do not reflect the burden of disease endured by the poorest people. In an accompanying commentary, Robert Black and his colleagues discuss the

---

[219] "8 Incredible Discoveries Developed by Professors at the University of Oxford"
https://oxfordsummercourses.com/articles/8-incredible-discoveries-developed-by-professors-at-the-university-of-oxford/
[220] Linsey McGoey, "No Such Thing as a Free Gift: The Gates Foundation and the Price of Philanthropy," Verso; Reprint edition (October 4, 2016).
[221] The Lancet, "What has the Gates Foundation done for global health?",
VOLUME 373, ISSUE 9675, P1577, MAY 09, 2009.
https://www.thelancet.com/journals/lancet/article/PIIS0140-6736(09)60885-0/fulltext

alarming lack of correlation between Foundation funding and childhood disease priorities… There is also a serious concern about the transparency of the Foundation's operations. What are its plans? It is difficult to know for sure. The first guiding principle of the Foundation is that it is driven by the interests and passions of the Gates family."

Linsey McGoey sheds light on the foundation's maneuvers and its unbridled power to influence. The professionals who spoke to her talk about the generalization of self-censorship at all levels within the world's health authorities, such as the WHO, which prevents any criticism of the Gates organization. This censorship even has a name in the field: *"Bill Chill Effect."* Officials disagree with the Gates's priorities and think he should fund health systems, but cannot say so publicly for fear of being sanctioned by a foundation that has enormous influence. Tensions and concerns are palpable within the WHO because of its growing interference. One official at the world body said on condition of anonymity: "You have a foundation that basically pays for the areas it wants to pursue, and also supports international agencies that are supposed to be independent or standards-setting agencies. Once you have them on the payroll, dissenting voices are silenced. That's why you're not going to get anyone to speak publicly … this reality has to be said."

Two striking examples are given by McGoey, confirmed by several well-placed sources at WHO and the NGO *Human Rights Watch*. In the first case, the WHO reportedly delayed its guidance on the early use of HIV treatment among serodiscordant couples, a term referring to a couple in which one partner is HIV-infected and the other is not. At *the International AIDS Society* meeting in Rome in 2011, guidance advocating for the early use of anti-HIV drugs among infected partners in serodiscordant couples was to be released. WHO abruptly chose to delay this. Many people attributed its reluctance to opposition from the Gates Foundation, which has been heavily involved in alternative studies exploring pre-exposure prophylaxis (PrEP), a new method of HIV treatment that involves taking a combination of drugs by negative individuals, those who have not tested positive for the virus. With simple and crude words, they are trying to make healthy people swallow chemical shit when simple and effective treatments exist...

There is no conspiracy in all this, but influence struggles whose collateral damage is catastrophic for health. An open letter to the WHO was circulated immediately after the Rome conference. "We write with concern following the *International AIDS Society* conference in Rome, where it appears that WHO has abandoned the publication of technical guidelines on HIV testing and treatment for serodiscordant couples," says the open letter signed by no less than seven international organizations involved in the fight against AIDS. The letter states that the treatment that was to be recommended manages to limit the transmission of the disease with 96% effectiveness and that "WHO is now failing in its responsibility to help countries and decision-makers translate science into health policy."

The second example McGoey gives relates to a decision in an African country [Lesotho] to ignore WHO guidelines in order to treat HIV-positive people at an early stage. Health practitioners in developing regions usually start treating HIV-positive people based on two criteria: if their CD4 count—CD4 being the white blood cell immune system—is below a certain threshold. This means that the immune system is weakened and needs to be strengthened with treatment. The other indication is the clinical status, so what we see in terms of what a patient is experiencing and what we are told about their symptoms. The WHO has a classification system by stages: stage 1, 2, 3, 4. Before WHO changed its guidelines at the end of 2010, people in developing countries would only start HIV treatment if their CD4 count was below 200 or if they were in stage 4, the last stage of the classification.

What is really important to know is that some countries were ahead of the WHO. This was the case in Lesotho, for example, which implemented new guidelines starting in 2008. The country simply did what seemed right for its population. If the WHO lacked ambition, it was because it gave in to pressure. "What we know—and we know it from people at the highest level—is that Bill Gates himself phoned the WHO to dissuade them from issuing new guidelines," says McGoey, "He intervened right up to the last hour," and that's how Lesotho got a two-year head start on the world body. But there was a silence and no one could say it publicly at the time.

Some courageous people have broken the silence. The head of the WHO malaria division complained in a 2007 memo that the foundation's growing dominance of malaria research was stifling a diversity of views among scientists and undermining the agency. That same year, the foundation began creating an institute that rivaled the WHO in some areas. "The Gates Foundation's presence has been at best an adjunct to the WHO and at worst a hostile takeover and usurpation," said Amir Attaran, professor of law and medicine at the University of Ottawa.

Let's go back to the AstraZeneca vaccine. The foundation invested some $55 million in September 2019 in BioNTech, the startup that developed Pfizer's vaccine. What would that company be worth if its vaccine is made obsolete by the Oxford competitor? Just after the Oxford-AstraZeneca deal was signed, the foundation advanced $150 million to an Indian company, *Serum Institute of India*, to produce the British university's vaccine. This shows that even less developed countries are capable of producing the vaccine…

And as for the argument of wanting to make it available to underdeveloped countries, the opposite is true in practice according to professionals in the field. Gates is doing everything he can to align himself with the interests of pharmaceutical executives. "Part of what they like about him is that he protects their way of life" with his "Big Pharma is great" message, said James Love, director of *Knowledge Ecology International*, the nonprofit organization that works for broad access to medicines already mentioned. Bill Gates has put himself in the spotlight more than ever, repeating over and over in interviews that the pandemic required an international response. "He's made a choice to become very public, very political, where he acts as a lobbyist," said Lawrence Gostin, a professor of global health law at Georgetown.

The Gates Foundation has supported the WHO's COVAX program to ensure that all countries have access to vaccines against epidemics. The foundation also provides funding to the International Vaccine Alliance (Gavi) and the Coalition for Epidemic Preparedness Innovations (CEPI), two organizations that were supported by Bill Gates from the beginning. Today, they are leading the COVAX program under the auspices of the WHO. According to the *New York Times*, the WHO would have liked to take on the governance of this program, but the Gates Foundation was the one to step in. "That's what I heard, too," Gostin said. "If that's true, it's a discouraging sign, based on the premise that the WHO should be in charge at the global level."

For Linsey McGoey this is due to Bill Gates's willingness to defend patents by applying a form of resistance to the lifting of property rights for COVID vaccines. Some countries (South Africa, India) have proposed to the World Trade Organization (WTO) to waive these patents in order to stimulate their production and delivery in poor and developing countries. Relaxation now supported by the United States, a country that was strongly opposed to this type of measure under the Trump era. But the business community as well as several countries, including Switzerland, and the EU, is resisting. "Surely Tedros Adhanom Ghebreyesus, director-general of the WHO, is himself in favor of liberalizing these patents, but he has certainly failed to influence Bill Gates, who is primarily defending a system on which he built his fortune," argues Linsey McGoey[222].

As calls for the lifting of patents on COVID vaccines multiply, U.S. President Biden favors a temporary suspension of rights while "philanthropist" Bill Gates is against it. On April 25, 2021, he explained on the British channel *Sky News* why he did not consider the proposal necessary, even to help developing countries. American vaccine manufacturers have all joined him in defending their patents, even going to the White House. According to the *Financial Times*, one of the arguments put forward was that messenger RNA technology could fall into the hands of China and Russia! However, this is not the technology used in the AstraZeneca vaccine, which is also easier to produce and store. This shows that a drug is ultimately just another weapon…

---

[222] Julia Crawford, "Does Bill Gates have too much influence over WHO?", www.swissinfo.ch, May 11, 2021.

Let's stay there and look at it from that perspective. When we give so much power to Bill Gates, what about national sovereignty? Is the case of Lesotho and the fight against AIDS not edifying? Can we delegate the health of our own population to an organization that is beyond our control? Doesn't the weapon risk turning against itself at any moment? So many questions that Le Monde has not yet asked itself and to which the social networks are responding with far-fetched and ridiculous theories of horns and other Satanist symbols…

## When Fear Numbs people

The mainstream media has ignored reality, but has done even worse. They have knowingly lied and terrorized the population to keep it under control. The goal is to grab attention and sell it as advertising. The quest for available brain time continues.

People who are afraid are not able of thinking. They are just trying to protect themselves. It is a primitive survival instinct in the face of danger. This can be seen in many automatic and uncontrollable physiological changes in the body. The response is naturally different from one person to another. There are three types of reactions in a stressful situation, which are called FFF[223]: Flight, Fight, or Freeze. The reaction begins in the amygdala, the part of the brain responsible for perceived fear, which responds by sending signals to the hypothalamus, which stimulates the autonomic nervous system (ANS). The body then releases adrenaline and cortisol, the stress hormone. These hormones are released fairly quickly, which can affect the following:

—Heart rate: The heart beats faster to provide oxygen to the major muscles in preparation for a possible escape or fight. During immobilization, the heart rate may increase or decrease.

—Lungs: Breathing speeds up to provide more oxygen to the blood. In the immobilization response, one may hold his breath or restrict his breathing.

---

[223] https://www.healthline.com/health/mental-health/fight-flight-freeze

—The eyes: Peripheral vision increases so that the environment can be perceived well. The pupils dilate and let in more light, which helps to see better.

—Ears: The ears "stand up" and the hearing becomes clearer.

—Blood: Blood thickens, which increases clotting factors. This prepares the body for possible injury.

—Skin: The skin may produce more sweat. You may look pale or have goose bumps.

—Hands and feet: As blood flow increases to the major muscles, the hands and feet may feel cold.

—The perception of pain: Fleeing or fighting temporarily reduces the perception of pain.

When we are confronted with a threat, not necessarily real, but just perceived, the brain deduces that we are in danger. As a result, the body automatically reacts with the FFF response to keep itself safe. Obviously, a person who sees on his screen parades of dead people on stretchers, or a person in charge who counts the number of deaths every day, naturally perceives the danger. People do not flee like a gazelle from a cheetah and do not throw themselves on their screen to break it like a lion from a buffalo. The person feels fear and remains mostly motionless (*Freeze*). Many things happen unconsciously in the body as we have seen, with consequences, of course, on the person's behavior. For example, the person no longer leaves the house and stays glued to his or her screen in search of information that could save him or her from danger... It is a vicious circle that slowly ruins health, without even realizing it. Fear induces cognitive biases such as the tendency to exaggerate the perception of risk and the overestimation of the effectiveness of an external intervention. When one is locked in one's home, this intervention can only come out of the screen, the only remaining link with the outside world. What is worse is that fear and cognitive biases are even transmitted from parents to their children, according to recent research[224].

One understands better why the consumption of antidepressants exploded during the lockdown and the malaise touched even in the children become suicidal. But all this is not the problem of the media and the Web. As long as there is brain time available…

To spread fear, the media manipulate information by exploiting many cognitive biases. For example, they never talk about the people who are cured and who get better, that is 99.5% of people who contract COVID and do not die. The picture is always bleak, because it changes everything in the perception of danger. This is the exploitation of a cognitive bias called the "framing effect" which means that the way in which information is presented, whether visual, verbal or textual, shapes its perception and therefore the decision. Let's see this on a concrete example with the following message:

*An epidemic breaks out and could kill 600 people if left untreated.*

- *Treatment strategy A will save 200 people.*
- *Treatment strategy B has a one-third chance of saving 600 people and a two-thirds chance of saving no one.*

Which of the two strategies would you choose? When asked this question, 72% of people choose option A, the one that will save 200 people.

Let's rephrase the question in another way while giving exactly the same information.

*An epidemic breaks out and could kill 600 people if left untreated.*

- *Under treatment strategy A, it is known that 400 people will die.*
- *Under treatment strategy B, there is a one-third probability that no one will die and a two-thirds probability that 600 people will die.*

---

[224] Danielle Remmerswaal, Peter Muris, and Jorg Huijding, "Transmission of Cognitive Bias and Fear From Parents to Children: An Experimental Study," Journal of Clinical Child & Adolescent Psychology, 2015, 45(5):1–13.

Which of the two strategies would you choose? When asked this question, 78% of people choose option B.

So, we see that there is a dramatic shift in responses when logic says that this should not be the case since the two strategies have not changed between the two questions. What has changed is just the framing of the question. The second scenario frames things in terms of loss, which people would rather avoid (loss aversion).

Biases related to group psychology were also used. The individual being attached to life in society, a survival factor, social pressure was pushed to its extreme. We used guilt (young people who are going to kill their grandparents), scapegoating (there will be a new wave, because some people do not want to be vaccinated), shame (we violated the recommendation of confinement), altruism (I vaccinate myself for others), denigration (he is selfish and refuses to be vaccinated because he is intellectually inferior), social belonging (vaccinated doctors wear a distinctive badge that mentions it, Internet users add the mention of "vaccinated" on their Twitter profile)…

The other cognitive bias exploited is the so-called anchoring bias. Everyone remembers the angry outburst by the Minister of Health in the National Assembly after a setback during a vote on the state of emergency. He got carried away and warned the deputies by telling them what he saw in a hospital intensive care unit: "In the first room, there was a young man of 28 years in a coma, intubated, ventilated. In the second room, there was an overweight 35-year-old man. That is the reality, ladies and gentlemen. If you don't want to hear it, get out of here." This statement inevitably provokes fear among many. Why? Because when you hear these words, you immediately make the comparison to your own age and say to yourself, "If a very young person can die, then I am at risk too." The number 28 unconsciously becomes the anchor point and we don't even pay attention to the rest of the speech, because the brain has already started thinking about the next step. It seeks to exploit this information to make itself safe as quickly as possible. Fear short-circuits the long process of reflection and logic. The minister just "forgets" to say that the person in resuscitation actually suffers from other serious illnesses and that the average age of the COVID deaths is 81 years old…

This biased way of presenting the facts has been pervasive during the Covid19 crisis. In March 2021, for example, the mainstream media reported the news that twenty parents of students at a school had died from Covid-19. Here are the headlines in Paris Match "Seine-Saint-Denis: 20 parents of students from the same high school died of Covid-19"[225], La Dépêche "The unusual case of Drancy High School, where Covid-19 killed 20 parents of students, closure requested,"[226] RTL "COVID: 20 parents of students of Drancy High School died, 22 classes close," France Bleu "Coronavirus at school: At Delacroix's high school in Drancy, 20 students have already lost a parent to COVID,"[227] LCI "It's agonizing: worry at Drancy High School, where 20 students have lost a parent victim of COVID"[228] … Two reporters from news channel BFM speak live to the mother of a student at this high school like this: "The school is facing a dramatic situation since we learn that 20 parents of students have died since the beginning of the epidemic, that the number of cases has been growing for a month. How do you live in the situation?"[229] On Twitter, it's the end of the world. A woman from the Paris region wrote: "I know this high school in Drancy and the commitment of its staff: it is dramatic to see that about twenty parents have died since the beginning of the epidemic. Currently, about fifty COVID cases have been reported in the school!" And responding to a skeptical comment, "This is a post from the SNES website[230], I don't think they would have endorsed *fake news*, that's why I shared it." She added links to the headlines of the major media to show that it is solid…

---

[225] https://www.parismatch.com/Actu/Societe/20-parents-d-eleves-morts-du-covid-19-le-drame-dans-un-lycee-de-Seine-Saint-Denis-1731216

[226] https://www.ladepeche.fr/2021/03/28/le-cas-hors-normes-du-lycee-de-drancy-ou-le-covid-19-a-tue-20-parents-deleves-la-fermeture-demandee-9454765.php

[227] https://www.francebleu.fr/infos/sante-sciences/au-lycee-delacroix-de-drancy-20-eleves-ont-perdu-leur-parents-du-covid-l-etablissement-reste-ouvert-1616775074

[228] https://www.lci.fr/societe/covid-19-c-est-angoissant-l-inquietude-au-lycee-de-drancy-ou-20-eleves-ont-perdu-un-membre-de-leur-famille-2181937.html

[229] https://www.bfmtv.com/replay-emissions/week-end-premiere/lycee-de-drancy-20-parents-d-eleves-decedes-28-03_VN-202103280047.html

[230] The SNES is the National Union of Secondary School Teachers, which advocated for the closure of classes during the COVID crisis.19

Some comments are sorry and others cry out indignation pointing to the responsibility of the Minister of Health in the tragedy: "It is necessary to close the schools urgently", "it is necessary to strike," "it is necessary to exercise the right of withdrawal"…

The far-left MP Éric Coquerel publishes to his 72,000 Twitter followers:

"When I hear 1 student from Delacroix's high school in Drancy (20 parents dead from #COVID19) say they are 26 in class it revolts me. @jmblanquer [Health minister] either you split ALL the classes in the schools, as we've been asking for months, or you close them! Doing nothing is becoming criminal." This message has been retweeted hundreds of times…

It's the apocalypse folks, all safe…

A person sitting on a couch and sees this on TV or reads this on the Web naturally thinks that 20 students in this high school have lost a mother or a father, as a result of contamination caused by their children. This is indeed the primary meaning of the word "parent," what the brain naturally chooses, by using shortcuts and laziness, if no other facts contradict it. It turns out that all of this is a vast manipulation. The Eugène-Delacroix high school in Drancy is a large institution of 2400 students located in the most precarious department of France, Seine-Saint-Denis. Many people have indeed lost their lives in this department, but the relatives mentioned in the media would be—I use the conditional, because even this is not proven—relatives in the broadest sense (grandfather, grandmother, aunt, uncle …). Libération, another newspaper which reported the information like everyone else, questioned the whole affair a few days later in an article[231] of *fact-checking* (under pressure from the Web?) in which one can read: "How, and by whom, was this count made? The Créteil school board and the high school, which seems to be the source of the figure, are passing the buck. When contacted on Monday, the school did not wish to speak to journalists, directing us to the school board. The latter invites journalists to check with the school, as it does not have any information itself. "We

---

[231] https://www.liberation.fr/checknews/covid-19-est-il-vrai-que-vingt-parents-deleves-sont-decedes-au-lycee-de-drancy-20210329_7P3AIQ6F4ZBYPAD5AOOS5A3CGQ/

are not in a position to confirm or deny. We do not have official records of parents of deceased students," he said. Le Figaro did the same about-face three days after its first publication, stating this time that "nothing confirms that these relatives from the family circle were contaminated by the young students."[232] All the articles published by the newspapers are still visible online without any correction at the time of writing, in May 2021…

But I have seen even better coverage of this event out of the blue. It was on the all-news channel that wants to be the French Fox New, CNews. A morning "debate" program questioned, rightly so as we saw, this information reported the day before in the press. But the program that followed it on the *same* channel, sensationalist as usual, brought up the subject of the twenty dead parents by repeating the information from another news channel of the previous day! It took a commercial break to make a 180-degree turn on the same channel…

CBS in the United States also did a lot of manipulation. It broadcast images of a New York hospital overflowing with Covid-19 patients. The problem is that some time before, the English channel Sky News, one of the most alarmist in the United Kingdom, broadcast the same images from an Italian hospital in Bergamo, Lombardy. A spokesman for the American channel acknowledged the blunder: "It was an editing error. We are taking every step to remove it from all our programs and broadcasts."[233] But a week later, the channel will reuse the same images to talk about a hospital in Pennsylvania this time!

It is, however, more difficult for CBS to make this mistake than to go on the *shutterstock* site and buy such a clip in a few clicks[234]. It's only 59 dollars for a 15-second-high-definition video. They could even choose music from a horror movie if they wanted to … unless it wasn't scary enough…

---

[232] https://etudiant.lefigaro.fr/article/a-drancy-20-parents-d-eleves-sont-ils-morts-du-coronavirus_30f9a494-912d-11eb-8804-00a9374ab700/
[233] https://nypost.com/2020/04/01/cbs-admits-to-using-footage-from-italy-in-report-about-nyc/
[234] https://www.shutterstock.com/fr/video/clip-1012593905-emergency-department-doctors-nurses-surgeons-move-seriously

But the golden palm of the *Terror Academy* undoubtedly goes to the French continuous news channel BFM. We have seen on its platforms self-proclaimed experts who wanted to lock up the whole population for months without bringing the least scientific argument. Without forgetting the columnists who cried scandal at the slightest image of young people going out to relax a little on the banks of the Seine. As soon as a Parisian street is filled with people, the cameras come in and they shout about the irresponsibility of the population. Alarmism is in full swing. One could really believe in the end of the world when listening to them. Except that a pebble is going to jam the machine. Under the title "BFMTV in the news business," the investigative Canard Enchainé reveals that a police raid took place on February 24, 2021, in a clandestine restaurant located a stone's throw from the headquarters of the channel. Twenty or so "journalists and medical consultants of the channel" would have been charged. In response, the channel's CEO Marc-Olivier Fogiel published a Tweet: "To close the day, contrary to the rumors of the last 24 hours, I would like to clarify that no journalist or consultant of BFMTV has been arrested in an illegal restaurant in Paris in late February." The satirical weekly put the cover back on two weeks later by catching him in flagrante delicto. The journalist of the Canard called the clandestine restaurant directly and asked to speak to Fogiel. The manager will rush to give him the phone and he will indeed answer according to the article. "It's good to see that the restaurants are not closed for everyone," says the journalist. Just to relax the situation, he punctuates with a "Bon appétit, Marc-Olivier Fogiel!"[235] When the story of the illegal restaurants starts to make a lot of noise, the chain's sets cry out for denunciation and castigate a climate that has suddenly become unhealthy…

After the previous episodes, the *blacklist of* channels on my TV got a little longer … even though I don't watch too much TV since the very first confinement.

That said, there is no shortage of similar examples elsewhere. The famous British journalist and presenter Piers Morgan, host of *Good*

---

[235] Christophe Nobili, "BFMTV, au four et au moulin de l'info", Canard enchainé, 03 March 2021.

*Morning Britain*, among others, has publicly called for tighter restrictions and even the cancellation of the 2020 Christmas party. This did not prevent him from walking down the street without a mask and especially from taking a first-class flight to the Caribbean to spend his winter vacations there! When an Internet user reminded him on Twitter that people were not able to see their deceased loved ones, because "it was not considered essential," he replied: "The government said it was possible to travel abroad if the route to the airport is direct."[236]

We will have seen, heard, and especially suffered in silence during this crisis while some privileged people had a good time…

## Fear, the curve, and me

It's late April 2020 and I'm on leave. Like everyone else, I was confined. I followed the news on the web and sometimes on TV. I was scrupulous in following the rules. I also took part in the circus of pots and pans at the windows[237]. I even dragged my children into it, in a sheep-like behavior, to explain to them how to be good citizens … while I have been trying since the beginning of the crisis to keep them away from anything that reminds them of the virus. I was scared inside, but I didn't show it. I even owed them an outing every day to the yard downstairs to play and let off steam when no one went out anymore. They got through the lockdown much better than I did. One sunny morning, we were out playing and suddenly paramedics came out of a nearby house pushing a girl in a wheelchair, coughing and spitting into a basin she was carrying on her lap. The scene was about 100 feet away

---

[236] https://www.huffingtonpost.co.uk/entry/piers-morgan-antigua-trip-lockdown-restrictions_uk_5ffd5222c5b691806c4c0f2d

[237] I actually changed my mind and considered it a crack when I learned later that even in the midst of a crisis, hospital beds were still being closed all over France without being denounced in chorus by the caregivers as I wanted to see. In reality, the health care personnel were subjected to excessive nudging. This applause is a way to flatter them, to make them heroes, but to make them forget the essential. Instead of paying them what they are worth and giving them the protections they needed in the midst of an epidemic, they have been concocted peanut salaries, such as the ability to cut a queue, as useless as the virtual badges offered by Uber to cabs. Moreover, they went from being heroes to pariahs because they refused vaccination. It was even imposed on them…

from us, but it terrified me. I took my two children and we quickly went home. This little anecdote is a testament to my stressful state at that time. I'm a cool-headed person by nature, but the terror of what I was seeing was so frightening that it took hold of me. The macabre count of the number of dead every day on TV and the alarmist information one after the other made me unconsciously weak. That's when I started to compulsively consult social networks in search of the slightest news. I fell into a kind of addiction that I talk about in the first volume of this book and in which I show how I got out of it. But that wasn't the only thing that hit me without me even realizing it.

One day, a Monday to be exact, I start to feel bad and have pains in my chest. I reassure myself as best I can and above all I rest. I stayed in bed for three days, then four, then five. I then felt some breathing difficulties. For me, there is no more doubt, I have contracted Covid-19. I had an oximeter, but it didn't show any oxygenation abnormalities. I'm not reassured, though, because I don't feel well. I am in pain. I'm thinking of going to the doctor, but I'm afraid I'll get the virus in the office…

At one point, I felt my heart racing. I was out of breath and had to lie down to keep from collapsing. The first time in my life that this has happened to me… I try to call the EMS, but it is saturated. I can hardly breathe and in my head it is too bad; I imagine the worst; I try to anticipate the next step; what will happen to my children without me? What could I do right now to ensure them a future? Fear, real fear, is getting to me. I think about them. The solution I saw in the time available is just to get well. All I have left is my primary care physician and it's already Saturday. It's now or never, because he doesn't work the next day. So, I go to see him, but without much conviction in my heart, because he didn't have, like all France (except Marseille!) a PCR test to confirm or deny the presence of the virus. He finally diagnosed me with stress and gave me a medication to take, three pills a day. When I got home, I took a pill. But I already started to distrust doctors, having heard everything and its opposite from their mouths, and this is probably the thing that affected me the most during the whole Covid-19 crisis. My own sister, with whom I am very close, is a doctor and I have a great respect for this profession. I decided to look at the package insert for the medication. To my surprise, I read this, "This medication is strongly contraindicated in cases of breathing difficulties." All my life I have been clicking and this was one of them. I took the box of medication and threw it in the trash. I go out for a jog right away. Same thing the following days. Everything quickly went back to normal.

I'm really not an anxious person by nature—I've lectured in front of 500 people—as I've mentioned before, but the stress ate me up from the inside out without me realizing it during the first lockdown. The pain I endured may have been due to Covid-19, but the stress, quite silent and pernicious, was there. There is nothing worse to weaken the immune system and prepare the ground for germs of any kind.

We are in the fall of 2020. After a relative summer truce in the media, the drums of fear are back and the shadow of the second wave that will overwhelm us all is on every TV set. The death toll of the famous first wave is 30,000, but all this is starting to make me wonder, because I heard somewhere that about 60,000 people die in France every month. And especially that the average age of the people who died from Covid-19—rather with Covid-19—exceeds 80 years. We are even talking about 84, which is the normal life expectancy of a French person, and the younger dead suffer from serious comorbidities. So, I decided to go to the source of the data, on the official site of INSEE, to see what was going on. The site contains the raw data of the number of deaths from all causes, therefore not subject to manipulation, recorded since 1946. With this, there is no room for cheating. I then select the year 2015 as the start date to display only the data of the last four years and compare them. The result is as follows:

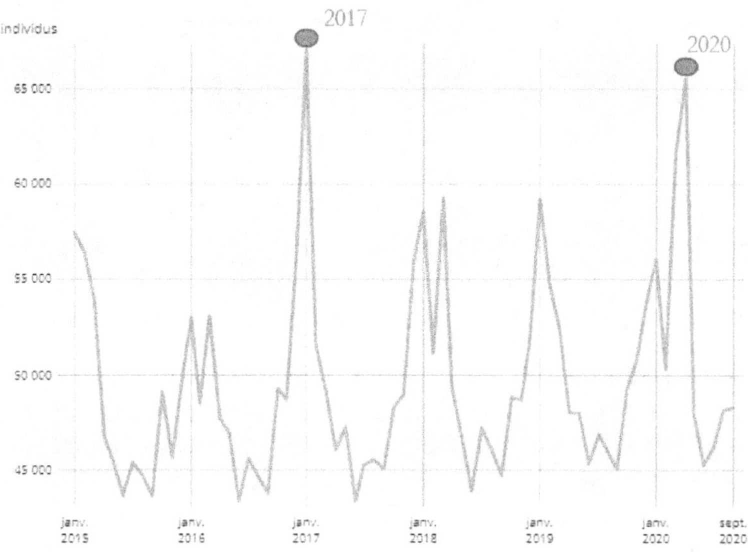



*Mortality in France between 2015 and September 2020 (INSEE data).*

When I see this curve, I think something is wrong. The 2017 flu death spike is higher than the Covid-19 spike! This is not something I would expect when I know the country is confined and life has stopped. This peak and the area under the curve are obviously not the only indicator to consider for a fine-grained analysis. But one thing is for sure for me, there is clearly no glaring difference between the last few years and the signal of an epidemic that was going to "kill us all" as hammered in all the media is clearly invisible in this data. When I saw this curve, I thought that the fear spread everywhere will probably kill more than the virus itself. I then sent this curve to a contact on LinkedIn, a doctor who has a large audience on this professional social network. He decided to post it and included my name. I think he exploded his counter of the number of views and comments with this publication. It was even picked up on Twitter as I would later discover by chance. It created a debate

171

and I was happy about it. My goal was to spread the information as widely as possible and see the reaction of as many people as possible. I must admit that some people surprised me, because I did not expect their reaction. One person, a pensioner who, after praising my intelligence even though I don't know him, reproached me for spreading the information and half-heartedly accused me of wanting to bring down the government… That's all! Some Internet users were trying to show that there was an overmortality in 2020 compared to 2019, but it was talking about 5000 to 10,000 people at the most. That's what dies in France in less than five days! Assuming that they are right, this figure clearly does not justify for me to arrest a whole country and to spread terror everywhere as we did for months. The discovery of this curve was the turning point for me. It pushed me to look for more information and what I learned reinforced my idea that everything was exaggerated.

Let's do a little flashback to a similar event that didn't stop the world from working. A virus, H3N2, appeared in China in the summer of 1968. It spread to Hong Kong and eventually reached the entire globe. In the winter of 1969, France was hit by what was to be called the Hong Kong flu. The newspaper France Soir, a mainstream media at the time, reported on December 14 that "for a minority of cases, the affair has taken a more worrying turn, with fatal cases among flu sufferers with vascular disorders. Doctors have noted quite a few cases of pulmonary congestion, otitis, conjunctivitis, resulting from superinfection." The days passed and alarmism grew in the press. One could read this: "At the SNCF [public train transportation], 15% of Parisian employees are affected. Parisian schools were affected one by one. In Toulouse, 25% of the population has the flu, and in Lyon, a quarter of the population is affected."[238] Other articles report on the extent of the flu, which is causing absences and closures of factories and schools all over France, where it is, in the Paris region, up to 20% of teachers and students who are sick. At the RATP [like SNCF but for buses and subways], 5,000 employees out of 30,000 were bedridden. The first estimates were made by IFOP and relayed on January 23, 1970, by France Soir: "36% of

---

[238] Jimmy Bourquin, "History of Forgotten Pandemics: the Hong Kong Flu in France (1969–1970)," www.franceinter.fr, May 13, 2020.

French adults were affected. The National Institute of Demographic Studies (INED), for its part, counted 40% more deaths than the average in December, due to the Hong Kong flu. This is equivalent to 20,000 additional deaths on average." Recalculations made by researchers in the early 2000s re-evaluated the figure at 31,226 deaths over a two-month period. The WHO speaks of one million deaths on the whole planet. These figures are more or less the same as those reported for Covid-19 in September 2020.

Below is the mortality curve in France on which we can see a very clear peak of 74,000 monthly deaths at the end of 1969, corresponding effectively to the Hong Kong flu, against the usual 55,000. This is therefore much more remarkable than the figure for spring 2020. The only difference is that the country was not confined and shut down as with Covid-19.

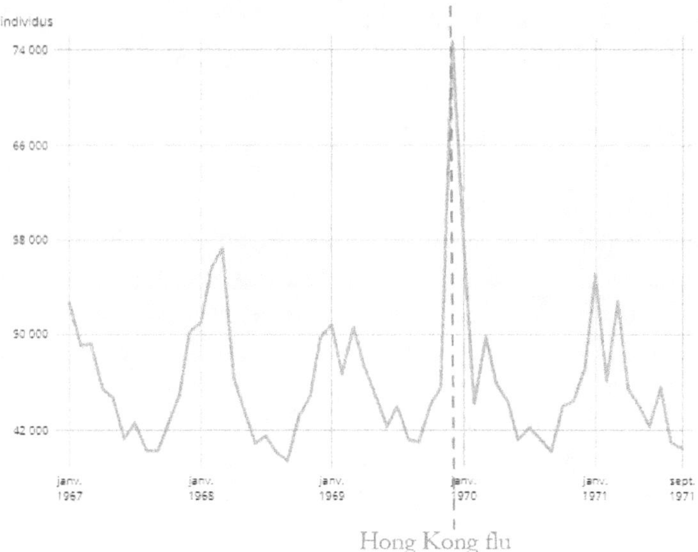

To put things in perspective, it is important to know that 1.3 million people die in road accidents worldwide every year. According to the WHO, tobacco alone causes more than 8 million deaths every year[239]. This is a far cry from the number of deaths caused by Covid-19. Yet, nobody stands up to ban cigarettes! All this does not seem too serious to me…

Another event further reinforced my doubts about the overuse of fear during the crisis. It was the publication on August 29, 2020, of a well-documented article in the *New York Times* entitled: "Your Coronavirus Test is Positive. Maybe not." The reporter gives voice to several epidemiologists. Dr. Michael Mina of Harvard says of PCR testing, "We use this for clinical diagnostics, for public health, for policy making." But that's not enough, he added. "It's the amount of virus that should dictate the next steps in patient management. It's really irresponsible, I think, to give up on recognizing that it's about the quantity [of the virus]," Dr. Mina said. Another doctor agrees. Any test with a cycle threshold above 35 is too sensitive, acknowledged Juliet Morrison, a virologist at the University of California. "I'm shocked that people think 40 cycles could represent a positive case," she said. Many laboratories amplify the samples they test up to 40 times (cycles). But that number detects anything and everything, and a positive result does not mean the presence of the virus." According to these doctors, the cycle should not exceed 30 and according to the CDC (*Centers for Disease Control*), the threshold should not exceed 33, in which case it would be extremely difficult to detect a live virus. The problem is that the FDA (*Food and Drug Administration*) does not set a threshold and leaves it to the manufacturers and laboratories. We're walking on thin ice. In Massachusetts, 85 to 90 percent of people who tested positive in July 2020 with a 40-cycle threshold would have tested negative if the threshold was 30 cycles, according to Dr. Mina. "I would say none of these people should be traced, not one," he said. Many other doctors have expressed astonishment at the way the tests are being used and

---

[239] https://www.who.int/fr/news-room/fact-sheets/detail/tobacco

completely questioned the official figures, which are, of course, repeated in chorus every day on the terror media. In France, there are no guidelines from the health authorities on the number of cycles to be applied. It is up to the laboratories to set it! The conflict of interest is serious. For me, this is too much. This is the straw that breaks the camel's back.

So, I decide to disconnect from the COVID news to live my life normally from fall 2020. I am passing the same message to my whole family. I rarely watch TV and when I do, it is only to analyze the evolution of the media coverage of the crisis in the context of writing this book. I hear about curfews and other government measures, but I have no idea what they are, when or how. I sometimes go out for a jog at 8 p.m. when apparently everyone else had to be home by 7 p.m... Many people asked me how I was coping with the crisis and were surprised when I replied, "Nothing special. The usual." I was willing to pay the fine. I told myself that my freedom is worth much more than 135 Euros! I don't regret anything and if I had to do it again, I would have even paid my fine earlier.

I don't know if my curve has been emulated on the web and has made others think. I haven't followed the rest of the story. But as I write this, in May 2021, I happened to listen to a person in this situation, a certain statistician named Pierre who runs a YouTube channel (Décoder l'Economie)[240]. In a video entitled "Covid-19: why so few deaths?" he made a clear demonstration using the INSEE data I mentioned above. The *fact-checkers* in some of the fear media have tried to discredit him, but their arguments are frankly fallacious. His reasoning is simple and logical. By taking into account the aging of the population with the increase in natural mortality since 2010 and by standardizing the data[241], his demonstration is without appeal. There is no remarkable difference in mortality between the different years. And incredible as it may seem, which did not even surprise me, the 2017 flu was actually a bit more

---

[240] https://www.youtube.com/watch?v=f0n3EdMDlcI

[241] Standardizing the data here means transforming the data to a configuration where all years show the same number of people in the population, making the comparison meaningful.

deadly than the spring 2020 COVID. Hospitals were actually overwhelmed in 2017 and the level 2 epidemic plan[242] was activated as seen in a news report still viewable online[243] titled, "Stretchers in the hallways, overcrowded ERs, overwhelmed GPs … the flu is back." But the phenomenon has actually been recurring for years precisely because of the increase in the number of elderly people in the population and the suppression of hospital beds. Yes, they have even continued to close beds in the midst of the crisis - 1,800 beds eliminated in 15 months[244]— and refused, despite the request of several doctors, to reopen the Val-de-Grâce hospital, which had been closed three years earlier "because rehabilitation work would take several weeks due to the humidity…"! I thought we were at war… The last time I checked[245], INSEE officially declared that there were fewer deaths in the under 65 age group in 2020 than in 2019 and a 10% increase for the older age groups. Assuming that this figure is true, which I don't believe, because the demonstration given by Pierre is once again unassailable, I don't think at all that this balance sheet deserves the terror spread everywhere and the confinement of the populations for several months…

With all the hindsight we have today on the disease, I sincerely think I did well to have detached myself completely from the media news on COVID. The collateral damage of the confinement was disastrous for the whole population, especially for the youngest deprived of any social link and sports activity. A study carried out on children showed "catastrophic figures" according to Martine Duclos, head of the service of sports medicine at the CHU Clermont-Ferrand who coordinated the work. "We have never seen anything like this," the specialist said with alarm. Children who were athletic, with no health problems or weight problems, gained 5 kg to 10 kg because they stopped playing sports. And not all of them have returned to physical activity. Worse still, their

---

[242] Level 2 of the epidemic plan is triggered as soon as signs of an impact on hospital activity appear. This is accompanied by the setting up of crisis units at the level of the 12 hospital groups and the general management of the APHP with daily monitoring of activity indicators and bed availability.

[243] https://www.youtube.com/watch?v=gBy04hOn_iY

[244] AFP, "Hospital: more than 1,800 beds closed or suppressed in 15 months, insists FO," June 23, 2021.

[245] https://www.insee.fr/fr/information/5013803

cognitive abilities would have decreased by about 40%. "One year of confinement was catastrophic, at an essential moment of neuronal plasticity," says Martine Duclos[246]. And this is unfortunately how a fertile ground for all kinds of chronic diseases is created for these poor children.

It is therefore not surprising to note the saturation observed everywhere in child psychiatry services. The number of children with suicidal thoughts has tripled and the number of acts of suicide has doubled[247]. Children of 10 years old who scarify themselves, take drugs and commit suicide. We are sacrificing the future of the country for an average age of 81 years of COVID deaths, for God's sake! And let's not forget the thousands of cancer patients and other serious pathologies who were not taken care of because of the deprogramming. They were dying in general indifference, and ironically, many of them with COVID as the cause of death! How many lives have been cut short because of a mass tipping into poverty? Everyone knows that precariousness is a risk factor for health and we have seen this during the crisis when the poorest department of France, in this case Seine-Saint-Denis (INSEE data[248]), is the most affected while its population is the youngest! France has lost 20 points of GDP and its debt has exploded to 2650 billion euros, a rate of 120%. It will take 67 years to pay back this increase alone and return to the pre-crisis level[249]. Contrary to what we hear from the politicians, it is not through the sluggish growth that we have known for years that we will try to reduce the debt, but through higher taxes and other anti-social measures (austerity). This means a decrease of the purchasing power and therefore of the consumption, and *in fine* an increase of the precariousness. It is like the Greek debt crisis. This is the vicious circle that will kill infinitely more people than the virus of fear… And the devastation has already begun, often without making a sound, as we have seen.

---

[246] Pascale Santi and Sandrine Cabut, "Confinements would have significantly reduced the physical and intellectual capacities of children," www.lemonde.fr, 06/28/2021.

[247] In the program Envoyé Spécial broadcast on France 2 on Thursday, June 3, 2021.

[248] Hajera Mohammad, "La Seine–Saint-Denis, département où les difficultés sociales persistent selon l'Insee," www.francebleu.fr, February 13, 2020.

[249] Florentin Collomp, "The French debt would not return to its pre-COVID level before … 67 years", www.lefigaro.fr, 20/05/2021.

I don't know if my story is a marginal case, but I know many people who have had a very bad experience with the confinement, especially with the media terror that accompanied it. People close to me have reported very serious depression with suicidal thoughts. A 25-year-old man was putting tape on all the windows of the house to make it as airtight as possible against the virus! A lady who took in a young girl close to my family, a young student who had come to study in France, refused to let her go to work for fear that she would bring the virus home. She then forced her to be vaccinated even though her own parents were against it! Fear has terrorized people. It is a weapon of mass destruction drawn in our interest according to the new fashion, *nudging...*

## When Nudging Goes Wrong

A serious investigative book by an English journalist and author, Laura Dodsworth, released in May 2021[250], has reinforced my hypothesis about the overuse of fear by design during the crisis. It is titled: "A State of Fear: How the UK government weaponized fear during the Covid-19 pandemic." She was able to gather testimony from several members of the SPI-B, the British scientific council charged with advising the government on policy during the crisis. Two members, who preferred to remain anonymous for obvious reasons, gave chilling accounts.

"In March, the government was very concerned about possible non-compliance and thought that people would not want to be confined. There were discussions that fear was necessary to encourage people to comply and decisions were made about how to amplify fear. The way we have used fear is dystopian. We have a totalitarian government when it comes to propaganda. But all governments engage in propaganda. The use of fear is completely ethically questionable. It was like a strange experience. In the end, it backfired because people became too afraid," he confesses. Another agrees, saying that the propaganda used reached "sinister" levels, especially when the health care workers were

---

[250] Laura Dodsworth, "A State of Fear: How the UK government weaponized fear during the Covid-19 pandemic," Pinter & Martin; 17 May 2021.

applauding in the windows. He confided: "I never joined the applause. I was relieved when it was over. I would say it was created, invented, I don't think it was spontaneous [...] We had never discussed it in SPI-B. It wasn't our policy or our recommendation, I just think somebody, somewhere, dreamed it up. It was ready to go. Something felt artificial to me. I bristled at this circus in people's windows. It seemed more like applause for Boris [Johnson] than applause for the NHS. I think the government used it as a shield. It may have been invented by one of the secret propaganda units of the SPI-B." The same scientist thought the balance was lost between protecting people from the virus and protecting what makes us human. He confessed, "I have a hard time accepting any of this. That we have allowed ourselves to be governed in this way." When the reporter reminds him that he is part of the propaganda machine, he clarifies, "It's on behalf of the cell I'm in—it's behavioral. You could refer to psychology as "mind control." That's what we do. Clearly, we are trying to do it in a positive way, but it has been used in a bad way. Psychology has been used for the wrong purposes. I don't want to get into that too much because it's dystopian and that's what wakes me up every day at 3 a.m."

When you read the book, you discover that the parallel with what happened in France, during all the phases of the crisis, is crystal clear. This is the case both in the media coverage and in the policy adopted by the authorities. And for good reason, it was not the scientific council that was actually guiding, but *nudge units* whose methods are the same in many countries, the United Kingdom being a pioneer and at the forefront in the field.

The SPI-B is a behavioral science-based pandemic analysis group. According to the official U.K. government website, the SPI-B "provides behavioral science advice to anticipate and help people adhere to recommendations made by medical experts or epidemiologists. Its role is "to provide independent expert behavioral advice to the SAGE (Scientific Advisory Group for Emergencies), which in turn advises ministers and members of government."[251] And the problem lies with these so-called independent experts.

In a document produced by SPI-B in March 2020[252], outlining options for "increasing public acceptance of social distancing measures," the second most important is "perceived persuasion," which states, "Many people still do not feel sufficiently threatened personally; they may be reassured by the low mortality rate in their demographic group, although levels of concern may vary. There is evidence that a good understanding of risk is positively associated with the adoption of social distancing measures. The perceived level of personal threat needs to be increased among those who are complacent, using powerful *emotional* messages […]" This paragraph points to an initial conflict of interest issues. It refers in particular to a survey conducted for the *Imperial College of London*[253], the same one that recommended the measures announced by the government a week earlier. In passing, the survey mentions that 77% of English people are afraid and 48% of adults who have never tested positive "think they are likely to contract the virus in the future." So, we are looking for new measures, as if that wasn't enough!

It is worth remembering that it is this same institute [Imperial] that has been making the recommendations and panicking the world for decades, notably through its spokesman Neil Ferguson. He is a member of the SAGE scientific committee and heads the *Imperial College* team in charge of the Covid-19 response. The pedigree of this professor of mathematical biology should, however, arose at least a little suspicion:

- o During the 2001 foot-and-mouth disease outbreak, Ferguson's mathematical models led British authorities to slaughter more than 6 million cows, sheep, and other livestock. This will have cost the country some 10 billion pounds. His recommendation to kill animals, even those that are not sick, will be questioned by

---

[251] https://www.gov.uk/government/groups/independent-scientific-pandemic-influenza-group-on-behaviours-spi-b

[252]

https://assets.publishing.service.gov.uk/government/uploads/system/uploads/attachment_data/file/882722/25-options-for-increasing-adherence-to-social-distancing-measures-22032020.pdf

[253] https://www.imperial.ac.uk/media/imperial-college/medicine/sph/ide/gida-fellowships/Imperial-College-COVID19-Population-Survey-20-03-2020.pdf

researchers who will speak of a "serious error" not taking into account the presence of several animal species in the farms[254].

- o Ferguson also predicted that between 50,000 and 150,000 people could die from "mad cow disease" and its sheep equivalent if it were transmitted to humans. To date, there have been fewer than 200 deaths from the human form of the disease. When reminded of this, he says, "Yes, but that hasn't changed government policy." Good thing we didn't listen to him for once…

- o In 2005, during the bird flu, he predicted that the disease would kill 200 million people worldwide. He said, "About 40 million people died from the Spanish flu in 1948. There are six times that many people in the world now. You can do the math to get to about 200 million." He also warned that if drastic measures are not taken immediately, it will be catastrophic for the UK. "If the disease comes to Britain, it will be too late," he assures. The disease will eventually kill 74 people worldwide!

- o During the 2009 swine flu, Ferguson and colleagues argued in a paper published in *The Lancet* that schools should be closed, travel between regions should be restricted, and antivirals should be used en masse, in order to stop the spread of infection and buy time before a vaccine could be found. The *Imperial* team estimated the lethality of this flu to be between 0.3 and 1.5%. Estimates made by the British government based on their models put the death toll at 65,000. The reality? Only 457 deaths in the whole kingdom, corresponding to the mortality of 0.026%, according to the *British Medical Journal*![255] The mathematician's apocalyptic models are off the mark once again. The day he will be right by accident, God forbid, he will be enthroned in history as a Nostradamus bis…

In 2020, the U.K. was going to adopt the Swedish strategy of no containment, but pressure from Ferguson, nicknamed "Professor

---

[254] Katherine Rushton and Daniel Foggo, "Neil Ferguson, the scientist who convinced Boris Johnson of UK coronavirus lockdown, criticized in past for flawed research," www.telegraph.co.uk, 28 March 2020.
[255] http://news.bbc.co.uk/2/hi/health/8406723.stm

Containment," scuttled it. The mathematician again predicted the apocalypse for the UK, "500,000 dead, if no containment measures are taken." When his model is applied to Sweden, the figure peaks at 85,000 deaths. The reality? At the end of May, there were 4350 deaths in Sweden compared to 39,045 in England! The Scandinavian country did not apply containment nor any of the recommended measures. Its economy and the minds of its people were preserved. Ferguson later acknowledged that, although Swedish authorities relied on "quite similar science, they went a long way towards the same result" without applying containment[256].

A BBC reporter[257], reporting from Sweden's capital of Stockholm, almost despairing of people living normal lives, asks the country's chief strategy officer, epidemiologist Anders Tegnell: "If you don't base your strategy on the same data as the rest of the world, what data do you use?" Unperturbed, Anders replies, "The question is mostly about what data the rest of the world uses to make decisions. We looked and found only a few things. There's the *Imperial College London* report, which is a non-peer-reviewed document. That's about all you'll find. In the majority of countries, there's nothing else." The interview ends there and the journalist reappears in a garden pretending to read a small notebook in which he would have collected anonymous confidences from a Swedish doctor who would have told him: "We are playing with people's lives and the lives of people who are trying to save lives…"

We have indeed heard here in France many cathodic doctors repeat the figures of *the Imperial College*. The latter has been the guide for most Western governments and their *nudge units*. We needed a reference, even if it is false…

I consulted the report of the French scientific council of October 26, 2020, entitled "A second wave leading to a critical health situation,"[258] and I was not disappointed. A paragraph justifying "the generalized

---

[256] Henry Bodkin, "'Prof Lockdown' Neil Ferguson admits Sweden used same science as UK," www.telegraph.co.uk, 2 June 2020.
[257] https://www.youtube.com/watch?v=pzzVxw5FyYs
[258] https://solidarites-sante.gouv.fr/IMG/pdf/note_conseil_scientifique_26_octobre_2020.pdf

containment of the whole territory" takes as a first reference to a paper published in June 2020 by … *the Imperial College of London,* Ferguson being one of its authors![259] This paper, which studied the effect of health measures such as containment and school closures in 11 European countries, concludes as follows: "Continued intervention [containment & school closures] should be considered to keep the epidemic under control." This is how fear rules and that a lockdown would have been instituted in France four days later, on October 30, 2020, without the Ferguson reference being questioned in the press or elsewhere. In fact, the opposite was done.

Libération's *fact checking* service wanted to verify the criticisms against Ferguson, as if the numbers didn't speak for themselves, by asking Antoine Flahault, an epidemiologist at the University of Geneva who is very present in the media. Here is his answer: "When dealing with an emerging, new disease, we have little choice but to resort to mathematical modeling, because we have no experience with this disease. Models can be used to build scenarios…"[260] I must say that this sentence alone closes all the absurdity of these pseudo-specialists of prediction. How can a scientist say such a thing? Predictive models are in essence based on past knowledge. Without this, everything that comes out of them is just wind without any scientific basis. One cannot predict anything new, except playing Mrs. Irma! Libération concludes that this is not a problem after all, and that scientists have told him that "Ferguson's job is mainly to imagine the worst." And when will the asteroid hit the Earth at full speed to decimate us all, *Mr* Ferguson? Then we wonder why none of the models of these pseudo-scientists fit reality…

---

[259] Flaxman S, Mishra S, Gandy A, Unwin HJT, Mellan TA, Coupland H, Whittaker C, Zhu H, Berah T, Eaton JW, Monod M; Imperial College Covid-19 Response Team, Ghani AC, Donnelly CA, Riley S, Vollmer MAC, Ferguson NM, Okell LC, Bhatt S. Estimating the effects of non-pharmaceutical interventions on Covid-19 in Europe. Nature. 2020 Aug; 584 (7820):257–261. doi: 10.1038/s41586-020-2405-7. Epub 2020 Jun 8.

[260] https://www.liberation.fr/checknews/2020/06/05/covid-19-neil-ferguson-l-epidemiologiste-pro-confinement-etait-il-trop-pessimiste_1790378/

None of Ferguson's projections will come true anywhere in the world. But that is not why he will resign "in disgrace" in May 2020 from the British SAGE scientific council. No, not for incompetence and health terrorism. While the kingdom is confined on his recommendations, this old sage violates himself the measure by receiving at home twice, clandestinely, of course, his 38-year-old mistress![261] He declared some time before this revelation that if the sanitary measures were lifted prematurely, 100,000 more deaths would be deplored! Welcome to the realm of the swindlers…

Elon Musk, the CEO of Tesla and SpaceX, posted a fiery tweet the same day calling the charlatan an "absolute moron" and declaring that "something more needs to be done about him" because "this guy has caused a lot of harm in the world with his fake science."

The Ferguson models have indeed provoked dramatic measures in the countries that followed it. If we take the official figures for the number of Covid-19 deaths per million inhabitants from[262], we can see that there are 1420 in Sweden, 1623 in France, and 1917 in the United Kingdom! The country of Ferguson is the worst, far from Sweden with 35% more deaths. This man probably deserves to be in prison in a country of justice. I know a person who lives in England who took his wife and children overnight and fled the country, because he was terrified of being forced into further action. He left behind his job and all his possessions… And meanwhile, Ferguson is living the *dolce vita* with his beau, as is the hellish British health minister Matt Hancock. Indeed, while the measure of "social" distancing of about six feet is recommended to the population, Hancock is caught with his finger in the honey pot, filmed within his ministry having a good time with his adviser, married like him and mother of three children like him! He apologized and Prime Minister Boris Johnson accepted his apology and considered the matter "closed,"[263] but Hancock ended up resigning as his

---

[261] Heather Stewart, "Neil Ferguson: UK coronavirus adviser resigns after breaking lockdown rules," www.theguardian.com, May 5th, 2020.
[262] Figures I have consulted in May 2021.
[263] BBC, "Matt Hancock affair: Health secretary apologizes for breaking social distancing guidelines," June 25th 2021.

position became untenable. I thought that fear was killing the libido unless these people watch TV and suffer from the terror they spread everywhere…

In neighboring Ireland, a scientific council launched in a "zero COVID" fight called ISAG (*Independent Scientific Advocacy Group*), has not deviated from the rule of terror. Documents and emails leaked to the press reveal that its founder, Professor Anthony Staines, has sent some rather peculiar instructions to other members of the group. He asked them to "internalize," to "look for ways to amplify insecurity, anxiety, and uncertainty," to "target people rather than institutions" since "people are affected faster than institutions," and to remember that "imagination and ego can draw far more serious consequences than any activist" since "the threat is often more terrifying than the thing itself." And all this has been recognized by Professor Staines[264], who is a former epidemiology researcher at the *Imperial College of London*[265]. It's a small world…

But *nudge units* have been very active everywhere in Western countries, not only in Great Britain, where fear has been used without gloves as a means of persuasion to enforce recommendations.

In Germany, the newspaper *Die Welt*, one of the country's three main newspapers, revealed how the German Minister of the Interior, Horst Seehofer, worked as early as March 2020, on scenarios aimed at artificially increasing fear of the virus among the population in order to gain acceptance for drastic measures. The minister was firmly opposed to lifting the restrictions on the date originally set by his government. Following a preparatory meeting he had with two scientists, Christian Drosten[266] and Lothar Wieler, a series of emails was sent to scientists and universities, asking them to draw up a plan that would allow the introduction of "preventive and repressive measures." The 200 email exchanges analyzed by *Die Welt were* obtained after several months of litigation with the Robert Koch Institute, the government agency responsible for coordinating the fight against the virus.

---

[264] Gary Kavanagh, "ISAG breaks silence as Founder admits to sharing 'increase insecurity, anxiety and uncertainty' note," https://gript.ie, Mar 15, 2021.
[265] https://dcu.academia.edu/AnthonyStaines/CurriculumVitae
[266] The virologist developed the PCR test.

The leads the researchers came up with in an initially classified report were terrifying: "manipulating the mortality rates of the virus by exaggerating it," "using images of people dying of suffocation," "showing seriously ill people being taken to hospital by their relatives, but being turned away and dying in agony at home, gasping for breath."… The report released weeks later presented a horror movie scenario that more than a million people could die from the coronavirus if life continued as before the pandemic. Suggestions were made on how to achieve the "desired shock effect" to avoid this. The information in *Die Welt* caused a scandal in Germany. Opposition members of parliament asked for clarification in the Bundestag, warning against "damage to the credibility of science and politics." One of them, Wolfgang Kubicki, stated that "anyone who wants to sow fear in the population in order to be able to better implement political measures is destroying the basic democratic order. Clearly, it is no longer a matter of explaining political decisions to mature citizens based on facts, but rather of imposing these decisions in a repressive manner."

In Belgium? It's even worse, with nudge mixing with serious conflicts of interest. Revisiting the decision to reopen non-essential shops from December 1, 2020, Health Minister Frank Vandenbroucke explained in an interview that "shopping does not really entail any risk when everything is well controlled." When asked by a journalist why these stores were closed on 30 October, he replied: "Because at some point we needed to take a shock decision, we needed an electroshock and that meant closing non-essential shops immediately." The Minister of Health also admitted that it was a mostly "psychological" measure[267]. His answers naturally provoked a reaction. Catherine Fonck, leader of the Centre Droit Humaniste group in the House, called it a "surreal" interview. "I have always advocated for strong and coherent measures given the seriousness of the epidemic. But this interview is surreal: businesses closed because a *shock decision* was needed. What cynicism in the face of all those who are now devastated by the loss of their business," Fonck wrote on Twitter. It must be said that the Belgian

---

[267] Marie Rigot, "Une interview surréaliste, De quoi ne plus donner envie aux Belges de suivre les règles: les propos de Frank Vandenbroucke après le Comité de concertation font réagir", www.dhnet.be, 30-11-20.

government was not advised by just anyone. The group of experts in charge of *the Exit Strategy*, a body created in April 2020 to help manage the crisis, has a very special member: Dr. Marc van Ranst. This advisor was, among other things, the chairman of the scientific committee of the inter-ministerial Influenza Commission, which recommended GSK's vaccine in 2009, even though he was receiving a salary from GSK. But he did even better. In a mind-boggling video of a talk given in January 2019 on pandemic management at the *Royal Institute of International Affairs*, also known as *Chatham House*, one of the most influential British *think tanks*, van Ranst quietly explains how he managed to scare the population during the H1N1 crisis ten years earlier. Michèle Rivasi, a member of the European Parliament for the Green Party, posted the video on her YouTube channel to denounce the instrumentalization of the media and of fear during the crisis[268]. In this video, we can see that after showing a slide listing his links of interest with the pharmaceutical industry, as long as an arm, van Ranst explains how to occupy the information space and get the media in the pocket during a pandemic: "You have to be omnipresent the first days. To get the media's attention, you make a deal with them. You'll tell them everything, and if they call you, you'll pick up the phone. By doing this, you can use the first few days to achieve maximum coverage. That way, they won't be looking for other voices. If you do that, it will be much easier." How do you distill fear? He explains shamelessly, sometimes eliciting laughter from a zombie audience, like this, "You have to say OK, we're going to have outbreak-related deaths, it's inevitable. I've used that in the media: 7 flu deaths a day at the peak of the epidemic would be realistic… That's true for every year, that's a very conservative estimate. But talking about deaths is very important, because people are going to start thinking, 'Wow, you mean people are dying of the flu?' And that was a necessary step." During the Covid-19 crisis, Van Ranst didn't let up on the Belgian government—it's very reminiscent of the French scientific council—which he sees as lacking responsiveness to slacking behavior. "With decision makers in slow motion, Belgium is heading for disaster," he thundered on Twitter.

---

[268] https://www.youtube.com/watch?v=U5i1h6WR5Q8

In France, the pandemic has not waited for the word "nudge" to become a means of communication. This word of all paradoxes even perfectly embodies the five-year term of President Emmanuel Macron with his "at the same time." Its use has just intensified during the crisis. On the eve of the first spring 2020 lockdown, the president announced to the nation that "we are at war," making sure to debrief the troops before engaging in combat by specifying everyone's role by referring to the "first, second and third front lines." To set the scene, a curfew was decreed, a measure that is actually applied in countries in conflict. As if the virus was nocturnal and preferred to surprise people in the dark like an enemy combatant! The effect was just monster traffic jams and crowded trains at rush hour like never before, as people rushed to get home to avoid a 135-euro fine. We have seen everything, of what scares us and certainly not the virus…

People who could not telework were even given a double whammy. Not only did they take crowded public transport with the fear of contracting the virus, but, as if that were not enough, they were frightened even more with anxiety-provoking messages in the stations. This is once again *nudge* at work, pushed to the point of abjectness. A noise is broadcast, that of a person coughing, followed by this message: "At this moment, someone who may be carrying the coronavirus is near you. To protect yourself, stay two steps away from other travelers." The head of the SNCF's *nudge unit*, Isabelle Collin, proudly declared in a video still visible online[269] this, "We play on the register of emotions, sensations, these noises that are a bit unusual for station announcements, help trigger attention … and then people look at each other." Crazy and mind-blowing!

Just before the second containment in October 2020, the President of the Republic suggested that "400,000 more deaths will occur if nothing is done." This figure, once again derived from models that have nothing to do with reality, justified the new restrictions. However, a collective of 200 researchers sounded the alarm in September 2020 on this anxiety-provoking management[270]: "We, scientists and academics of all

---

[269] https://www.francetvinfo.fr/sante/maladie/coronavirus/video-transports-et-deconfinement-comment-tenir-la-distance_3950967.html

disciplines, and health professionals, exercising our free will and freedom of expression, say that we no longer want to be governed by and in fear. The French society is currently in tension, many citizens are panicking or, on the contrary, do not care about the instructions, and many decision makers are panicking. It is urgent to change course. We are not at war, but confronted with an epidemic that caused 30 deaths on September 9 [...] This is why we call on the French political and health authorities to stop instilling fear through an anxiety-provoking communication that systematically exaggerates the dangers without explaining the causes and mechanisms. Enlightened responsibility should not be confused with moralizing guilt, nor should citizen education be confused with infantilization. We also call on all journalists to stop relaying without distance a communication that has become counterproductive: the majority of our fellow citizens no longer trust the official speech, conspiracies of all kinds abound on social networks and extremists take advantage of this [...] We also call on the government not to use science as an instrument. Science has for *sine qua non* transparency, pluralism, contradictory debate, precise knowledge of the data and the absence of conflicts of interest. The Scientific Council of Covid-19 does not respect all of these criteria and should therefore be reorganized or abolished..." There is only one word missing from this article, *nudge*!

The *nudge* was more than ever blatant when Macron decided to impose the "health certificate" in almost all social places, justifying this life by using false figures and curves just as false, taken from imaginary models! We were told that vaccination was not compulsory, following the principle of *nudge*, but the constraints imposed on the population were such that we are not far from it finally. Moreover, a million French people, overcome by fear, made an appointment even before the end of the presidential speech! This is how fear rules and how a whole population falls into darkness...

The *nudge is* not a plot, but it is not a democratic process either, far from it. It is even unethical, and in a health context where the population

---

[270] "Covid-19: we no longer want to be governed by fear", published in Après-demain, 2020 (No. 55, NF), pages 27 to 28.

needs a strong immune defense that fear weakens as it is commonly admitted, it is even criminal. The choices that impact the life of the city must be discussed in all transparency in a self-respecting democracy. Divergent opinions must be listened to and taken into consideration. My fear is that nudge will become the new normal, as there is no shortage of pretexts to use it in the name of the collective interest, whereas it completely flouts the foundations of democracy.

In the aftermath of the French Revolution, on February 5, 1794, Robespierre declared: "If the mainspring of popular government in peace is a virtue, the mainspring of government in revolution is both virtue and terror: virtue without which terror is fatal; terror without which virtue is powerless." So, have we not made progress since then? The answer is clearly yes.

The French Prime Minister has already warned that masks will become a standard, especially in case of flu. The "health certificate" may also become standard. In response to the question about the problems that these measures could pose for society, a journalist replied: "If it's to get back to a normal life, why not?" We see in this answer how people lose all bearings when confronted with fear. This is a cognitive bias called the "anchoring effect." Over time, the life before COVID has been forgotten and the new reference point (anchor) is that of the crisis. After a few loose ends have been tied up, the shortcut is to think of a complete return to the old life. Living masked and stalked is therefore the new normal for this lady journalist. I have heard much of the same speech from many Chinese who are satisfied with the concept of social credit. This is their new normal, which may soon be ours…

Will the climate, for example, be another pretext, always in the name of our interest, to decide to lockdown the planet at any time to reduce the greenhouse effect of gas emissions? Where will they stop? Who are they anyway to decide for us, the others? The saying "The road to hell is paved with good intentions" has never been more valid than for our sad era…

Let us note that I avoid talking about the agreement of any authority or group whose purpose is to cause harm. I keep a certain optimism about the possible goodness of humans. I avoid considering all this as a *conspiracy*, a term that I completely refute for several reasons.

## The Ecosystem of Triple Ignorance

Let's first go back to the definition of the word *conspiracy*. This term refers to "a secret design, concerted between several people, with the intention of harming the authority of a public figure or an institution, possibly to attack his life or his safety." This definition obviously fits perfectly with a number of historical events such as all the attacks planned or committed by terrorist groups. This is also the case, for example, of the American intervention in Iraq in 2003 following the lie about Saddam Hussein's imaginary weapons of mass destruction. History is full of real examples, but the recent use of the term *"conspiracy"* on the web and in the media in general is often a mistake that testifies above all to what I call "an ecosystem of triple ignorance" in which the various protagonists who use it are immersed. Of course, I am not giving a negative connotation to the word *ignorance* here. The world of knowledge is like an adventure game that consists of collecting keys to open doors and access to certain levels unknown to everyone. Not having the keys doesn't mean being stupid, but just not having had the opportunity to find them. What I am going to try to explain in this chapter, without any pretension, is part of this register. I don't pretend to have all the keys, but I just want to share the few that I have. I will try to explain this notion of triple ignorance by using concrete examples for each of them.

*1) The dictators of thought...*

The first of the ignorance is that of the contradictors who use the term *conspiracy* as soon as they run out of arguments. They do this to mock, denigrate and impose the unique thought. This became so obvious during the COVID crisis that this argument is now immediately turned against the one who uses it. When Professor Luc Montagnier, Nobel Prize winner, put forward the hypothesis that the virus might be the result of a laboratory manipulation, all the media fell on him and called him a conspiracy theorist. However, a laboratory accident is not an impossible thing. Zero risk does not exist in any field. To claim the opposite is to lie or be ignorant. Without going back very far in time, the anthrax that terrorized the United States in the aftermath of the World Trade Center attacks in 2001 leaked from the military laboratory at Fort Derick[271]. And without going far back, in France, on April 12, 2014, the Pasteur Institute issued a statement reporting that 2348 tubes containing SARS had been misplaced! There have been so many other problems like this in the past[272].

A year and a half after the start of the COVID pandemic, all the media without exception are reviving the hypothesis of a laboratory leak after a letter published in the journal *Science* by some twenty world-class scientists. Even the newspaper Le Monde headlined: "Origins of Covid-19: the hypothesis of an accident at the Wuhan Institute of Virology revived after the disclosure of unpublished work." The same newspaper wrote a few months earlier in a *fact-checking* article: "The idea that the virus could have been created by scientists has been formally denied by the Wuhan Institute of Virology, and rapid advances in the scientific community lend credence to the Chinese laboratory's defense." To take up the defense of the institute as an argument is still not serious. As if the Chinese could do otherwise… And what scientific community? It is clear that there is no consensus. In the interest of intellectual honesty, we should not reduce the scientific community to the one that defends one thesis and excludes the other. It is this way of contradicting a thesis with fallacious arguments that becomes counterproductive and turns against the press. Le Monde did an about-face following the researchers' article in *Science*: "The hypothesis of a laboratory accident as a possible origin of the Covid-19 pandemic is neither the majority nor the most probable, but it is not a conspiracy theory."[273] This is an example of what undermines the confidence of readers and strengthens the cults on the Web. A few days later, President Joe Biden officially requests a serious

---

[271] https://www.nti.org/gsn/article/fbi-anthrax-investigation-shuts-fort-detrick-labs
[272] Martin Furmanski, "A Brief and Terrifying Story of Viruses Escaping the Labs," http://www.slate.fr/, April 16, 2014.
[273] Stéphane Foucart, "Origins of Covid-19: the hypothesis of an accident at the Wuhan Institute of Virology revived after the disclosure of unpublished work", www.lemonde.fr, 14 May 2021.

investigation from the American intelligence services in order to establish the true origin of the virus. This is a good thing if it is carried out with scientific objectivity, not with geopolitical ulterior motives in the context of the Sino-American trade war. Let's not be fooled either… But the only way to get to the truth, which is so essential to avoid problems recurring, is to keep the debate open. Let's let science do its work in all serenity.

The best way to respond to a far-fetched thesis is however simple: demonstrate by facts that it is false. If it is just a hypothesis of some researchers and not yet contradicted by science, it must be presented as such like all the others without exclusion. And even there, one must be careful not to be too certain, because science is not fixed and progresses. Otherwise, all laboratories will be closed and every scientist will go and do something else. Isaac Newton was right until Albert Einstein demonstrated something else with *general relativity*, thanks to which we can use a GPS with a good precision today… Fortunately, we have not stopped looking. It's a good thing we didn't stop looking. Isn't it?

*2) Distracted paranoids…*

The second kind of ignorance is that of people who explain that the politicians behind a fiasco, as well as the media who support them unreservedly, are in a conspiracy pattern. This is just ignoring how institutions and bureaucracy work. In reality, it is often a system, a kind of gear with many cogs, in which decision-makers have been immersed for many years and make decisions mechanically without even thinking. When the government spokeswoman says that "the mask is useless and people don't know how to put it on anyway," she really means it. And I am convinced of that. The shortage of protective measures had to be justified in some way, and if science and transparency are not used, ignorance is often an argument that passes without too much trouble. It is La Fontaine's fable of the fox and the grapes. One can hardly blame the animal, although cunning, for denying reality. It should be remembered that the sale of masks has been forbidden to pharmacists and many have been condemned for not following the directive. The hardest thing was to make the same population swallow, less than three months later, without any scientific proof, the obligation to wear the mask, under penalty of a 135-Euro fine and even imprisonment at the third repetition! Obviously, there was no lack of masks at that time and the grapes were sweet again, especially if they are useful to consolidate the strategy of fear. What is extraordinary is that few voices were raised against the absurdity that was unfolding before our eyes. But fear has undoubtedly inhibited any power of reflection. The majority of people, immersed in the screens of terror, were tetanized.

In other cases, the decisions of those in charge, incomprehensible and sometimes serious in consequence, are just the result of influence struggles to keep interests or impose a certain ideology. We have seen this with the Gates Foundation, which is playing the pyromaniac fireman.

Sometimes decision-makers act in good faith thinking they are doing things for the collective good when they are just taking the wrong path to get there. Like everyone else, they are humans with their biases and limitations. During the crisis, some politicians were terrified and acted on emotion. The British health minister Matt Hancock quietly explained on TV that he was inspired by a movie, *Contagion*, to manage the vaccination campaign in his country! Yet the film tells the story of a pandemic that kills 30% of those infected, which has nothing to do with Covid-19. This is "disturbing" as the British newspaper Guardian[274] writes, but one cannot blame the minister for bad intentions. But it is obviously problematic to give power to people who give in so easily to emotion. The psychologist Marie-Estelle Dupont, one of the few people to look at the crisis with composure and who has earned my admiration and respect by warning very early on about the damage of containment, explained this on the very cathodic doctor Karine Lacombe—decorated with the Legion of Honor for I don't know what service to the nation during this crisis, but who has received from the pharmaceutical industry according to the official government website Transparence Santé[275] some 379 benefits, 61 remunerations, and 149 conventions since 2015 for a total of €212,209, including €28,412 from Gilead alone (seller of

---

[274] Stuart Heritage, "Matt Hancock's vaccine rollout was inspired by Contagion. Here's what he should watch next," www.theguardian.com, 4 Feb 2021.
[275] https://www.transparence.sante.gouv.fr

the famous Remdesivir)—which has sown terror on all the TV sets since the beginning of the epidemic and pushed to lock up everyone without mercy. She even went so far as to support the idea that people should be paid to get vaccinated! Ms. Dupont had this to say about her[276]: "Karine Lacombe says something very interesting. She says that she consults a shrink because she is afraid that life will end. And here we see how fear that has been used to heighten the threat to get people to obey the recommendations is not only being governed by fear, but it is also those who decide who are themselves governed by their own fears… It's all the studies about what is called "fear appeal" in psychology by heightening the threat and increasing the personal sense of vulnerability, including advertising campaigns that play up intimacy like this grandmother on a romantic song reunites with her son, etc. All of this is quite distressing. What's interesting is to see that when you have power, if you haven't worked on your own fears, your fear of death, your fear of illness, your relationship to reality, you set it up as a law and you're spinning around as if in a jar on a reward-punishment system that's totally infantilizing, for once again a disease that's not the black plague."

One should not be naive either and think that decision-makers are choirboys, as I have seen with many people. While watching a "debate" program on a 24-hour news channel, I listened to a former investigating judge and public prosecutor turned into a columnist say this: "I consider that everything proposed to us [by politicians] is by definition for our own good." Yet this is a person who has worked in the justice system and has seen it all for forty years! I just mentioned that some policy makers do act in good faith for a just cause, but to think that this is the case by definition is at best naive and at worst a lie.

*3) The zealits…*

The third type of ignorance is that of people accused of plotting. Such a scheme requires a certain intelligence and strategy in action. People who are accused of all kinds of machinations are in reality not even capable of keeping a secret for more than ten minutes! Everything can be found

---

[276] During the program Brunet Direct on LCI of 25/05/2021.

in the press, including the contents of text messages exchanged between senior government officials! You just have to read some newspapers to see it.

When doctors invade the TV sets to put pressure on the government to impose a confinement to the population, it is not in an obscure scheme to kill people, but just by ignorance. These pseudo-experts simply don't read the scientific literature anymore and don't know that several scientific publications advocate the opposite, in the United States[277] as in Germany[278] to name only these two. How do you expect them to do this if they are always on TV sets looking for light? It takes time and intelligence to read and understand science.

The worst thing is that the press confirms the denial of these extremists. Here is what the newspaper Le Monde published on June 18, 2021, which was taken up by all the media: "By delaying until the beginning of April the measures demanded by scientists at the end of January, the government has increased the toll of the pandemic in France. And the newspaper advances figures to quantify this increase: "More than 14,000 deaths, nearly 112,000 hospitalizations, including 28,000 in intensive care, and about 160,000 cases of Covid-19 long additional, according to calculations of Le Monde."[279] This same scientific council called for the tightening of containment in the spring without which it would be the apocalypse. Its cathode ray soldiers have obviously invested the media en masse to spread their terror. Here is what Gilles Pialoux, columnist for L'Express and head of the infectious and tropical diseases department at Tenon Hospital in Paris (AP-HP), said on France Inter on March 30, 2021: "In any case, the weeks that are going to pass are already written, for reasons of natural history, whatever the political decision, in any case we will go to the wall […] We go from crisis cell

---

[277] Eran Bendavid, Christopher Oh, Jay Bhattacharya, John P. A. Ioannidis, "Assessing mandatory stay-at-home and business closure effects on the spread of Covid-19," European Journal of Clinical Investigation, Volume51, Issue4, first published 05 January 2021.

[278] Justin Huggler, "Lockdown 'had no effect' on coronavirus pandemic in Germany," The Telegraph, 3 June 2021.

[279] Nathaniel Herzberg, "The Heavy Human Cost of a Third Late Containment in France," www.lemonde.fr, June 18, 2021.

to crisis cell. That's why I come to this microphone to get out curves, figures […] I belong to a very large hospital group [AP-HP], we exchange, we have alerts by WhatsApp and short circuits. We know the reality of this wave and this wall we are going into." Dominique Costagliola, an epidemiologist and researcher at INSERM, agreed a few weeks later: "I don't see how we can expect a massive drop in cases by the end of May."[280]

The rest is common knowledge. None of this will happen and the epidemic curve will flatten out like the previous year with the arrival of summer. The comments of Internet users on these alarmists are cruel, but understandable as these people have not missed an opportunity to terrorize the population. The government spokesman, pressured by economic actors suffering from the previous drastic measures, did not fail to remind them either: "We see today that the signals are green […] this proves all the prophets of doom wrong…" It will have been noted that doctors are organizing on WhatsApp groups to coordinate and put pressure on the government…

For the record, when the government started listening to dissonant voices on containment, we got a directive that will go down in history, probably as a result of the contradictions inherent in *nudge*: "lock yourself out! And don't forget to fill out the certification before you go out…"

Another example of mutual political-media blindness can be cited. It is the case of the Minister of Health saying that Covid-19 variants do not exist and all the media relaying his speech without changing a comma. The "scientific" council certainly dictated this to him. They simply did not know that real researchers in the world, including a few kilometers away, at the IHU in Marseille, had been manipulating these variants for three months already and had even communicated and published on them. I was flabbergasted when I saw the show. However, one should have just followed the question a little seriously and trusted the people in the field. The lab assistants who had been playing with the variants for months must have laughed at the ignorance. We know what happened

---

[280] https://www.youtube.com/watch?v=nuDEdJh10ZA

next. The media and the ministers were only talking about these variants … which were going to kill us all and exterminate the planet like the original strain!

When some alarmist doctors from Paris hospitals were squatting on TV sets in packs at the same time, thanks to WhatsApp we saw, it was also in order to blackmail a President of the Republic who did not listen to them several times. They believe that the world revolves only around them. This is also the smallness of these circles that have nothing of an elite. They are not driven by the collective interest, but by their oversized hubris, moreover, more than ever during this crisis. They are undoubtedly the biggest losers of the crisis, as they have lost all credibility. We will come back to this.

There is another explanation for the incomprehensible decisions of politicians, that of escalating commitment. They have gone so far down certain paths that it is very difficult for them to go back. It is mentally difficult to take. Also, in a crisis like COVID, there are lives at stake. The fear of lawsuits following an admission of mismanagement adds to the discomfort of cognitive dissonance.

The media are also accused of being part of a conspiracy scheme, because they do not, for example, invite the rare discordant voices. My explanation, certainly not valid in all cases, is quite similar to what I said in *volume 1* of the current book about artificial intelligence algorithms using the example of a brothel manager. Today, the media is looking for an audience like this manager. Selling available brain time to *Coca Cola* and other *Nutella*. When you invite an alarmist doctor who announces worrying news, he naturally scares the audience. As a result, they stay in front of the screen and the channel in question increases its audience. Fear sells. And this is, of course, captured by the TV channel managers thanks to the audience measurement tools. At the end of the month, when the guests who have effectively exploded the meters will be assessed, the alarmist doctors will be found in the high scores. As a result, they are invited back, not with the aim of explicitly scaring people, but just to go hunting for more viewers once again. The worst part is that these sales guests—they are called "good customers" in journalistic jargon—play along, consciously or unconsciously. I heard the epidemiologist Martin Blachier, the French Ferguson, the "third-wave reassurer" as he has been nicknamed, say: "Some alarmist doctors have become addicted. They are dying to be invited back by the media. And since they are careful about the success of their statements on the stage and the controversies they create, they fall into the trap of buzz and one-upmanship. So, they use fear over and over again to get people talking about them without realizing the damage they are causing."

I have a rather striking example in mind that demonstrates this mad race for ratings. It is the case of the polemicist Éric Zemmour who spends his airtime beating up on the justice system, because it would let delinquents get out of prison too soon. I share this observation, as do many of his opinions, but he himself is a recidivist offender, sentenced several times by the courts. This does not prevent the channel CNews from giving him a live platform with the risk of drawing his outrageous remarks at any moment and thus committing another offense. What I mean by this is that as long as the polemicist makes audiences and sells, the channel lets it go, without having as first intention to support racism, for example. On the other hand, journalists or hosts who have spent years loyally serving certain channels are fired overnight, because they no longer get ratings. There is no conspiracy in the story, just companies like others trying to make money, without worrying too much about the way. The end justifies the means for them.

In more serious cases, such as the fatal fall of a cable car in Italy, the manager and his employees who tampered with the brakes were convicted of "manslaughter" because their intention was not to kill people, but primarily to make money. Again, the bad intention is not explicit and it is difficult to condemn people in this sense. In politics, the media, and everywhere else, it is the same thing. Greed is often the primary motive, far from any intelligence or conspiracy. The paper of the wallet is closer to the brain of the man than any book…


## Help, Dr. Knock is back!

We have just seen how information is manipulated, oriented, truncated, and exploited in the political-media system. But it would be unfair of me to put everything on their backs, because without our complacency and complicity, none of this would be possible. People like the comfort of inertia and don't try to dig for information. When a journalist hands a microphone to people in the street, he does not force them to answer. In the evening, the TV news filters the answers to orient the information, but does not invent those who have answered. These people therefore participate in the manipulation, consciously or unconsciously. Without them, it would, of course, be impossible, unless you pay for the services of extras…

The COVID crisis was particularly interesting in terms of information. It's true that fear has paralyzed people, but I didn't understand the fact that people remained so inert in front of a number of absurd decisions. We still closed restaurants and cinemas and let the Parisian subways run full of people. We closed the bookstores and left the shelves of reality magazines open in the supermarkets. We considered toilet paper essential, but not books! We applauded caregivers and closed hospital beds at the same time. We did all this without shocking people. I made a post on LinkedIn expressing my astonishment at all the actions, but the response was minimal. I didn't understand the silence of people. So, I tried to find out more to understand. The answer really lies in a kind of omerta at all levels of society. Before I explain myself, I would like to mention that the situation of confinement is convenient for me personally, because I work from home and this saves me more than two hours a day, which I lose in the tiring Parisian traffic jams. That's as much time as I spend with my family and enjoy my children. But I don't want to lie to myself and think only of my own little self. This situation that suits many of us is made at the expense of many others, and all of us in fact as I will explain later. It is abnormal and so is the omerta that accompanies it.

—Social peace has been bought with "whatever it takes" by paying people to stay. Two out of three French people are bored at work according to surveys[281] and it is probably the same in other developed countries. So many of them want the confinement to last as long as

---

[281] "More than 60% of French people are bored at work," www.lepoint.fr, 02/25/2019.

possible, to get a salary and to be able to watch Netflix from morning to night. This is the only explanation I could find for a number of comments posted on the web that were pushing for continued lockdown and school closures.

The manipulation of the school in Seine-Saint-Denis where we were told that 20 parents of students died is particularly edifying. Once the information came out and spread like wildfire on the Web and the media, not a single teacher from that school stood up to deny it. I understand that they are terrified of what is being reported in the media and are afraid of contracting the disease, but this information was false and they should not have kept it quiet. Instead, it was used to pressure the Minister of Education…

—The restaurant owners, for example, are not protesting, because many of them, not all of them, of course, are actually finding their account and even better in this crisis. Some of them were doing takeaway sales while receiving state aid. I know some of them… And on TV I must not be the only one to have seen a restaurant owner, who is very present in the media and who is certainly not suffering from the crisis, accuse another restaurant owner on the verge of the abyss who "can't manage to feed his children" and who wants to reopen in spite of the directives, as irresponsible.

—Medical laboratories have earned billions with PCR tests. That's $54 for each screening, completely covered by the public health insurance. For the year 2020 alone, this expense item amounted to about 2 billion euros[282]. It is therefore not surprising that a biologist will tell you to get lost if you ask him to give you the number of cycles used to perform the COVID analysis. A false positive is a godsend for him, because it means that you will have to come back a week or ten days later to do another test to check that the "virus" is gone.

—Lines as far as the eye can see are visible everywhere in front of the medical biology laboratories. The "free" health care that has been hammered home since the beginning has attracted crowds, including

---

[282] Marie-Cécile Renault, "Covid-19: la facture salée des tests et des arrêts de travail," www.lefigaro.fr, 28/01/2021.

young people in good shape. It's just incredible. The loss aversion bias says that "it would be a loss not to take" the test when it's free" and if the test turns out to be positive and allows people to save ten days of work and stay at home, it's all good! It is easy to forget that nothing is free in life. The country's debt has exploded and it will have to be paid somehow…

—Journalists are caught in the trap of the race for clicks on articles published online. They are paid by the number of views and this pushes them to solicit, even if it means putting terrifying headlines or even dealing with reality. Some articles relaying information that turned out to be completely false are still present on the Web…

Journalists and columnists of TV and radio stations have their jobs well protected and do not even wear masks on closed stages. Why do you want them to worry about others? Why contradict the official guidelines when the fall in advertising revenue is compensated by all kinds of health campaigns broadcast in the millions? They and many other people are happy to do so…

—Caregivers received salary increases and few dared to denounce the closing of hospital beds, which continued even during the pandemic. The population was confined using the argument of hospital saturation, but beds continued to be cut. When the criteria for admission to intensive care were changed, which artificially lowered the average age of patients, not because of the Delta virus variant, as one could hear in the media, almost no one came to denounce the manipulation, except for two or three doctors. The caregivers contributed with their silence to the idea of containment, believing that this is what will lighten their workload. Just like the pots and pans in the windows, the hammering of this fact has just diverted their attention. It will later be a rude awakening for them…

—In order to amplify the vaccination effort, private doctors were called to work in centers opened for the occasion. They were paid on a fee-for-service basis and earned about 750 euros per hour! It is once again, omerta obliges, the naughty newspaper Canard Enchainé with an article entitled "Doctors who are well looked after to prick") which has shed light on this fact[283]. This has obviously surprised and even shocked the hospital community, especially the nurses who face the crisis sometimes without protection and for miserable wages. How then can we be surprised by the surreal comments about vaccines made by some doctors on the plateaus? I have even heard several say without batting an eyelid that the vaccine was "100% safe." It is not possible to say that when serious side effects such as anaphylactic shock, Bell's palsy, thrombosis …, and death have been reported since the very first reports. I quote, without changing a comma, an official pharmacovigilance report from the ANSM (the French FDA) concerning, for example, the AstraZeneca vaccine[284]—without forgetting that this is very underestimated and the figures are in reality certainly even higher, as with all drugs—, over a period of 15 days corresponding to 451,584 injections: "During the study period (2021/04/23 to 2021/05/06), 1,875 cases were validated (3,300 adverse events) and reported. These cases included 1193 women and 677 men (unknown 5) with an average age of 58.6 ± 13.4 years (median 61 years and extremes 20 to 84 years [not stated in 20 cases]. *Of these cases, 28.4% were serious with 21 deaths, 38 life-threatening, 176 hospitalizations, 9 disabilities, and 296 medically significant.*" The other vaccines are no safer when you look at the official ANSM reports. Pfizer's report is even far ahead in terms of the number of side effects reported[285]. The pharmacovigilance center in Toulouse, for example, has recorded five times as many reports as in normal times, a third of which are serious, as reported in the regional press[286]. And there, they only talk about very short term effects. But there is another lie, that of asserting that the vaccine protected 100% from severe forms. Unfortunately, this is not the case and this inaccurate statement creates a feeling of security that puts fragile people in danger and makes them think they are safe. I have heard this so much from those who have been vaccinated.

---

[283] Canard enchainé, " Des toubibs bien soignés pour piquer ", 1er April 2021.

[284] https://ansm.sante.fr/uploads/2021/05/17/rapport-n11-covid-19-vaccine-astrazeneca-12-05-2021-vfa.pdf

[285] https://ansm.sante.fr/uploads/2021/06/04/20210604-covid-19-vaccins-rapport-hebdomadaire-16-pfizer-2.pdf

[286] Nicolas Mathé, "Toulouse. Vaccins Covid-19 : les déclarations d'effets indésirables explosent", www.lejournaltoulousain.fr, 25 May 2021.

To encourage young people to get vaccinated, the Minister of Health said on live TV that the phase 3 clinical trials of the vaccines "are well underway and anyone who says otherwise is spreading *fake news.*" When I heard this, I must say that I thought I was dreaming. The Web was rightly inflamed after these declarations to denounce unbelievable statements. The fact-checkers of the newspaper Le Monde came to the rescue of the Minister the next day to say that it was a simple "misunderstanding" on his part and finally to say, after confirmation given by the Pfizer laboratory, that the trials were indeed running until May 2023[287].

To claim that the vaccine is 100% safe or that the trials have been completed is a serious lie. It creates mistrust among the population, which could unfortunately bury vaccination in general for the next century if more side effects appear in the coming years. This would be catastrophic, because it is important to remember that vaccines are useful to stop many serious diseases, some of them fatal, like diphtheria or tetanus. But for a salary of $2000 a half-day or an excessive political ambition, some people quickly forget the notion of ethics and collective interest…

—On Friday, June 11, 2021, was played a legendary semi-final between Rafael Nadal and Novak Djokovic at the Roland Garros Grand slam tennis tournament. The problem was that the public had to leave the court before the end of the match because of the curfew set at 11 p.m. for "health reasons." But at the last minute, the Elysee [President Macron] gave an exemption to the delight of the Roland Garros audience who chanted, "Thank you Macron." This decision is cynical, because at the same time young people who were having fun at the Place des Invalides in Paris were dispersed by the police with tear gas canisters. One cannot invoke the health reason and apply it at two speeds. What bothered me most, even though I love this sport and my children are enrolled in a tennis club, was the attitude of the public at Roland Garros who did not leave as planned even though the decision to grant an exemption was made. We cannot accept that people do not bury

---

[287] Les Décodeurs, "Covid-19: Are phase 3 vaccine trials over 'for months' as Olivier Véran claims?", www.lemonde.fr, 08 July 2021.

their dead in dignity by invoking the COVID and take advantage of the *fait du prince* to watch a match after the limit set for the rest of the population! Compromising behavior is one of the worst failings during crises…

—There is no shortage of war profiteers. An order of May 2020 made it easier for managers to file for the takeover of a company in bankruptcy. It was a godsend for some who took advantage of this to pay off their debts and sometimes to separate from their employees. This is the case, for example, of the children's clothing company Orchestra, which was crumbling under a debt of 650 million euros. It was taken over by its boss for 71 million euros, leaving 200 employees on the floor…[288]

—In Germany, a big scandal has shaken the country after revelations made by the famous newspaper *Bild* in which hospitals are accused of having made false declarations by underestimating the number of unoccupied intensive care beds[289]. It all started with a letter written by the Robert Kock Institute to the Ministry of Health raising suspicions about this issue. Any establishment whose rate of these available beds is less than 25% of its capacity receives state funding. And it was noted that there was a sharp drop in the figures reported just after the passage of the law concerning this compensation, even though the number of Covid-19 cases did not increase[290]. A total of 10.2 billion euros will be distributed to German hospitals in 2020 alone[291] to cope with the crisis … or not.

The motive is obviously financial, but a secret report by the *Federal Audit Office* shows that the German Minister of Health was aware of the manipulation of the figures, but continued to sound the alarm about the collapse of the hospital system. The use of fear again and again. Let us remember that in France, the same number of available beds was used as

---

[288] Guillaume Mollaret, "Orchestra Prémaman taken back to court by its boss", www.lefigaro.fr, 19/06/2020.
[289] https://www.bild.de/bild-plus/politik/inland/politik-inland/rechnungshof-bericht-enthuellt-der-grosse-betrug-mit-den-intensivbetten-76696870
[290] Johannes Hillig, "Scandal in Germany, Hospitals Allegedly Manipulate ICU Occupancy Rates," www.blick.ch, 11/06/2021.
[291] https://www.n-tv.de/panorama/Lauterbach-vermutet-Abrechnungsbetrug-in-Kliniken-article22615147.html

a criterion for reconfiguring the country in the spring of 2021, and some doctors did not fail to evoke a possible artificial filling of beds, pointing out in particular the oddity of the sudden decorrelation in March 2021 between the curves of the number of admissions to intensive care and the number of deaths[292].

As we have just seen, the omerta and the compromising behavior are at all levels. The self-censorship of information is not only the work of journalists. The crisis allows many people to earn easy money. It is profitable for them today, but it is destructive for the country in the medium and long term. The debt will be a deadly burden for the present and future generations. A society that lives a lie is doomed to die … and the COVID is just an excuse to finish it.

I cannot resist the idea of recalling here the play "Knock or the Triumph of Medicine" written by Jules Romains and first performed in Paris in 1923[293]. This comedy denounces manipulation, in medicine as elsewhere, at a time when the use of excessive advertising across the Atlantic was beginning to spread to Europe. The play has remained famous for, among other things, Dr. Knock maxim "Every healthy man is a sick man who doesn't know it." This play has been adapted several times to the cinema and an excellent version (French) from 1951 can be seen on YouTube[294]. I strongly invite the reader to watch it. It is incredible to see how perfectly it fits the current crisis.

The play is performed in three acts and is summarized as follows:

*First act:* Dr. Parpalaid has sold Dr. Knock an almost non-existent clientele in the canton of Saint-Maurice. Knock accepts the challenge and gives his interlocutors (Parpalaid and his wife) a pompous picture of his medical pretensions. He does not tell them his secret, because "it would be seen as propaganda" according to him. When the act ends, we don't know if Knock will win his bet, but we have already witnessed the

---

[292] Cécile Thibert, "Covid: Is it normal for hospitalizations to increase, but not deaths?", www.lefigaro.fr, 3/30/2021.
[293] https://fr.wikipedia.org/wiki/Knock_ou_le_Triomphe_de_la_m%C3%A9decine
[294] https://www.youtube.com/watch?v=U-NtO0uKhyo

first step of his project: estimating the incomes of his future clients and identifying everything that could hinder his project.

*Second act:* we witness Dr. Knock's demonstration of cunning, that is to say all the most formidable manipulation techniques of marketing. He parades all the social groups (KOL) of the canton on which he can rely, starting with the teacher whom he flatters and gives him back the place he deserves in the education of the people. Then comes the crier with his drum to announce free consultations, the *freemium* of medicine, not to say "foot in the door" or "finger in the gears." Knock has not forgotten the pharmacist to whom he promises considerable profits. The act ends with two "patients" whose control Knock takes with vigor, reminding us of his power of persuasion.

*Third act:* Dr. Parpalaid, who mocked Knock in the first act, now witnesses his success. Stunned, he is manhandled by Knock's "disciples." Knock has managed to take control of the entire township and those who are not bedridden are working for him. He watches his followers act for him like a guru in a cult. When Knock finds himself alone with his colleague Parpalaid, he launches into a speech in which he displays his will to power, which approaches madness. Dr. Parpalaid says to him: "If people are tired of being healthy and want the luxury of being sick, they should not be shy." But Knock does not let himself be destabilized. On the contrary. In the last line, he even manages to convince his colleague to be sick himself. In one of the final scenes of the comedy, we see the whole group of patients accompanying Doctor Parpalaid to his room, following him up the stairs with an air reminiscent of the worst horror films. The climax is reached when Knock says: "What do you want, it is done in spite of me. Whenever I'm in the presence of someone, I can't help but make a diagnosis ... even if it's completely unnecessary and irrelevant. So much so that, for some time now, I have avoided looking at myself in the mirror."

Knock has succeeded in getting the whole township, the "patients," the teacher, the town crier, the pharmacist, and the hotel owner, who has no more rooms available, because they are all occupied by patients treated by Knock. When Knock announces his departure from the canton to be replaced by the returning Parpalaid, everyone is stunned. Nobody wants him to leave…

The coronavirus crisis, without denying the seriousness of the disease on fragile people, is for me a giant play. All the ingredients were there, including the drums of media terror, for a Knock-like result. And nobody wants to end it. During a program on France Info radio that featured Labor Minister Elisabeth Borne[295], a listener called in and told her, "It's scary the idea of having to stop what [telework] we've acquired." I tell you no one wants to end it…

## The indelible stain of the white coat and the death of authority

The covid19 crisis has revealed something very interesting about authority in general and that of physicians in particular. It's like a life-saving reminder to everyone that medicine is not a science, but just a discipline that sometimes uses science. Unfortunately, we've all discovered that those who actually use science before speaking are quite rare, at least in the media. We have heard everything and its opposite, sometimes from the same people in the space of only a few days! I was personally stunned, because I did not understand how a person who respects himself and has a minimum of self-esteem can assume such reversals and can return without shame on the plateaus. And sometimes their actions contradict what they say *live*, which naturally undermines their credibility. And there is no lack of examples.

---

[295] Broadcast on June 16, 2021, at 7 pm.

The most flagrant case was the case of doctors who castigated people who did not wear their masks outside, but they themselves did not wear them when they were indoors on TV sets. The nephrologist (kidney specialist) Gilbert Deray, with strong links of interest with the pharmaceutical industry (€160,649 on Transparence Santé website), who predicted the apocalypse every day and wanted to confine everyone for months, wore a mask on TV, but intermittently, as if the virus was taking days off! Not to mention that he was touching his flap at nose level every ten seconds. The television show was frankly distressing… *No doubt that thinking hurts the kidneys and one cannot carry both burdens and ideas*[296].

How can we find an ounce of credibility in an alarmist doctor, also president of the Ligue against the Cancer, present on all TV channels at the same time—one wonders about the validity of the fundamental laws of physics during this crisis—who pleads for a confinement during the end of the year 2020—even announcing that he will celebrate Christmas in June! —Then, at the beginning of 2021, he comes back to announce that because of Covid-19, almost 100,000 cancers have not been detected? This same doctor, coming back from a media tour in Belgium, is arrested by the police at the Gare du Nord for not presenting a PCR test as the rule of the moment requires it in France for anyone coming from abroad. He gets angry and uses his authority and his name as a public figure, "don't you recognize me?" The police officer reminds him that the rule is valid for everyone. The doctor retorts, "I don't care!" Charitably, a police commander ends up letting him go…[297]

And how can we not reject vaccination, which I do not do, but try to do almost on principle against stupidity and not the medical act, when we see a pseudo-psychologist on a TV set shamelessly telling us that the resistance of nurses to the new messenger RNA vaccines is due to the fact that they would be, according to him, "less intellectually equipped"? Yesterday's heroes have suddenly become less than nothing in the media. Yet they are the ones who see the Covid-19 patients every day and are in the best position to judge what is good for their health. It is

---

[296] Quote from the French writer and critic Rémy de Gourmont (1858–1915).
[297] Canard enchainé, "Axel Kahn skids on the platform", 28/04/2021.

even healthy to have fears about a new technique never tested on humans on a large scale and still in phase 3 clinical trials. Does this psychologist know that Pfizer, the laboratory that markets the best-selling RNA vaccine, has been sentenced by the American authorities to the highest fine of all time, 2.3 billion dollars, for falsifying data?[298] This laboratory has been sentenced to six times since 2000, for a total of 3.3 billion dollars, second only to GSK with its 3.7 billion! The others are no better. Johnson & Johnson was sentenced to 2.3 billion and AstraZeneca to 520 million[299]. You have to stop for a second and look at these astronomical figures to get a sense of the gravity of the matter. Does this psychologist even have any idea about the opioid scandal in the United States, where hundreds of thousands of people, mostly young, have become drug addicts and are collapsing in the streets from heart attacks because of a drug (OxyContin) promoted by the Purdue Pharma laboratory, helped in its marketing by a large consulting firm [McKinsey] sentenced to pay 574 million dollars for the occasion[300], the same firm that oversees the Covid-19 vaccination strategy in France and elsewhere?[301] Isn't it healthy not to trust these people blindly now?

It should be noted in passing that a study[302] made concerning new molecules approved by the FDA between 2001 and 2010 shows that one third of these drugs are accompanied by serious side effects[303]. Also, it is useful to remember that the average time elapsed between the first alert concerning a serious side effect and the first effective withdrawal of the drug in question is 6 years! This is shown by a large study of 2016 conducted on all drugs marketed between 1953 and 2013. In passing, the

---

[298] Gardiner Harris, "Pfizer Pays $2.3 Billion to Settle Marketing Case," www.nytimes.com, Sept. 2, 2009.
[299] https://violationtracker.goodjobsfirst.org/prog.php?agency_sum=FDA
[300] Andrew Edgecliffe-Johnson, "McKinsey to pay almost $574m to settle opioid claims by US states", Financial Times, FEBRUARY 4 2021.
[301] RYM MOMTAZ AND ELISA BRAUN, "Sluggish coronavirus vaccination rollout poses risks for Macron," www.politico.eu, January 4, 2021.
[302] Onakpoya, Igho J et al. "Post-marketing withdrawal of 462 medicinal products because of adverse drug reactions: a systematic review of the world literature." BMC medicine vol. 14 10. 4 Feb. 2016.
[303] Nicholas S. Downing, Nilay D. Shah, Jenerius A. Aminawung et al, "Postmarket Safety Events Among Novel Therapeutics Approved by the US Food and Drug Administration Between 2001 and 2010," JAMA, 2017.

study notes that withdrawals are much less frequent in Africa, five times less than in Europe or North America. So, is this pseudo-psychologist smarter than the doctors in Scandinavian countries, which are otherwise the least corrupt and have the best health systems in the world, who have suspended certain vaccines against Covid-19? And if it was so safe, why put vaccines under "conditional MA" (market authorization) and not under definite MA as is done for any drug with sufficient safety guarantees? It is distressing to see the arrogance of ignorance…

But we have seen worse with this doctor who is afraid that life will stop and who proposes on live TV to pay people to accept to be vaccinated. I "understand a little" some American brands, like all the crisis profiteers, who seize the opportunity and offer on presentation of a vaccination certificate vouchers, burgers, donuts, or even cannabis [304]… but a doctor who proposes to use money as a means of persuasion is just dramatic. It's undermining confidence in medicine for the next 50 years. Where is the Hippocratic Oath? What about informed consent? Shouldn't people be convinced in all transparency before taking any medication? Doctor, it is a very serious issue to fall so low!

Another thing I realized during this crisis. We are no longer training doctors who must have a human connection with their patients, but robots who must apply rules dictated by health agencies that cannot be contradicted. It is easy to forget that each patient is unique and must be treated individually accordingly. If it's just a matter of rules, then let's give the job of doctors to any technician who has gone through three years of higher education and learned to apply rules.

A little anecdote that I experienced in the fall of 2020 illustrates this well. I contracted an otitis that was hurting me after a trip to the beach and went to the emergency room, my attending physician being absent. When the young lady doctor starts to examine me, she asks me if I took Paracetamol and I told her yes, "a 500 mg pill." She looked at the nurse next to her with a smile and then said, "But the 500 is for children who weigh a few pounds, not adults." I retorted that no, and that despite my

---

[304] Charles Passy, "The Best Coupon In Your Wallet? Your Vaccination Card," www.wsj.com, March 28, 2021.

80 kilos I am not used to taking more, because 500 is enough to relieve me. She kindly agreed and I thanked her. I don't even blame her, it's the training that dehumanizes the profession. By the way, the overdose of "even a small amount of Paracetamol," the most sold drug and the most used in the composition of many medicines (Doliprane, Dafalgan, Actifed...), is the first cause of liver transplantation for severe hepatitis in France[305]. So be careful, less is better…

The most striking example of this dehumanization appeared during the COVID crisis with the famous recommendation that can be summarized in 3D: Doliprane-Dodo-Die. My aunt, who contracted Covid-19, confirmed by a PCR test, was sent home from the hospital (Paris) with the only indication "take Doliprane and stay home." She suffers from many very serious diseases and the symptoms of Covid-19 are obvious on her. She has lost her sense of taste and smell and has difficulty breathing. She has not even been provided with an oximeter, which costs about $25, a third of a single PCR test! I was the one who had to alert my uncle to the danger of hypoxia[306] and pushed him to get one urgently. It's so sad…

The thing that transpired the most in the information conveyed by the doctors and other experts on the TV sets during the crisis was the cruel lack of monitoring and reading of research works. I rarely heard them put forward a fact and refer to any scientific study. I take a rather flagrant example concerning the abject instrumentalization of the issue of children. They have been masked and made to feel guilty without any science to back it up.

Some alarmist doctors declared that "many children were ill with Covid-19" with "severe symptoms reminiscent of Kawasaki disease." However, it has been known for a long time that this is just not true, according to several published studies[307]. An English study published as

---

[305] https://sante.lefigaro.fr/actualite/2011/11/25/16133-meme-faible-surdosage-paracetamol-est-dangereux

[306] Hypoxia occurs when the amount of oxygen delivered to the organs and muscles by the blood is insufficient.

[307] Ross Clark, "Children who died of Covid-19 were already seriously ill, new study shows," https://www.spectator.co.uk/, 28 August 2020.

early as August 2020, conducted on 69,516 people hospitalized in 260 British hospitals, counted only six deaths of people under the age of 19, all of whom had "very severe comorbidities."[308] Another study conducted at the Necker Hospital in Paris raised a suspicion of a link with Kawasaki disease, but there were no deaths among the children[309]. The same result, no deaths, is reported in an Italian study of May 2020[310].

The other thesis that has been put forward on TV shows since the beginning, including in abject ads paid for by our money, is the risk of death of grandma because of her little girl or boy who would contaminate her. Numerous studies have shown that this is not the case and that it is the adults who transmit the virus to the children, who do not risk anything. This is what prompted no less than 20 learned societies of pediatrics to call for the return of children to school in May 2020[311]. The statement read: "It is urgent to control our fears and move forward for the sake of children [...] Children are now paying a heavy price for the initial assumption that they were the main vector for the circulation of the Covid-19 virus, by analogy with other viruses. We know today that this is not the case, and that almost all children who were infected by Covid-19 were infected by adults [...] It is urgent to recall that children's communities, nurseries or classrooms, continued to exist during the containment, in particular for the children of caregivers. No outbreaks were noted in these groups of children, while viral circulation was high among adults." Much later, but better than nothing, Martin Blachier, who is very present on TV, wrote an op-ed on June 19, 2021, entitled "Save our honor: immediately lift the wearing of masks in elementary school!"[312] Once again, he uses several references and publications to back up his point.

---

[308] https://www.bmj.com/content/370/bmj.m3249

[309] Julie Toubiana, Clément Poirault, Alice Corsia, Fanny Bajolle, Jacques Fourgeaud, François Angoulvant, Agathe Debray, Romain Basmaci, Elodie Salvador, Sandra Biscardi, Pierre Frange, Martin Chalumeau, Jean-Laurent Casanova, Jérémie F Cohen, Slimane Allali, "Kawasaki-like multisystem inflammatory syndrome in children during the covid-19 pandemic in Paris, France: prospective observational study", BMJ, 3 June 2020.

[310] https://www.ncbi.nlm.nih.gov/pmc/articles/PMC7219028/

[311] Contributed, "Covid-19: 20 presidents of pediatric learned societies call for children to return to school," Le Quotidien Du Médecin, 5/13/2020.

But the worst is never far away, as the media terror continues to push at all costs to vaccinate children who do not get sick from Covid-19 again. We just risk having an unprecedented health scandal if serious side effects were to occur in the long term. Where is the basic logic in this? The case of *Dengvaxia*, a vaccine against dengue fever, suspended following the death of several hundred *healthy* children in the Philippines is still ongoing[313]. We are seriously playing with fire…

There is no shortage of profiteers of misfortune who use the worst manners, especially in times of a pandemic. So many Drs. Knock came to light during the coronavirus crisis. The play that was performed for real was so true to the original that it felt like a play.

Professor François Raffi, head of the department of infectious and tropical diseases at the University Hospital of Nantes, made anonymous phone calls to Professor Didier Raoult to threaten him and ask him to stop talking about treatment against Covid-19. This professor admitted the facts and was condemned by the justice. It is useful to recall the far-reaching links of interest of this doctor with the pharmaceutical industry. They amount to 541,729 euros, including 52,812 euros with Gilead. As a reminder, this American laboratory is the manufacturer of Remdesivir, a drug that has been authorized as a treatment for Covid-19 and ordered by Europe for 1.2 billion euros, even though there was no lack of evidence of its ineffectiveness, and even advised against by the WHO! It must be said that the war against chloroquine has been so intense and ruthless even within the scientific council[314] and the groups of researchers in charge of the clinical studies, according to a serious investigation by the newspaper Marianne[315].

This treatment war has had an episode that shows the limitless greed of some. In July of the year 2020, the world's media relayed a scientific

---

[312] Martin Blachier: "Let's save our honor: let's immediately lift the wearing of masks in elementary school!", www.lejdd.fr, June 19, 2021.

[313] Carol Isoux, "Dengue: Sanofi at heart of deadly vaccine case in the Philippines," www.nouvelobs.com, November 27, 2018.

[314] Etienne Campion, "Ambiguïté gouvernementale, liens d'intérêts au sommet de l'État : enquête sur la guerre secrète de la chloroquine", www.marianne.net, 09/04/2020.

[315] Etienne Campion, "Discovery: are the French experts seeking a treatment for COVID under the influence of the labs?", www.marianne.net, 18/05/2020.

publication in the *European Respiratory Journal* that would demonstrate the beneficial effect of smoking on Covid-19. It talked about the "smoker's paradox," the principle according to which smoking does indeed damage the lungs (thanks, we didn't know that!), but smokers are more protected against the coronavirus thanks to nicotine! A year later, the study was withdrawn in disgrace, because two authors of the publication failed to mention conflicts of interest with ... the tobacco industry! José M. Mier is a consultant and Konstantinos Poulas is the main instigator of the NGO NoSmoke, an organization supported by large companies in the tobacco sector[316]. The cynicism of the name NoSmoke (no tobacco) is noted, as it is a counter tactic often used to distract and control any movement of opposition to a product.

This is very reminiscent of the so-called NoFakeMed, a movement of people who present themselves as advocates of evidence-based medicine, but who are in reality a lobby of the pharmaceutical industry. Its members, most of whom have vested interests, have fought hard against any treatment that has fallen into the public domain, even against *vitamin D,* even though the French Academy of Medicine recommended it in a communiqué in May 2020[317]. It states: "The National Academy of Medicine recalls that the administration of vitamin D orally is a simple measure, inexpensive and reimbursed by the Health Insurance; confirms its recommendation to ensure vitamin D supplementation in the French population in a report in 2012; Recommends promptly measuring vitamin D levels in people over age 60 with Covid-19, and administering a loading dose of 50,000 IU to 100,000 IU in case of deficiency, which could help limit respiratory complications; recommends providing vitamin D supplementation of 800 IU to 1,000 IU/day in people under age 60 as soon as the diagnosis of Covid-19 is confirmed." These same NoFakeMed people supported tooth and nail the famous fake *Lancet* study that denigrated chloroquine and later turned into LancetGate after the manipulation scandal was revealed!

---

[316] https://erj.ersjournals.com/content/57/3/2002144.article-info
[317] https://www.academie-medecine.fr/communique-de-lacademie-nationale-de-medecine-vitamine-d-et-covid-19/

The coronavirus crisis has been like a spotlight on many aspects of information dissemination, including in the field of research, which have remained in the shadows for the ordinary person until now. We have discovered that publications, even in prestigious international journals, can be not only false, but manipulated on purpose. I have personally done academic research and published in many journals and know this world. Serious proofreading is normally a condition before accepting any paper. I myself have been involved in the proofreading of many papers, a demanding process that often takes several months. I thought this was the case in all fields, but I discovered during this crisis that this is not the case in the medical field, a sensitive field that should instead raise the standards. Following the *LancetGate* affair, I watched a doctor saying quietly on a continuous news channel that some papers are published without even being reviewed! I must say that I fell out of my chair. And obviously the phenomenon is not isolated, but very widespread. Here is what Richard Horton, editor of one of the most prestigious international medical journals, The Lancet, wrote[318]: "Much of what is published is wrong. I'm not allowed to say who made that remark because we were asked to observe the *Chatham House* rules of silence. We were also asked not to take pictures of the slides. Those who work for government agencies pleaded that their comments not be quoted… Why the paranoid concern for secrecy and non-attribution? Because this symposium—on the reproducibility and reliability of biomedical research, held at the Welcome Trust in London last week— addressed one of the most sensitive issues in science today: the idea that something has gone fundamentally wrong with one of our greatest human creations." Richard Horton drives the point home, "The case against science is simple: much of the scientific literature, perhaps half of it, may simply be wrong. Plagued by studies with small sample sizes, tiny effects, invalid exploratory analyses, and blatant conflicts of interest, as well as an obsession with pursuing fads of dubious importance, science has fallen into obscurity." I must admit that reading this statement gave me the chills. I really didn't expect this. It simply means that the medicines we consume, which are supposed to heal us,

---

[318] Richard Horton, "Offline: What is medicine's 5 sigma?", VOLUME 385, ISSUE 9976, P1380, APRIL 11, 2015.

are for the most part fake and probably poisonous at times. I have heard about this before and even gave a book—*The Guide to 4000 Useful, Useless or Dangerous Medicines*[319]—to my doctor sister, but I did not imagine this magnitude. I should have read it before I gave it to her…

Regarding the medical and political handling of the Covid-19 crisis, Kamran Abbasi, the chief editor of the prestigious *British Medical Journal* (BMJ), wrote an editorial with a title that leaves little room for nuance: "Covid-19: politicization, corruption, and the suppression of science."[320] It states, "Politicians and governments are suppressing science. They do it in the public interest, they say, to speed up the availability of diagnostics and treatments. They do it to support innovation, to bring products to market at unprecedented speed. Both of these reasons are partly plausible; the greatest frauds are born from a grain of truth. But the underlying behavior is troubling. Science is being suppressed for political and financial gain. Covid-19 has unleashed state corruption on a massive scale, and it is harmful to public health. Politicians and industry are responsible for this opportunistic misappropriation of funds. So are scientists and health experts. The pandemic has revealed how the medical-political complex can be manipulated in times of emergency—a time when it is more important to safeguard science […]" He concludes: "When good science is suppressed, people die."

An investigation conducted by the Washington Post in 2012 (we have already talked about it with the Avandia affair of GSK[321]) sheds a particularly good light on the subject of conflicts of interest. The analysis of articles on new drugs published in the world's most prestigious medical journal, the *New England Journal of Medicine* (NEJM), is particularly enlightening. Over a one-year period, the NEJM published 73 articles on original studies of new drugs, either approved by the FDA or still in the experimental phase. Of these articles, 60 were

---

[319] Philippe Even, Bernard Debré, "Le Guide des 4000 médicaments utiles, inutiles ou dangereux," Le Grand Livre du Mois (September 13, 2012)

[320] Kamran Abbasi, "Covid-19: politicisation, 'corruption,' and suppression of science," BMJ 2020;371:m4425

[321] Peter Whoriskey, "As drug industry's influence over research grows, so does the potential for bias," www.washingtonpost.com, November 24, 2012.

funded by a pharmaceutical company, 50 were authored by employees of a pharmaceutical company, and 37 had as lead author, usually an academic who had previously received external compensation from the pharmaceutical company in the form of consulting or speaking fees! And this is counted in hundreds of thousands of dollars, sometimes millions, with stock market shares as a bonus…

And when they appear in the media, even though the law requires them to declare their links of interest, none of the doctors on the sets do so!

There is another point that is worth making: corruption does not necessarily mean huge sums of money or dream trips on a cruise. It actually takes much less to influence a person's opinion or actions, including in the medical field. An American study on medical students has shown that even small gifts such as mugs or pens with a pharmaceutical company logo have an effect[322]. "Our study finds that subtle exposures to branded pharmaceutical promotional items influence medical students' implicit attitudes toward these brands," it states. While the article demonstrates that "there is no gift too small" to be influential, it points to a recurring bias among medical professionals, "Many physicians, because they are medical experts, believe they are not susceptible to these influences."

The boss of a previous company I worked for forbade employees to keep any gifts from suppliers, even the smallest ones. All items are given to the executive assistant and then randomly redistributed to employees at the Christmas party during a friendly lunch and a raffle…

I mean to say that the generalization of "all rotten" would certainly be unfair and it is not the object of my speech. But one rotten tomato unfortunately does a lot of damage to the whole.

---

[322] Grande D, Frosch DL, Perkins AW, Kahn BE. Effect of Exposure to Small Pharmaceutical Promotional Items on Treatment Preferences. Arch Intern Med. 2009; 169 (9):887-89.

## The New Guardians of a Ruined Temple

In a previous book on digital sovereignty[323], I mentioned a GAFAM putsch on the fourth estate. They now control information and do not hesitate to censor dissenting voices. One can think whatever one wants about Trump and one has seen that I have no affection for him, but closing his Twitter account is extremely serious. But what personally shocked me the most was the closing of the accounts of doctors who simply called for treating COVID patients instead of leaving them at home with Paracetamol at the risk of seeing their condition worsen. Many people have unfortunately died in this way. It is unbelievable that Facebook or Twitter decides what a doctor or researcher with more than ten years of higher education can or cannot say! Ironically, one year after the censorship of these doctors, there is a 180-degree turnaround in the official recommendations concerning treatments. The Minister of Health himself asks people during a press conference on March 20, 2021, to consult their doctor at the slightest alert. He states: "Some patients were admitted to the hospital in a hurry yesterday. They had stayed at home with their symptoms and had not realized that they were in hypoxia and lacked oxygen. They realized too late that their condition warranted a transfer for heavy resuscitation care. In some cases, you may be offered medication, treatment … oxygen, blood thinners, antibiotics…" In light of what I have just related, my question is simple: how many people have died because of the censorship applied by Facebook, Twitter, YouTube and the others?

The other edifying example of this new kind of dictatorship, which has become a common practice on the Web, is the possibility of a leak from a Covid-19 laboratory, which we have already mentioned. Any post that raises the issue has been systematically deleted by Facebook. But who the hell is Zuckerberg to impose the scientific debate? It is worth noting in passing that the medRxiv platform[324] on which scientific articles in the medical field are pre-published is financed to the tune of 2 million dollars by the *Chan Zuckerberg Initiative* Foundation[325], just like

---

[323] Boussad Addad, Souveraineté numérique européenne : Innovations, échecs et espoir de 1900 à nos jours, VA Press Editions, juillet 2021.
[324] https://www.medrxiv.org
[325] https://chanzuckerberg.com/newsroom/2-million-to-medrxiv-top-source-breaking-

BioRxiv dedicated to the field of biology[326]. This foundation created by Zuck and his wife is even the only sponsor visible on the home pages of the websites of these platforms[327]. This is obviously problematic when we see the censorship imposed on scientific debate.

After the publication of several researchers in the journal *Science* mentioning the possibility of a laboratory leak of Covid-19, as well as on the mainstream media, it is the reversal at Facebook. A spokesperson for the social network said in a statement this, "In light of ongoing investigations into the origin of Covid-19 and in consultation with public health experts, we *will* no longer *remove the* claim that Covid-19 is man-made from our applications."[328] Experts? But what experts? Rather, they are a new breed of consultants paid directly by Facebook.

These new guardians of the information temple are what we now call *fact-checkers*, verifiers or decoders of information. They are in charge of checking the news published on the Web. The problem is that they all come from the mainstream media and they have no more credibility than their parent companies. "In a context of mistrust of the media, *fact-checking* will allow us to reinforce our credibility and our legitimacy," declared Yannick Letranchant, the head of information at France Télévisions in the columns of Le Parisien[329]. Not sure that this attempt to redeem a virginity with Internet users is successful. Especially since these new services are funded in part by Facebook with a program launched in late 2016. A partnership has indeed been concluded with several media, including Le Monde, France 24, 20 Minutes, Libération or even AFP. The AFP Factual service is the world leader "with three quarters of the market of what has become a business for the media" dixit the president of the French news agency[330]. This service employs

---

covid-19-research/

[326] Ewen Callaway, "BioRxiv preprint server gets cash boost from Chan Zuckerberg Initiative," Nature, vol. 545, no. 7652, 26 April 2017, pp. 18-18

[327] https://www.biorxiv.org

[328] CRISTIANO LIMA, "Facebook no longer treating 'man-made' COVID as a crackpot idea," www.politico.com, 05/26/2021.

[329] M.Z., "Les 20 heures se mettent au *fact-checking*," www.leparisien.fr, February 3, 2019.

[330] https://www.europe1.fr/emissions/L-invite-medias/fabrice-fries-president-de-lafp-4042543

more than 100 full-time journalists in 30 different countries. This does not fail to worry some unions like the SNJ (National Union of Journalists), pointing to a partnership that relies on the financing of a single private player [Facebook] who is trying to restore its image after all the scandals it has experienced. It is not sure that this union will be heard given the stakes, especially after the AFP has landed a new contract with the social network for an extension of its service in the Middle East and North Africa. There is still talk of a contract worth one million euros for 2018 alone[331]. Go and ask these media to criticize Zuckerberg after that!

At the end of 2020, Twitter also launched a pilot of another approach to news verification called *Birdwatch[332]*. It aims to moderate content on the platform based on "context notes" provided by a community of *fact-checkers* among subscribers. But if any Internet user can do this, it will be back to square one. If it's a handful of people, how are they selected? *Quis custodiet ipsos custodes,* but who will guard these guards? *Fact-checking* journalists from the mainstream media as for Facebook? Maybe so. Wait and see…

Freedom of expression is already regulated by law. Why not just apply it? Hate, racism, call to murder … are all forbidden and it is the duty of the platforms to remove them. Yet, that's all we see on news feeds. When Facebook lets the Christchurch killer broadcast his massacre, but censors a doctor who saves lives, one has to wonder about the inertia of justice. Not to mention the phenomena of harassment, blackmail, mockery … on Twitter that lead to depression and sometimes suicides. What are politicians and other human rights associations doing? The GAFAM putsch is finally on all powers, not only on the fourth…

---

[331] Laure Croiset, "What's behind the media's interest in fact-checking," www.challenges.fr, 08.02.2019.
[332] https://blog.twitter.com/en_us/topics/product/2021/introducing-birdwatch-a-community-based-approach-to-misinformation.html

## When the blue bird sings Parole… Parole…

Chris Wetherell, the designer of the retweet, the feature that allows you to repost a tweet with a simple click, is now more than bitter. "We handed a loaded gun to a four-year-old," he confides in an interview with online media outlet BuzzFeed[333]. He watched helplessly as the Gamergate harassment case unfolded and could do nothing. When he told a circle of Silicon Valley social networking engineers about it, he was simply told, "It's not our business." Twitter CEO Jack Dorsey himself, however, admits in 2019 in a TED Talk[334] that "it's very easy to abuse and harass on a large scale" on his platform and that "people spend their time there reporting abuse and responding to attacks instead of just learning useful things." He clearly questions the way Twitter works. In particular, his teams are thinking about the mass use of AI to flush out fake news. "Thirty-eight percent of *fake news* are already detected automatically" by the algorithms, while it was "zero a year ago," he says. He's also thinking about changing some features. "A lot of our work has to do with technology, but we're also considering the incentives of the service: what does Twitter encourage you to do when you open it? Previously, it strongly encouraged outrage, mob behavior, collective harassment. We need to look deeper at some of the fundamentals of what the service does to generate greater progress. We can make small changes about the technology, but fundamentally we need to look deeply at the dynamics in the network itself, and that's what we're doing." He admits, "One of the choices we made at the very beginning was that we had this number showing how many subscribers you have. We decided that this number should be big and bold, that anything on the page being big and bold mattered and was what you should aspire to drive. Was that the right decision at the time? Probably not. If I were to relaunch the service, I wouldn't value the number of subscribers as much. I wouldn't value the number of *likes* as much. I don't think I would create *likes* at all, because that's not a driver of what

---

[333] "The Man Who Built the Retweet: 'We Handed a Loaded Weapon to 4-Year-Olds,'" interview with Alex Kantrowitz, BuzzFeed, July 23, 2018.

[334] https://www.ted.com/talks/jack_dorsey_how_twitter_needs_to_change?language=en#t-148672

we believe today is the most important thing." Jack Dorsey's interviewer doesn't let it go to sleep: "To many, you seem to be an enigma. Maybe it's unfair, but I woke up the other night with this image that made me think of you and the following situation: we were on a trip with you on a boat called "Twittanic" and there are people on deck expressing discomfort and you, unlike many captains, say to them, 'Tell me, talk to me, listen to me, I want to hear. They talk to you and they say, "The iceberg in front of us is worrisome." And you tell them, "That's a very good point and our boat was not made properly to turn as much as it should." We say, "Do something about it." You go out on deck and we wait and watch and you're extraordinarily calm, but we're all out there saying, "Jack, come on, turn the rudder!" You see? My point is that democracy is at stake."

These words resonate surprisingly well when we think of the dramatic turn taken by the bluebird boat after the American elections and the closure of Donald Trump's account and those of his many supporters. It is not the iceberg and the ocean of *fake news* that finally sank democracy, but the brutal maneuver of its captain who threw all his opponents overboard! I don't like Trump, but I will never agree with his muzzling…

## The AI of hope, really?

When we listen to or read the media, we would think that artificial intelligence is the panacea, the solution to all the world's problems. Let's be clear, AI will be what we make of it. It is a powerful tool, it is true, but it is also a double-edged sword. I have already explained in a previous book[335] how AI can be used to generate fake news by manipulating images, sound and text. I also pointed out the different research works that are working on the fight against *fake news*. It's an arms race really, but I'm afraid it's a difficult one for the truth seeker, for various reasons.

---

[335] Boussad Addad, "La face cachée de l'intelligence artificielle," VA Editions, May 2020.

Humans are creative, both in good and bad ways. When a word is blacklisted on a platform, for example the term—the reader will excuse me—"shit," you only have to write "sh1t," for the reader to read exactly the same thing. And, no matter how strong the algorithm behind the moderation system is, man will always find loopholes to exploit.

But what I really have a problem with, because I am convinced that the efficiency of the algorithms will be greater and greater to detect offensive sentences or words, is the bias introduced in the learning process on the veracity of the information. I remind you that AI, like a baby, only learns from what we feed it. The question is therefore who defines what is true or not true in the data to be used for the learning of the AI? Can we seriously entrust, for example, Facebook or Twitter with the task of saying what is true or not and that the algorithm will then reproduce? We saw the absurdity of the decisions taken by these platforms during the COVID crisis where doctors were censored before time proved them right! They have nevertheless invited themselves into the scientific debate, even though this is far from their role. What about conflicts of interest or facts that affect these platforms or their partners in any way? Will a case of harassment or something else occurring within one of these firms, relayed by an Internet user, be considered as fake news and censored? What about state affairs? Can we seriously expect these platforms, which collaborate with American intelligence services, to let information that affects the strategic interests of the United States pass through?

What about the sovereignty of countries in all this? This is for me the most sensitive point, because the stakes are enormous. Let's suppose tomorrow another Colin Powell brandishing a vial and accusing a third country of having weapons of mass destruction. It is logical to expect that the American platforms, like the mainstream media in their time, would support preventive intervention and censor all dissenting voices from other countries. As a result, the opinion on the Web is in favor of punishing the targeted country and people, manipulated without their knowledge, will pressure their governments to ally themselves with the Americans. Even a de Villepin will give in under the current gigantic pressure of the Web. And here we really touch on the sensitive subject of the pure and simple independence of states. When the truth comes out five or ten years later, the war will have already devastated a region of the world and a precarious calm will have returned, and everyone will have forgotten…

One should never entrust the monopoly of truth to a liar, just as the shepherd never adopted a wolf to watch over his sheep…

## The right information exists

Information will inevitably be digital and paper newspapers are likely doomed to disappear. Technology and the ease it induces pushes to new behaviors that are naturally adopted by a man won by laziness. We only have to look at Scandinavian countries like Norway or Sweden where the media have almost entirely switched to digital formats. Yet these are the countries where the population's trust in the media is the highest in the world.

The problem with the Web is that the number of possible sources of information is almost infinite. So, you have to learn how to sort out the information. This is not an easy task and unfortunately it is not at school, although it should be, that one can learn this. The educational system forms, let's say it, machines with a critical thought no higher than that of a parrot in a cage. And the trainers who are supposed to educate them no better.

It is June 2020 and here is the surreal dialogue held live on a crowded set of the Swiss channel RTS[336], between a regular guest, Sebastian Dieguez, clinician reconverted into a researcher at the University of Fribourg, and a journalist, without anyone stopping them:

- o Dieguez: "What the conspiracist does, he's going to research, think for himself. He wants to see for himself."
- o Reporter: "Thinking for yourself, but how is that possible? But it's pathological to think for yourself."

---

[336] https://www.rts.ch/play/tv/infrarouge/video/quel-vaccin-contre-le-complotisme?urn=urn:rts:video:11373235

- o Dieguez: "But you can't think for yourself, that's an idea that's been demolished since … it doesn't make sense. You can't think for yourself."
- o Reporter: "I think that phrase, you have to remember it, you can't think for yourself."

What can we seriously expect from an academic who tells people not to think for themselves? This gentleman alone embodies the defeat of thought and the decadence of a certain elite. Isn't it precisely because of ignorance and the end of reflection that people end up believing in everything and anything? This crisis has had the merit of showing so many things unimaginable within our pseudo-media elite. Plato must be turning in his grave…

Let's get back to our topic. The most trivial way to avoid bad news is to educate yourself and diversify your sources of information. The problem, as we have seen, is that most of the media in a country often repeat the same information, an AFP or Reuters dispatch, for example. The so-called alternative media are sometimes a good source, but they easily fall into far-fetched theories. There too, it is necessary to make the sorting under penalty of falling into sectarianism and other dogmatism. Not all media content, mainstream or not, is to be discarded. There is good and bad everywhere. You just have to know how to separate the wheat from the chaff. And this is not easy.

The good news—one of the few that emerged during the coronavirus crisis—is that there are more and more people doing this work of sorting out information. These groups are gathering in so-called reinformation collectives and proposing quality content. Each one in his field of expertise brings his stone to the informational edifice with a good popularization within the reach of the general public. We must take advantage of this. I can cite the Reinfo COVID collective whose slogan is *question, understand and act*[337]. It was born during the crisis to bring the voice of many doctors, artists, caregivers …, who do not agree with the consensus of the TV sets and the media in general around the measures taken during the crisis. Still on the subject of the crisis, we can

---

[337] https://reinfocovid.fr

also mention the media *Bas les masques*[338], made up mainly of doctors and health professionals, who relay alternative information far from the terror of the mainstream media. Unfortunately, these dissonant voices often fall victim to social network censorship for completely spurious reasons that can be summed up in a hollow phrase: "Contrary to the rules of our community." Since nature abhors a vacuum, I am confident that more free speech-friendly platforms will flourish to remedy this problem. Moreover, most alternative media have websites where you can find all their productions. It is enough to know them. A simple search on the Internet will find them. But once again, be careful not to take everything as truth.

If one is forced to go on a social network to get information, which is my case for example concerning the news of my region of origin (Kabylia) where I have a family, my recipe is quite simple. I have identified some interesting sources, alternative media and people, and from time to time I go to them to see the news. I refrain from endless scrolling and just look at these sources. I go straight to the point and don't look for anything else. I avoid comments and *likes* and greatly reduce my interaction with the social network. I try to get rid of all the biases and other filter bubbles. The targeting of the social network concerning me is thus reduced to almost nothing. This prevents me from wasting time with useless or secondary information. You have to focus on the essential.

Also, I avoid any attachment to a YouTube channel for example and do not hesitate to stop watching a video at any time if the content does not suit me. I don't hesitate to stop a video after five minutes on whatever channel. Conversely, I can listen with interest to the end of a person whose ideas go against mine if I find his or her words useful on a particular subject. I don't care about labels on people. Authority is not after the COVID story! I have no problem changing my opinion on a given topic if the person gives me solid arguments. There is nothing rational about escalating commitment and cognitive dissonance, and one should not give in to it. This openness allows me at least to know the

---

[338] https://baslesmasques.com

diversity of opinion in the society in which I live and this is not anything. Any truth is good to take, even bitter. You have to go out and explore to survive; otherwise you die of boredom and ignorance.

My other advice is simple: go back to that animal instinct that allowed man to survive in hostile environments: curiosity. We must search, explore the lands of the Web. There are priceless treasures to be found there. Automatic translators are not perfect, but we can use them to go even further. In a globalized world, understanding what is happening in Germany or the United States can sometimes help to decipher current events in France or elsewhere. You have to read books and above all diversify your subjects to be well educated and never get bored. I never imagined I would like cognitive psychology, but I loved it once I discovered it. You have to look at specialized journals from time to time, even on subjects that don't seem to concern you. The information you find there is often valuable.

Finally, we need to get back to real life and communicate with real people. This has become a real luxury, because it is the first-hand source of what is going on in society. And the people available are few and far between, the majority being sucked into the web and screens. If we can't do that, we should at least take the time to sit down, reflect, and communicate with ourselves. Because when we know ourselves well, we know how to lead ourselves smoothly towards the destination we have chosen and that has not been imposed on us. This is the meaning of freedom.

Be free, be the authors of your own stories.

# CONCLUSION

*"The powerful will continue to distract others, sometimes making them believe they are informing them,"*

—Jacques Attali

One thing to keep in mind, information is power. From time immemorial, man has run after news to improve his chances of survival. To be informed of the presence of a source of drinking water in the immensity of the desert was and still is vital for the nomadic man. Finding the right information today in the cognitive chaos of the Web is just as vital.

The protagonists of the "triple ignorance" play put on a *show*. Some of them surrender their brains to Lucifer 2.0 by spending hours on the Web scrolling, liking, and writing comments on more or less far-fetched theories. They forget the real issues of life such as family, education, and democracy, for example. Others, like zeteticians and journalists, spend their time trying to *debunk* or decode theories and "forget" to conduct serious investigations on real problems. Still others, politicians and other decision-makers, are locked up in their ivory towers and are comforted in their ideas by a press under orders. They continue to peacefully carry out their dirty work of dismantling everything that is in the collective interest. When they need a little intelligence to carry out a task, they hire a consulting firm with millions of public money to come up with a *nudging* technique. The politicians will, of course, present the curves and figures at the end to show the people that the job has been done.

All the while, the attention merchants are enjoying their platform and filling their pockets. They have the real information. They hold the real power. Jacques Attali, in his book on the media, writes: "The powerful will continue to distract others, sometimes making them believe that they are informing them. The most precious information, political, economic, technological, sanitary, biological, will continue to circulate in very small circles."

Real information is expensive now. Being informed is more tiring than ever. But everything has a price and nothing is free. You just have to know what you want to do with your life and be ready to pay the right price. You can take your destiny into your own hands, like a determined nomad, and go explore the immense desert to find water for infusion. This is what being free is all about. One can also choose the easy way out, be satisfied with the can of *Coca Cola* delivered by Uber at regular intervals while watching the latest Zombies series on Netflix. But when the deadly fiction comes out of the screen and becomes reality, we'll have more than tears to drink before we die.

So be free, be the author, the real author, of your own story.

# THANK YOU

*Dear reader,*

*Thank you very much for taking the time to read this book. I sincerely hope you find it useful. I hope you learned something from reading it as I did from writing it.*

*You can send me your criticism on my email box, it will please me. And don't hesitate to ask me if some explanation is not clear enough. I will do my best to correct it for the next edition.*

*Finally, your encouragement is my fuel to keep moving forward. A review posted on Amazon or elsewhere will therefore be welcome. You can do it simply by scanning the QR code below.*

*See you soon for new adventures.*

*—Boussad*

Email: boussad83@yahoo.fr

# Table of contents

# ABOUT THE AUTHOR

Boussad ADDAD is the author of several books and a researcher in a private laboratory of artificial intelligence. He holds a PhD degree from the École Normale Supérieure de Paris Saclay and is a laureate of the best thesis in France, awarded in Strasbourg in 2013.
Boussad is also passionate about psychology and neuroscience, two disciplines that inspire his research.

# FROM THE SAME AUTHOR

### English books

o   *Encyclopedia of cognitive biases, the ultimate guide to making better decisions, Independently published, 2023.*

o   *Digital Heroin, the magic secrets behind screen addiction Independently published, 2023 (original French edition published in 2021).*

### French books

o   *La souveraineté numérique européenne : Innovations, échecs et espoir de 1900 à nos jours, VA PRESS, juillet 2021.*

o   *La Face cachée de l'Intelligence artificielle, VA PRESS, mai 2020.*